CARLOS SAURA

INTERVIEWS

EDITED BY LINDA M. WILLEM

UNIVERSITY PRESS OF MISSISSIPPI / JACKSON

www.upress.state.ms.us

Publication of this book was made possible in part by a grant from the Program
for Cultural Cooperation between Spain's Ministry of Education and Culture and
United States Universities.

10   09   08   07   06   05   04   03   02   4   3   2   1
∞

Library of Congress Cataloging-in-Publication Data
   Saura, Carlos, 1932–
      Carlos Saura : interviews / edited by Linda M. Willem.
         p.   cm.—(Conversations with filmmakers series)
      Filmography: p.
      Includes index.
         ISBN 1-57806-493-7 (alk. paper)—ISBN 1-57806-494-5 (pbk. :
      alk. paper)
         1. Saura, Carlos, 1932–   2. Motion picture producers and
      directors—Spain—Interviews.   I. Willem, Linda M.   II. Title.   III.
      Series.
   PN1998.3.S28 A5   2003
   791.43′0233′092—dc21   2002003009

British Library Cataloging-in-Publication Data available

CARLOS SAURA

INTERVIEWS

CONVERSATIONS WITH FILMMAKERS SERIES
PETER BRUNETTE, GENERAL EDITOR

© agencia efe

CONTENTS

Introduction *vii*

Chronology *xvii*

Filmography *xxv*

From Black Spain to Silver Bears: Part One 3
AUGUSTO M. TORRES AND VICENTE MOLINA-FOIX

New Interview with Carlos Saura on *La prima Angélica* [Cousin Angelica] 17
ENRIQUE BRASÓ

Interview with Carlos Saura 22
JUAN CARLOS RENTERO

Carlos Saura: An Individualist in Conversation 32
VICÉN CAMPOS

Interview with Carlos Saura on *Cría cuervos* [Raise Ravens] and *Elisa, vida mía* [Elisa, My Life] 42
ENRIQUE BRASÓ

Interview with Carlos Saura 52
ANTONIO CASTRO

Interview with Carlos Saura 65
ENRIQUE ALBERICH

Antonieta, Carlos Saura Between the Past and the Present   72
VALERIA CIOMPI

Los zancos [The Stilts] by Carlos Saura: Interview   84
ESTEVE RIAMBAU

The Flamenco Trilogy   88
PATRICK SCHUPP

Carlos Saura: The Culmination of a Dream   96
PEDRO CALLEJA

Continuity, Rupture, Remembering: The Spanish Cinema During Franco's
Time   103
MECHTHILD ZEUL

Interview: Carlos Saura   115
ANTONIO CASTRO

The Apprenticeship of Life: Interview   144
ANTONIO CASTRO

Tango According to Saura   150
PAULA PONGA

The Image and the Word: A Conversation with Filmmaker and Novelist
Carlos Saura   156
LINDA M. WILLEM

Interview: Carlos Saura   167
JOSÉ ENRIQUE MONTERDE

Index   171

INTRODUCTION

CARLOS SAURA HAS BEEN A prominent figure within the international film community for over forty years. His works frequently appear in
worldwide competitions and have garnered multiple awards at such prestigious venues as Cannes, Berlin, and Montreal. Film scholars and critics con-
sistently join his name with that of Luis Buñuel and Pedro Almodóvar to
form a triad of Spain's most renowned filmmakers. But whereas Buñuel
belonged to the generation of Spaniards who pursued their careers in exile,
and Almodóvar is of the generation which came to artistic maturity after
Franco's death, Saura embodies the generation of liberal filmmakers who
lived under the thirty-six year dictatorship and creatively circumvented its
censorship restrictions. Despite the challenge that his early films posed to
official Francoist ideology and the idealized view of society seen in Spain's
mainstream cinema of the dictatorship, Saura has never been an overtly
political filmmaker. Rather, he has cultivated a style which is highly personal
yet has a universal quality that transcends nationalistic boundaries. The wide
distribution and favorable reception of his films throughout Europe and the
United States attest to the effectiveness of that style. Although Saura is recognized as one of the most significant oppositional directors of the Franco era,
his importance extends far beyond that time period. Indeed, some of his
most innovative work and greatest international acclaim has been achieved
after Spain's transition to democracy. With a distinguished film career that
began in 1957 and continues to the present, Saura has worked under a diverse
set of political and social situations, and as such, he can lay claim to being
the filmmaker of Spain's twentieth century.

Given Saura's international reputation, it is surprising that very few of the interviews he has given over the course of his long career have been translated into English. And those that are in translation tend to be brief and/or excerpted. A notable exception is the excellent interview with Silvia Lemus in the subtitled Films for the Humanities series, but its frequent translation errors unfortunately diminish its usefulness for those who do not understand Spanish. My aim in this volume has been to bring the English-speaking reader in contact with the substantial and informative interviews published in the foreign press. All seventeen of the interviews contained within these pages appear in English for the first time, and as such, they represent a treasure trove of comments by Saura on his own work which have thus far been unavailable to readers without foreign language fluency. These interviews—from Spain, France, Germany, and Canada—cover the entire range of Saura's career as a filmmaker: his early contributions to the New Spanish Cinema; his documentaries and documentary-like urban films; his Flamenco trilogy and other dance films; his historical films; his cinematic adaptations of literary and theatrical works; and the films rooted in his personal reminiscences. In addition, these interviews touch upon Saura's efforts as a photographer, opera director, and novelist. Together these interviews discuss each of Saura's films to date and present his views on a wide variety of issues.

In keeping with the policy of the Conversations with Filmmakers series, these interviews are printed in their entirety so as to preserve their integrity for the scholarly reader. Consequently, in selecting the interviews to be included in this volume, I tried to avoid undue repetition. While some redundancy does occur, more prevalent is Saura's ongoing elaboration of certain themes of importance to him and his work. Concepts merely mentioned in some interviews, for example, are fleshed out in others. What emerges is Saura's amazingly consistent approach to his cinema and his role as a director. But this does not imply either rigidity or stagnation. Rather, it reveals a set of principles which forms the foundation upon which his creativity and intuition can build in diverse directions and innovative ways. This is not to say that contradictions never arise, nor does it suggest a complete clarity of expression in Saura's responses. Sometimes his comments are vague or confusing, and he frequently avoids certain questions by redirecting his answers to areas he prefers to discuss instead. But throughout his interviews he conveys a sincere desire to explain his craft to the best of his ability.

Above all, Saura's cinema is a personal one. "I can't separate cinema from my life," he told Pedro Calleja. "The two things are interrelated and enrich or impoverish each other." Indeed, experiences from Saura's life do work their way into his films, sometimes in subtle ways (such as the inclusion in *Cría cuervos* [Raise Ravens] of the "Little Almond" fairy tale that his mother used to tell him as a child), and sometimes more directly (as in the homage to his Murcian relatives in *Pajarico* [Little Bird]). But more than any other aspect of his life, what colors his work the most are his remembrances of his early years during the Spanish Civil War. Several of the interviews in this book allude to these childhood experiences; however the extent of their influence is better seen in his "Memories of the Civil War," which was published in the Spanish edition of *Penthouse* magazine in 1978. Its status as an essay rather than an interview precluded its inclusion in this volume, but some of its contents are worth mentioning. Of particular interest are the examples Saura gives of how he used incidents from the war years in his films: the fear he felt on the first day of the war while watching his family anxiously listening to the radio behind the shuttered windows of their Madrid apartment is relived by Luis in *La prima Angélica* [Cousin Angelica], as is the horror of the surprise bombing attack on Saura's school that wounded his classmates; the vulnerability Saura felt during the war and its aftermath is expressed in the monologue given by the adult Ana in *Cría cuervos*, where childhood is defined not as a time of happiness, but rather as one filled with sadness and lack of comprehension; the character of Paulina in the same film is Saura's "belated revenge" on the despotic aunt he briefly lived with in Barcelona; and the brutal and unjust punishment Saura suffered at the hands of a teacher near the end of the war is echoed in *El jardín de las delicias* [The Garden of Delights]. Furthermore, events chronicled by Saura in this 1978 essay appear in his later films as well, most notably in *Dulces horas* [Sweet Hours] where the nocturnal air raids that frequently disturbed Saura's sleep are vividly shown from a child's perspective and the accidental injury Saura received while his father was chopping furniture to use for fuel is reenacted. Despite the numerous references in his films to events in his life, Saura adamantly insists that none of his films is autobiographical. In response to questions by interviewers on this matter, he carefully explains that he portrays only portions of the events in his life and that he does not always present them as they actually occurred. In his films there is what he described to Mechthild Zeul as a "decoding of memories." He fictionalizes specific elements in his life and places them within the larger context of a film's plotline. Similarly, he assures interviewers that none of his characters *is* Carlos Saura even though some characters may share a few of his personality traits.

Saura often describes himself in interviews as being very permeable, taking his inspiration not only from his personal experiences, but also from everything around him: news reports, conversations, literary works, movies, paintings, photographs, historical accounts, songs, etc. Perhaps the most direct result of this is *Los ojos vendados* [Blindfolded Eyes], based on testimony he heard while serving on a tribunal investigating political torture in South America. But more often what sparks his imagination is incorporated into a particular film but does not become its main thrust. This is especially the case with literary references: a Renaissance poem by Garcilaso de la Vega provides the title for *Elisa, vida mía* [Elisa, My Life], a statement by novelist Ramón del Valle-Inclán establishes the perspectivism of *La prima Angélica*, the spectacle of Rambal's theater gives visual definition to *Mamá cumple cien años* [Mama Turns One Hundred], etc. Sometimes a combination of ideas come together in a single film, as in *El jardín de las delicias*, which arose out of a news report of a car accident coupled with a comment made by a neurologist friend of Saura's concerning one of his patients. Indeed, outside influences are evident in the technical terminology from fields such as medicine, philosophy, and theology which Saura employs at times in his responses to interview questions. In 1996 Saura told Antonio Castro that "Our obligation is to 'vampirize' everything and make it our own," and eight years earlier in an interview with Mechthild Zeul he said, "I advocate the theory that one is morally obligated to forget nothing." Saura fulfills both these obligations through a highly personalized cinema that draws from his own life as well as from the social, political, and cultural life of Spain's past and present.

"I always want to tell *my* story, not a story." This statement made to Pedro Calleja succinctly captures the essence of Saura's philosophy toward filmmaking. Saura's personal vision permeates the films he directs, and he considers himself to be responsible for all creative decisions. He is closely involved in the various aspects of his films—especially editing, cinematography, and music—and he likes to use the same crew members from one film to the next because they know what he wants and can give it to him. He usually writes his own scripts, but when he does use a collaborator, his opinion carries the most weight. Having been exposed early in his career to *la politique des auteurs* being posited in *Cahiers du cinéma*, Saura unabashedly defines himself in those terms. Throughout his interviews he refers to himself in Spanish as an *autor*, the equivalent of the French word *auteur*. "What interests me is being an *auteur*. I've wanted to be one all my life," he told Valeria Ciompi in 1981, adding, "I've always considered myself to be an *auteur*, good or bad, but an *auteur*." While this assertion is widely accepted with regard to the bulk of Saura films, interviewers have questioned its validity for his adaptations of literary or theatrical works and for his historical films based on the lives of famous individuals. But Saura defends these as also belonging to his work as an *auteur* because of the strong personal stamp he puts on them. In his cinematic adaptations he is not merely what he calls an "illustrator" of a completed text, but rather, he appropriates the authorship of it by reworking the material to conform to what he wants it to be. Similarly, in his historical films he creates what he described to Antonio Castro as "a type of cinematic essay of a particular person." "And rather than an essay about his entire life," Saura added, "it always is a fragment of his life that seems essential to me and which in some way explains his life and allows me to use the imagery of the era, and above all, imagination, inquiring into the truth about what the character was like." And in the case of his film on Buñuel, he even disregards the past in order to fabricate fictional and contemporary versions of historical figures engaged in events of his own devising. In these films Saura transcends the historical facts to provide his own subjective biographies of individuals that are of interest to him.

Despite the control that Saura exercises over the entire filmmaking process, he incorporates a great deal of flexibility into the making of each individual film. "What I detest the most," he told Paula Ponga, "is knowing what I'm going to do. People think that my mind is very structured, but it's not true. Perhaps I do indeed know what I'm going to do, but I don't want to know. What I like best is having the sensation that I'm going to invent something new every day." Consequently, Saura considers scripts to be merely approximations of what will eventually be seen on the screen, and he prefers to shoot his films in story order so he can make changes along the way. He primarily works from intuition, and for that reason he often is unable to give interviewers any reason for why he did something in a film other than because it felt right to him. While this answer may seem unsatisfying at times, it conforms to Saura's belief that the interpretation of films is the job of the critic not the director. He applauds the efforts of serious critics who expend the time and energy necessary to examine the complexity of his films. But he also is outspoken in his condemnation of critics who blithely toss off negative reviews and simplistic interpretations of his films without much thought involved.

Given his frankness, it is not surprising that Saura's relationship with the press has been a stormy one at times. He has a reputation for not wanting to be interviewed, and he openly expresses his frustration with reporters who fail to see his films before coming to discuss them with him, or with critics who attempt to place his films into neat categories. He especially speaks out when interviewers chastise him for not making more overtly political films. "To make political films is very good for someone who wants to do that. That doesn't interest me very much," he told Vicén Campos, adding, "To propose that we all should make political films 'of the first degree' seems nonsense to me. I advocate the existence of this political cinema, as long as it can coexist with whatever other type in which the politics are secondary." Saura always defends his cinema in very personal terms: he simply makes the films that he wants to make. He explained this to Antonio Castro in 1996, saying, "For me, each film is a new adventure, and perhaps for that reason I have embarked on adventures that seem foolish to some people, but I hope to continue doing it anyway." Saura frequently expresses bewilderment and dismay at seeing which of his films have appealed to audiences over the years and which have not. "I would really like to know the secret—if there is one—to 'communicating' with a large number of people," he confided to Enrique Brasó, "but since I don't know this secret, I have to content myself with telling stories that interest me, in the hopes—sometimes I'm not very optimistic—that others will like or be interested in the same things that appeal to me." In his interviews he often mentions that some of the films he cared for the most were very poorly received by the public, and he laments that movie-goers primarily see films for passive entertainment rather than intellectual stimulation. "My films are complicated perhaps, but I believe that they are within the reach of anyone," he said to Vicén Campos.

Saura's films are indeed complicated. As he told Antonio Castro in 1976, "I'm totally against limiting cinema to a simplistic way of telling a story that is easily understandable, with a beginning and an end, that has clearly defined characters, and is easily identifiable with everyday reality." Rather, Saura favors nonlinear narration and innovative expressions of time and space. Instead of using traditional flashbacks to signal different time periods, he often conflates all times into one time by having characters and events exist on several temporal planes simultaneously. He reflects the subjective points of view of his characters by fusing reality with fantasy, past with present, and memory with hallucination. He employs multiple-character casting of actors to capture the dynamics involved in the concept of the double. He explores the relationship between representation and life through theatrical performances embedded in his plotlines. He suggests ideas through metaphor and allegory. "Nothing that's in my films is accidental," he told Juan Carlos Rentero. "The smallest details have a meaning." Overall, the visual ambiguity and narrative confusion occurring on the surface of his films elicit the viewer's active participation in piecing together its covert elements. This was particularly important during the Franco dictatorship when censorship restrictions required oppositional directors to express their criticism of the government indirectly. But Saura is quick to note that his films are complicated out of choice not just necessity. "Dealing with things in an indirect manner has always been something that I've liked a lot," he told Antonio Castro in 1996, adding, "I like that way of narrating, and that's why I have continued to use it after censorship ended." Explaining this preference, he went on to say: "It seems richer, more interesting, more fertile. It makes you think more. Taking an oblique approach to something not only doesn't seem to me to be a defect, but on the contrary, it is an extraordinary virtue, making things more complex, not so direct and simple. And if I haven't always used it, it's because the producers don't like it all."

As a self-proclaimed "investigator of images," Saura is known as a visual filmmaker. But the music that accompanies these images is of no less importance to him. American audiences are most familiar with the masterful use of tango and flamenco songs in his dance films, but music forms an integral part of his dramas and comedies as well. In his ongoing discussion with Antonio Castro over the years about the music in his films, Saura explains that he prefers using existing music instead of having musical pieces composed for his films. This gives him the freedom to choose exactly those pieces he wants. He usually selects compositions he personally likes, frequently drawing on the classical repertoire that his mother used to play in his home. "Music is a tyrant," Saura said in 1996. "It can destroy something for you or it can give you tremendous power." Saura respects that power and plans his scripts accordingly. "When I write or when I'm shooting, I see the scenes with music. The music almost always comes first." And that music is not just there for the benefit of the viewer who eventually will see the film on the

screen. Saura also takes advantage of the evocative quality of music by playing it while shooting his scenes in order to establish the mood for the actors
portraying their roles. Rock songs, folk tunes, hymns, operas, and military
marches are all part of the eclectic mix Saura includes in his films. But as
with everything else he uses, Saura takes over the music and makes it his
own by manipulating it to suit his needs: the musical compositions may get
shortened, the measures repeated, the order of things changed, or a small
phrase of music can be taken out of a larger passage and used as a leitmotif
throughout a film. Music is part of the personal vision that Saura projects on
the screen through a collaboration of sound and image, creating what he
described to me as "a complex chorus."

During my interview with Saura in the summer of 2000 I was struck by
the sense of wonder that cinema still holds for him. "The imagination can
be explored in fantastic ways through film," he told me. Readers of this volume will have the opportunity to share in Saura's enthusiasm for cinema
through the various discussions he has had about his work since he career
began.

Although the material compiled here does not reproduce the exact words
that were exchanged between Saura and his interviewers, their original state-
ments have been translated as faithfully as possible into conversational
English. I wish to thank Paula Willoquet-Maricondi and Vernon A. Chamberlin for translating the French and German interviews, respectively. I myself
translated the Spanish ones. I also am greatly indebted to Margarita Lobo at
the Filmoteca Española Nacional in Madrid for making arrangements for me
to access materials not available in the United States. Without her help this
book literally would not have been possible. She, along with Miguel Soria,
Javier Herrera, Alicia Potes Vargas and Trinidad del Río Sánchez made each
day I spent in those archives as pleasant as they were productive. In addition,
I'm grateful to Butler University for the research grants that allowed me to
travel to Spain. My thanks also go to my friend and colleague Wayne C.
Wentzel for the countless hours he spent answering my questions about the
music in Saura's films, to Florence Redding Jessup for using her retirement in
Spain to perform the many and varied tasks I requested of her over the course
of this project, and to Antonio Menéndez-Alarcón and Francisco Sánchez
Roca for helping me to translate some particularly difficult political terminology and slang expressions. I also want to acknowledge the guidance provided by Peter Brunette and Anne Stascavage from the University Press

of Mississippi. Furthermore, the assistance I received from my husband, Stephen Asunto, in the preparation of my manuscript was invaluable. Finally, I wish to express my appreciation to Carlos Saura for taking the time to meet with me in Madrid for the delightful conversation that is recorded in this book.

CHRONOLOGY

1932 Carlos Saura Atarés is born on January 4 in Huesca, Spain. His father, Antonio, is secretary to the Minister of Finance and his mother, Fermina, is a concert pianist. He is the second of four children, including an older brother, Antonio, and two younger sisters, María del Pilar and María de los Angeles.

1936 At the outbreak of the Spanish Civil War Saura and his family are living in Madrid, where they subsequently experience the aerial bombings of the city as well as the severe food and fuel shortages.

1938 Following the route of the Republican government, Saura's father moves with his family to Valencia and then to Barcelona.

1939 As soon as the war ends, Saura is sent to live with his maternal grandmother and aunts in Huesca while his parents and siblings return to Madrid. The conservative Catholic atmosphere of this household contrasts sharply with his previous liberal upbringing.

1941 Saura is reunited with his family in Madrid, where he soon becomes an avid movie fan, sometimes seeing several films—mostly American—in a single day.

1948 Saura's family buys a house in Cuenca to use as a summer residence.

1949 Saura completes his secondary education, and due to his aptitude in math and drawing, he decides to pursue a university degree in industrial engineering. He also develops an interest in photography.

1950   Saura performs his military service as an aviation volunteer.

1951   Exhibitions of Saura's photographs are held by the Royal Photographic Society of Madrid and by the city halls of Madrid and Cuenca.

1952   At the urging of his brother, Saura leaves his engineering studies to enroll in the I.I.E.C. national film school (Instituto de Investigaciones y Experiencias Cinematográficas). He also briefly enrolls in the School of Journalism. He buys a 16mm camera and plans to make a documentary about Madrid's annual pilgrimage of Saint Isidro, which would incorporate aspects of Goya's paintings. This project is abandoned.

1953   Saura exhibits his photographs in Madrid's Bucholz gallery as part of the "Tendencias" artists, a group which includes his brother. His photographs also are shown at the International Exhibition of Abstract Art in Santander and at the Exhibition of Fantastic Art in Madrid's Clan gallery. Saura develops an interest in literature and writing through his social contacts with such authors as Jesús Fernández Santos, Rafael Sánchez Ferlosio, Carmen Martín Gaite, and Ignacio Aldecoa.

1954   Saura is introduced to Italian neorealistic cinema during a week-long screening of films by Visconti, Antonioni, Germi, Fellini, and De Sica at the Italian Institute of Culture.

1955   Saura attends the politically-charged Conversations on National Cinema colloquium in Salamanca, where director Juan Antonio Bardem condemns Spanish cinema for being "politically futile, socially false, intellectually vapid, apathetically void, and industrially paralytic."- Saura makes a short documentary, *Flamenco*, showing his brother engaged in creating a work of Action Painting.

1957   With his medium-length film, *La tarde de domingo* [Sunday Afternoon], Saura earns his diploma from the I.I.E.C. with a specialization in directing. He is the only student to be approved for graduation for 1956–57. He is put on the faculty of the school, where he continues to give classes until 1964. He attends the Hispanic Cinema Meeting in Montpellier where he sees many of Luis Buñuel's films for the first time. He marries Adela Medrano. He is commissioned by the government of Cuenca to make a 10–15 minute documentary of the city and its province; he extends the length to 40 minutes and uses footage acquired over a year of shooting. The film receives an Honorable Mention at the 1958 San Sebastián Film Festival and the Silver Medallion at the 1959 Bilbao Festival.

1958   Saura's son, Carlos Saura Medrano, is born.

1959   Saura makes his first full-length feature film, *Los golfos* [Hooligans], which uses natural locations and a cast of largely nonprofessional actors. He appears uncredited in the final sequence as a spectator at the bullfight.

1960   *Los golfos* is presented at the Cannes Film Festival, where Saura meets Luis Buñuel. This is the beginning of a close friendship between the two men that will last throughout the remainder of Buñuel's life. At Saura's urging, Buñuel returns to Spain to make *Viridiana*. Saura's son, Antonio Saura Medrano, is born.

1961   Saura's directing career is temporarily halted by his association with the "*Viridiana* scandal" brought about by the Vatican's condemnation of the film as blasphemous.

1963   The Spanish government sets explicit censorship norms for the review and classification of Spanish films. Saura makes *Llanto por un bandido* [Lament for a Bandit], which is selected for the 1964 Berlin Film Festival.

1964   The Spanish government establishes a new "special interest" subsidy for high-quality cinema. Saura collaborates on the script for Mario Camús's *Muere una mujer* [A Woman Dies].

1965   Saura makes *La caza* [The Hunt], thereby beginning his long professional relationship with producer Elías Querejeta.

1966   Saura wins his first international award, the Silver Bear, at the Berlin Film Festival for directing *La caza*. While attending the festival, Saura meets Geraldine Chaplin.

1967   Saura makes *Peppermint frappé*, his first color film. This marks the beginning of a professional and personal relationship with Geraldine Chaplin that will last until 1979.

1968   *Peppermint frappé* is selected to be presented at the Cannes Film Festival, but Saura prevents it from being shown as a protest in solidarity with the "May of 68" French revolt. Saura wins the Silver Bear award at the Berlin Film Festival for directing *Peppermint frappé*. He makes *Stress es tres, tres* [Stress Is Three, Three], which is shown at the Venice Festival.

1969   Saura makes *La madriguera* [The Burrow], which is shown at the Berlin Film Festival.

1970   Saura makes *El jardín de las delicias* [The Garden of Delights], his first film with direct sound. Upon its completion, the film is banned by the censors and held by the Spanish government for seven months, during which time it receives invitations for the Cannes, Berlin, and Venice film festivals. Although Saura and Querejeta decline these invitations, they show the film illegally at the New York Film Festival, where it is critically acclaimed. Afterwards, Spanish censors allow the film to be shown domestically with some cuts.

1972   Saura makes *Ana y los lobos* [Ana and the Wolves], which is presented at the 1973 Cannes Film Festival.

1973   After numerous censorship problems, Saura makes *La prima Angélica* [Cousin Angelica], which provokes a strong negative reaction from both the right-wing press and the right-wing public. Theaters screening the film in Madrid and Barcelona are subjected to street protests, disruptive behavior during performances, stink bombs, a failed attempt to steal a copy of the film, and a fire causing extensive property damage. The selection of *La prima Angélica* for the 1974 Cannes Film Festival further fuels protests.

1974   Saura receives the Jury Prize at the Cannes Film Festival, awarded to him personally rather than to *La prima Angélica*. Shane, Saura's son with Geraldine Chaplin, is born.

1975   Saura makes *Cría cuervos* [Raise Ravens], in the months preceding Franco's death. It is the first of Saura's films to be written exclusively by him. It is chosen for the 1976 Cannes Film Festival, where it wins the Special Grand Jury Prize. It also receives a 1977 César nomination for Best Foreign Film.

1976   Saura makes *Elisa, vida mía* [Elisa, My Life]. Fernando Rey wins the Best Actor Award at the 1977 Cannes Film Festival for his performance in this film.

1977   Government censorship is abolished by Royal decree. Saura is a member of the Bertrand Russell Tribunal in Madrid, which documents accounts of political torture in South America. Saura's son Antonio is attacked and beaten by right-wing youths.

1978   Saura makes *Los ojos vendados* [Blindfolded Eyes], which is presented at the Cannes Film Festival.

1979   Saura makes a comedy, *Mamá cumple 100 años* [Mama Turns One Hundred], for which he receives his first Oscar nomination. The film wins the Silver Shell award at the San Sebastián film festival.

1980   Saura makes *Deprisa, deprisa* [Hurry, Hurry], which wins the Golden Bear award at the 1981 Berlin Film Festival. Manuel, Saura's son with Mercedes Pérez, is born.

1981   Saura makes the first of his dance films, *Bodas de sangre* [Blood Wedding], which is presented at the Cannes Film Festival. He also makes *Dulces horas* [Sweet Hours], his last film with Elías Querejeta.

1982   Saura makes *Antonieta*, his first film shot outside of Spain. Saura marries Mercedes Pérez.

1983   Saura makes what will become the most internationally successful film of his career: *Carmen*. In addition to receiving nominations for an Oscar, a Golden Globe, and a César, *Carmen* wins awards at various venues throughout the world, including the Best Foreign Film awards in England, Japan, and Germany, and two awards at the Cannes Film Festival: the Best Artistic Contribution Prize and the Technique Grand Prize.

1984   Saura makes *Los zancos* [The Stilts]. Fernando Fernán-Gómez wins the Special Critic's Prize at the Venice Film Festival for his performance in this film. Along with Antonio Gades, Saura mounts a theatrical version of *Carmen*, which premieres in Paris. Adrián, Saura's second son with Mercedes Pérez, is born.

1985   Saura makes *El amor brujo* [Love, the Magician], which is presented at the 1986 Cannes Film Festival.

1986   The Academy of Motion Picture Arts and Sciences presents a tribute to Carlos Saura at the Samuel Goldwyn Theater in Beverly Hills, and UCLA holds a public film festival in conjunction with the event, screening all of Saura's films from *Los golfos* through *Los zancos* along with selected works by other Spanish directors. Saura also receives the Special Prize at the Montreal Film Festival for his flamenco trilogy.

1987   In Costa Rica Saura shoots *El Dorado*, the most expensive film to date in the history of Spanish cinema. It is selected for presentation at the 1988 Cannes Film Festival. Diego, Saura's third son with Mercedes Pérez, is born.

1989   Saura makes *La noche oscura* [The Dark Night].

1990   Saura makes *¡Ay, Carmela!*, which is nominated for fifteen Goya Awards (Spain's Oscar), winning thirteen of them, including Best Picture, Best Director, Best Actress for Carmen Maura, and Best Actor for Andrés Pajares. For their performances Carmen Maura and Andrés Pajares also win, respectively, the Best Actress Felix Award from the European Film Academy and the Best Actor Award from the Montreal Film Festival. Spain submits *¡Ay, Carmela!* to the Academy of Motion Picture Arts and Sciences for its Foreign Language Film Award, but it does not receive an Oscar nomination. Saura shoots *Los cuentos de Borges: El sur* [The Borges Tales: The South] in Argentina, a film made for Spanish television. Along with Antonio Gades, Saura mounts a theatrical version of *El amor brujo*—entitled *Fuego* [Fire]—that premieres in Paris.

1991   Saura and his brother collaborate on an opera production of *Carmen* in Stuttgart, with Saura directing and Antonio—an internationally recognized artist of the Spanish vanguard—designing the sets. Saura makes *Sevillanas*, a documentary commissioned by EXPO'92. He is honored by the King and Queen of Spain with the Gold Medal for Fine Arts.

1992   Saura shoots *Maratón* [Marathon], the official film of the 1992 Olympics in Barcelona. He receives the Spanish Film Academy's Gold Medal.

1993   Saura makes *Dispara* [Shoot, aka Outrage].

1995   Saura makes *Flamenco*. At the Montreal Film Festival Saura receives the Special Grand Prize of the Americas (along with Michelangelo Antonioni, Jean-Luc Godard, and Zhang Yimou). Anna, Saura's daughter with Eulalia Ramón, is born.

1996   Saura shoots *Taxi*, which receives a Special Jury Mention at the San Sebastián Film Festival. He also shoots *Pajarico* [Little Bird] for which he wins the Best Director Award at the 1997 Montreal Film Festival.

1997   Saura publishes his first novel, *Pajarico solitario* [Solitary Little Bird], upon which his film *Pajarico* was based. In Argentina Saura shoots *Tango*, for which he receives his third Oscar nomination. It is presented at the 1998 Cannes Film Festival, where it wins the Technique Prize for Vittorio Storaro.

1998   Saura's brother dies.

1999   Saura completes *Goya en Burdeos* [Goya in Bordeaux], which wins five Goya Awards in 2000, including Best Actor for Francisco Rabal. It also wins the Best Artistic Contribution Award at the Montreal Film Festival. For his work on this film Vittorio Storaro is named Cinematographer 2000 by the European Film Academy.

2000   Saura publishes his second novel, *¡Esa luz!* [That Light!], which is set in the period of the Spanish Civil War. A major exhibition of photographs taken by Saura between 1949 and 1962 is held at the Círculo del Arte cultural center in Barcelona.

2001   Saura premieres *Buñuel y la mesa del rey Salomón* (Buñuel and King Solomon's Table) at the San Sebastián Film Festival.

FILMOGRAPHY

1955
FLAMENCO, documentary
Director: **Saura**
Cinematography: **Saura**
Cast: Antonio Saura
16mm, color
8 minutes

1956
EL PEQUEÑO RÍO MANZANARES [The Little Manzanares River], documentary
INFIES (Spain)
Director: **Saura** (listed on the credits but not recognized by him because he only collaborated briefly on the project at the request of his professor Serrano de Osma)
Screenplay: Ignacio Aldecoa and **Saura**
Cinematography: Alfonso Nieva
35mm, color
9 minutes

1957
LA TARDE DEL DOMINGO [Sunday Afternoon], I.I.E.C. graduation film
Director: **Saura**
Screenplay: **Saura** (based on a story by Fernando Guillermo de Castro)

Cinematography: Enrique Torán
Production Design: José Antonio Marqués
Music: Rafael Martínez Torres
Cast: Isana Medel, Julia M. Butrón, Francisco Herrera, Carlos Polac, Soledad
Perucha, Leopoldo Anáis, Luis Marín, José María Ramonet, Rafael Vera, José
Marqués, and the collaboration of Carmen Lozano, María Carrero, Pilar
García Fauré
35mm, B&W
32 minutes

1958
CUENCA, documentary
Moro Studios (Spain)
Director: **Saura**
Screenplay: **Saura**
Cinematography: **Saura** and Antonio Alvarez with the collaboration of Juan
Julio Baena
Editing: Pablo G. del Amo
Music: M. Ramírez and J. Pagán
Cast: Francisco Rabal (narrator)
35mm, color
44 minutes

1959
LOS GOLFOS [Hooligans]
Films 59 (Madrid)
Producer: Pedro Portabella
Director: **Saura**
Screenplay: **Saura**, Mario Camús, and Daniel Sueiro
Cinematography: Juan Julio Baena
Production Design: Enrique Alarcón
Editing: Pedro del Rey
Music: Antonio Ramírez Angel and J. Pagán; "Petenera" performed on the
guitar by Perico el del Lunar
Cast: Manuel Zarzo (Julián), Luis Marín (Ramón), Oscar Cruz (Juan), Juanjo
Losada (Chato), Ramón Rubio (Paco), Rafael Vargas (Manolo), María Mayer
(Visi), Arturo Ors, Teresa González, Lola García, Angel Calero, Miguel

Merino, Carmen Sánchez, Maruja Lázaro, Abelardo Díaz Caneja, Francisco
Bernal
Premiere: July 7, 1962 (Madrid)
35mm, B&W
88 minutes (released at 72 minutes)

1963
LLANTO POR UN BANDIDO [Lament for a Bandit]
Agata Films (Madrid), Atlántica Cinematografía (Rome), Mediterranée Cin-
éma (Paris)
Producer: José Luis Dibildos
Director: **Saura**
Screenplay: **Saura** and Mario Camús
Cinematography: Juan Julio Baena
Production Design: Enrique Alarcón
Editing: Pedro del Rey
Music: Carlo Rustichelli; popular Spanish music adapted by Pedro del Valle
and performed by Rafael Romero and Luisa Romero
Cast: Francisco Rabal (José María "El Tempranillo"), Lea Massari (María Jeró-
nima), Philippe Leroy (Pedro Sánchez), Lino Ventura ("El Lutos"), Manuel
Zarzo ("El Sotillo"), Silvia Solar (Marquesa de los Cerros), Fernando Sánchez
Polack (Antonio), Antonio Prieto ("El Lero"), José Manuel Martín ("El
Tuerto"), Agustín González (Capitán Valdés), Venancio Muro (Jiménez),
Rafael Romero ("El Gitano"), Luis Buñuel (executioner), Antonio Buero Vallejo (magistrate), Rafael Azqueta (priest), Pablo Runyan (Lewis, the English
painter), José Hernández (boy)
Premiere: September 17, 1964 (Madrid)
35mm, color
95 minutes

1965
LA CAZA [The Hunt]
Elías Querejeta P.C.
Producer: Elías Querejeta
Director: **Saura**
Screenplay: **Saura** and Angelino Fons
Cinematography: Luis Cuadrado

Artistic Director: Carlos Ochoa
Editing: Pablo G. del Amo
Music: Luis de Pablo; "Tu loca juventud" by Huerta Navarro; "Snob ye ye" by C. Núñez de la Rosa; "Te veré" by Reguerio y Llorente; "Española, abanícame" by Morell y Ceratto
Cast: Ismael Merlo (José), Alfredo Mayo (Paco), José María Prada (Luis), Emilio Gutiérrez Caba (Enrique), Fernando Sánchez Polack (Juan), Violeta García (Carmen)
Premiere: November 9, 1966 (Barcelona)
35mm, B&W
93 minutes

1967
PEPPERMINT FRAPPÉ
Elías Querejeta P.C.
Producer: Elías Querejeta
Director: **Saura**
Screenplay: **Saura**, Rafael Azcona, and Angelino Fons
Cinematography: Luis Cuadrado
Artistic Director: Emilio Sanz de Soto
Production Design: Wolfgang Burman
Editing: Pablo G. del Amo
Music: Luis de Pablo; "El misterio de Elche" transciption by Oscar Esplá; "Peppermint frappé" performed by "Los Canarios"
Dedication: To Luis Buñuel
Cast: Geraldine Chaplin (Ana/Elena), José Luis López Vázquez (Julián), Alfredo Mayo (Pablo), Ana María Custodio (Julián's mother), Emiliano Redondo (Arturo), Fernando Sánchez Polack (patient), Janine Cordell (teacher)
Premiere: October 9, 1967 (Madrid)
35mm, color
92 minutes

1968
STRESS ES TRES, TRES [Stress Is Three, Three]
Elías Querejeta P.C.
Producer: Elías Querejeta
Director: **Saura**

Screenplay: **Saura** and Angelino Fons
Cinematography: Luis Cuadrado
Production Design: Emilio Sanz de Soto and Tadeo Villalba
Editing: Pablo G. del Amo
Music: Jaime Pérez
Cast: Geraldine Chaplin (Teresa), Juan Luis Galiardo (Antonio), Fernando Cebrián (Fernando), Porfiria Sanchís (aunt), Fernando Sánchez Polack (guard), Humberto Semper (boy), Charo Soriano
Premiere: November 4, 1968 (Madrid)
35mm, B&W
94 minutes

1969
LA MADRIGUERA [The Burrow]
Elías Querejeta P.C.
Producer: Elías Querejeta
Director: **Saura**
Screenplay: **Saura**, Geraldine Chaplin, and Rafael Azcona
Cinematography: Luis Cuadrado
Production Design: Emilio Sanz de Soto and Tadeo Villalba
Editing: Pablo G. del Amo
Music: Luis de Pablo
Cast: Geraldine Chaplin (Teresa), Per Oscarsson (Pedro), Emiliano Redondo (Antonio), Teresa del Río (Carmen), Julia Peña (Agueda), María Elena Flores (Rosa), Gloria Berrocal (aunt)
Premiere: July 15, 1969 (Madrid)
35mm, color
102 minutes

1970
EL JARDÍN DE LAS DELICIAS [The Garden of Delights]
Elías Querejeta P.C.
Producer: Elías Querejeta
Director: **Saura**
Screenplay: **Saura** and Rafael Azcona
Cinematography: Luis Cuadrado
Production Design: Emilio Sanz de Soto

Editing: Pablo G. del Amo
Music: Luis de Pablo; "Recordar" by Richard Witting and performed by
Imperio Argentina; "Concierto de Aranjuez" by Joaquín Rodrigo; "Alexander
Nevsky" by Sergei Prokofiev; "Fis e verays" performed by José Vivo Eggers
Dedication: To Geraldine
Cast: José Luis López Vázquez (Antonio), Francisco Pierrá (Don Pedro), Luchy
Soto (Luchy), Lina Canalejas (aunt), Julia Peña (Julia), Alberto Alonso (Tony),
Mayrata O'Wisiedo (nurse), Charo Soriano (actress), Esperanza Roy (Nicole),
José Nieto, Luis Peña, Antonio Canal, Eduardo Calvo, Ignacio de Paúl, and
Antonio Sánchez (Antonio's friends), Marisa Porcel (maid), Jamil Omar
(chauffeur), Luis de Pablo (organist), Geraldine Chaplin (communion guest),
Gloria Berrocal, the voice of Porfiria Sanchís
Premiere: November 5, 1970 (Madrid)
35mm, color
90 minutes

1972
ANA Y LOS LOBOS [Ana and the Wolves]
Elías Querejeta P.C.
Producer: Elías Querejeta
Director: **Saura**
Screenplay: **Saura** and Rafael Azcona
Cinematography: Luis Cuadrado
Production Design: Elisa Ruiz and Francisco Nieva
Editing: Pablo G. del Amo
Music: Luis de Pablo; "El misterio de Elche" transciption by Oscar Esplá; "El
dos de mayo" by Federico Chueca
Cast: Geraldine Chaplin (Ana), Fernando Fernán-Gómez (Fernando), José
María Prada (José), José Vivó (Juan), Rafaela Aparicio (mother), Charo Sori-
ano (Luchy), Marisa Porcel and Anny Quintas (maids), María José Puerta,
Nuria Lage and Sara Gil (girls)
Premiere: June 4, 1973 (Seville)
35mm, color
102 minutes

1973
LA PRIMA ANGÉLICA [Cousin Angelica]
Elías Querejeta P.C.

Producer: Elías Querejeta
Director: **Saura**
Screenplay: **Saura** and Rafael Azcona
Cinematography: Luis Cuadrado
Production Design: Elisa Ruiz and Francisco Nieva
Editing: Pablo G. del Amo
Music: "Rocío" by Rafael de León and Manuel L. Quiroga and performed by
Imperio Argentina; "Rosario de la aurora"; "Música de los romanos";
"Dolor" by Father José Antonio de San Sebastián; "El Señor es mi pastor";
"Change It All" by J. Fishman and A. Baldan Bembo
Dedication: To Oona and Charlie
Cast: José Luis López Vázquez (Luis), Lina Canalejas (Angélica), Fernando
Delgado (Anselmo), Lola Cardona (young Aunt Pilar), Encarna Paso (Luis's
mother), Pedro Sempson (Luis's father), María Clara Fernández de Loayza
(young Angélica), Julieta Serrano (nun), Josefina Díaz (Aunt Pilar), José Luis
Heredia (Felipe Sagún), María de la Riva (grandmother), Luis Peña (priest),
Marisa Porcel (maid), Antonio Canal (soldier), Trinidad Rugero (maid from
1936)
Premiere: April 29, 1974 (Madrid)
35mm, color
107 minutes

1975
CRÍA CUERVOS [Raise Ravens]
Elías Querejeta P.C.
Producer: Elías Querejeta
Director: **Saura**
Screenplay: **Saura**
Cinematography: Teo Escamilla
Production Design: Rafael Palmero
Editing: Pablo G. del Amo
Music: "Canción y danza No. 6" by Federico Mompou (mistakenly cited as
No. 5 in the film credits); "¡Ay, Maricruz!" by Valverde, León, and Quiroga
and performed by Imperio Argentina; "Porque te vas" by José Luis Perales
and performed by Jeanette
Cast: Ana Torrent (young Ana), Geraldine Chaplin (Ana/Ana's mother), Mónica Randall (Paulina), Florinda Chico (Rosa), Héctor Alterio (Anselmo), Ger-

mán Cobos (Nicolás), Mirta Miller (Amelia), Josefina Díaz (grandmother),
Conchita Pérez (Irene), Maite Sánchez (Maite)
Premiere: January 26, 1976 (Madrid)
35mm, color
107 minutes

1976
ELISA, VIDA MÍA [Elisa, My Life]
Elías Querejeta P.C.
Producer: Elías Querejeta
Director: **Saura**
Screenplay: **Saura**
Cinematography: Teo Escamilla
Production Design: Antonio Belizón
Editing: Pablo G. del Amo
Music: "Schiarazula Marazula" by Giorgio Mainerio; "Gnosienne No. 3" by
Erik Satie; "Fatal amour" from "Pigmalion" by Jean Philippe Rameau
Dedication: To Lucienne Mardore
Cast: Geraldine Chaplin (Elisa), Fernando Rey (Luis), Norman Brisky (Anto-
nio), Isabel Mestres (Isabel), Joaquín Hinojosa (Julián), Arancha and Jacobo
Escamilla (children), Francisco Guijar (doctor)
Premiere: April 4, 1977 (Madrid)
35mm, color
117 minutes

1978
LOS OJOS VENDADOS [Blindfolded Eyes]
Elías Querejeta P.C.
Producer: Elías Querejeta
Director: **Saura**
Screenplay: **Saura**
Cinematography: Teo Escamilla
Production Design: Antonio Belizón
Editing: Pablo G. del Amo
Music: 17th-century music by Henry Purcell; "Norma la de Guadalajara" by
Dámaso Pérez Prado; "La lirio" by León, Ochaita, and Quiroga and per-
formed by Conchita Piquer; Philip Green

Dedication: To my son Antonio
Cast: Geraldine Chaplin (Emilia), José Luis Gómez (Luis), Xabier Elorriaga (Manuel), Andrés Falcón (lawyer), Lola Cardona (aunt), Manuel Guitián (uncle), Carmen Maura (nurse), C.E.T. actors (theatrical group)
Premiere: May 18, 1978 (Madrid)
35mm, color
110 minutes

1979
MAMÁ CUMPLE CIEN AÑOS [Mama Turns One Hundred]
Elías Querejeta P.C.
Producer: Elías Querejeta
Director: **Saura**
Screenplay: **Saura**
Cinematography: Teo Escamilla
Production Design: Antonio Belizón
Editing: Pablo G. del Amo
Music: "El dos de mayo" by Federico Chueca; "Duet of Mignon and the Harpist" D. 877 by Franz Schubert; "Sevillanas de colores" by Manuel García and Manuel Garrido; popular Iranian music
Dedication: To Catherine and Alberto Portera
Cast: Geraldine Chaplin (Ana), Amparo Muñoz (Natalia), Fernando Fernán-Gómez (Fernando), Rafaela Aparicio (mother), Norman Brisky (Antonio), Charo Soriano (Luchy), José Vivó (Juan), Angeles Torres (Carlota), Elisa Nandi (Victoria), Rita Maiden (Solange), Monique Ciron (Anny)
Premiere: September 17, 1979 (Madrid)
35mm, color
95 minutes

1980
DEPRISA, DEPRISA [Hurry, Hurry]
Elías Querejeta P.C.
Producer: Elías Querejeta
Director: **Saura**
Screenplay: **Saura**
Cinematography: Teo Escamilla
Production Design: Antonio Belizón

Editing: Pablo G. del Amo
Music: "Ay, qué dolor"; "Caramba, carambita"; Me quedo contigo"; Yo le
pido al Dios del cielo"; "Hell Dance with Me"; "Gorgeous Things"
Dedication: To Merce
Cast: José Antonio Valdelomar (Pablo), José María Hervás Roldán (Sebas),
Jesús Arias Aranzeque (Meca), Berta Socuéllamos Zarzo (Angela), María del
Mar Serrano (María), Consuelo Pascual (Sol), Joaquín Escolá (doctor), Ives
Arcángel (guard), Andrés Falcón (cashier), Suzy Hannier, Ives Barsacq, Alain
Doutey, Matias Prats Jr.
Premiere: April 2, 1981 (Madrid)
35mm, color
99 minutes

1981
BODAS DE SANGRE [Blood Wedding]
Emiliano Piedra P.C.
Producer: Emiliano Piedra
Director: **Saura**
Screenplay: **Saura**, Antonio Gades, and Alfredo Mañas (adapted from a play
by Federico García Lorca)
Cinematography: Teo Escamilla
Production Design: Rafael Palmero
Editing: Pablo G. del Amo
Music: Emilio de Diego; "La nana"; "Ay, mi sombrero"
Choreography: Antonio Gades
Dedication: To Emma Penella
Cast: Antonio Gades (Leonardo), Cristina Hoyos (bride), Juan Antonio Jimé-
nez (groom), Pilar Cárdenas (mother), Carmen Villena (woman), Pepa Flores
"Marisol" (woman who sings), Pepe Blanco (man who sings), El Güito, Lario
Díaz, Enrique Esteve, Elvira Andrés, Azucena Flores, Cristina Gombau, Marisa
Neila, Antonio Quintana, Quico Franco, and Candy Román (wedding
guests), Emilio de Diego and Antonio Solera (guitarists), José Merce and
Gómez de Jerez (singers)
Premiere: March 9, 1981 (Madrid)
35mm, color
72 minutes

1981
DULCES HORAS [Sweet Hours]
Elías Querejeta P.C.
Producer: Elías Querejeta
Director: **Saura**
Screenplay: **Saura**
Cinematography: Teo Escamilla
Production Design: Antonio Belizón
Editing: Pablo G. del Amo
Music: "Recordar" performed by Imperio Argentina; "La Valse" by Maurice Ravel; "Symphonie Fantastique" by Hector Berlioz; Sonata in Re [D] minor opus [Longo] 423 by Domenico Scarlatti; "Sevillanas" performed on the guitar by Emilio de Diego; "Mírame" performed by Celia Gómez
Dedication: To my sisters Pilar and Angeles
Cast: Iñaki Aierra (Juan), Assumpta Serna (Berta/Teresa), Pablo Hernández (Juanico), Magdalena García (Martita), Alvaro de Luna (Uncle Pepe), Alicia Hermida (Aunt Pilar), Luisa Rodrigo (grandmother), Alicia Sánchez (maid), Pedro Sempson (father), Isabel Mestres (Marta), Clara Marín (Lucía), Antonio Saura (painter), Ofelia Angélica (Sofi), Jaques Lalande (Uncle Angelito), Marion Game (Amparo), Julián Thomast (Pablo)
Premiere: February 15, 1982 (Madrid)
35mm, color
106 minutes

1982
ANTONIETA
Gaumont, FR3 (Paris), Conacine (Mexico), Nuevo cine (Madrid)
Producer: Samuel Menkes, Benjamin Kruk, Pablo Buelna
Director: **Saura**
Screenplay: **Saura** and Jean-Claude Carrière (based on the novel by Andrés Henestrosa)
Cinematography: Teo Escamilla
Production Design: José Tirado and Benedict Beaugé
Editing: Pablo G. del Amo
Music: José Antonio Zavala; "Clair de lune" by Claude Debussy
Cast: Isabelle Adjani (Antonieta Rivas Mercado), Hanna Schygulla (Anna), Carlos Bracho (José Vasconcelos), Ignacio López Tarso (Vargas), Gonzalo Vega

(Manuel Lozano), Diana Bracho (Juana), Héctor Alterio (León), Bruno Rey
(Obregón), Fernando Balzaretti (secretary), Víctor Junco (Porfirio Díaz), José
Lavat (Antonieta's husband), Víctor Alcocer, Narcisco Busquets, Gustavo
Ganen, Fernando Palavicini, María Montano, George Belanger, Edward
Clark, Sylvie Favre, Claude Merlin, Guylene Péan, Carina Barone, Guy
Louret, François Marthouret
Premiere: October 21, 1982 (Madrid)
35mm, color
104 minutes

1983
CARMEN
Emiliano Piedra P.C.
Producer: Emiliano Piedra
Screenplay and Choreography: **Saura** and Antonio Gades (inspired by the
novella by Prosper Mérimée and the opera by Georges Bizet)
Director: **Saura**
Cinematography: Teo Escamilla
Production Design: Félix Murcia
Editing: Pedro del Rey
Music: Paco de Lucía; fragments of Bizet's opera "Carmen" sung by Regina
Resnik and Mario del Monaco; "El gato montés" by Manuel Penella; "Deja
de llorar" by Paco Cepero
Dedication: To Albert S. Larios
Cast: Antonio Gades (Antonio), Laura del Sol (Carmen), Paco de Lucía (Paco),
Cristina Hoyos (Cristina), Juan Antonio Jiménez (Juan/husband), Sebastián
Moreno (Escamillo), José Yepes (Pepe Girón), Pepa Flores "Marisol" (Pepa),
Gómez de Jeréz and Manolo Sevilla (singers), Antonio Solera, Manuel
Rodríguez, and Lorenzo Virseda (guitarists), Enrique Esteve, Antonio Quint-
ana, José Luna "Tauro," José Antonio Benítez, Ernesto Lapeña, Carmen Villa,
Rocío Navarrete, María Fernanda Quintana, Ana Yolanda Gaviño, María José
Gaviño, Stella Arauzo, Mayte España, Conchita España, María Jesús Pages,
Blanca Navarro, Angela Granados, María Jesús Sandoval, Sonia Camara, Mar-
garita Becerra, Esperanza Becerra, Carolina Becerra, Angela Santamaría, Julia
Guzmán, Mayte Saez, Mercedes Saez, Esther Montoro, Estrella Casero, Vivi-
ana Avila, María Lurasch, Teresa Vallejo, Carmen Losada, Victoria Boris,

María Magdalena, La Bronce, El Fati, Enrique Ortega, Diego Pantoja, Enrique
Pantoja, El Moro, Ciro, Diego Amaya
Premiere: May 6, 1983 (Madrid)
35mm, color
102 minutes

1984
LOS ZANCOS [The Stilts]
Emiliano Piedra P.C.
Producer: Emiliano Piedra
Director: **Saura**
Screenplay: **Saura** and Fernando Fernán-Gómez
Cinematography: Teo Escamilla
Production and Costume Design: Tony Cortés
Editing: Pablo G. del Amo
Music: "Por amor una doncella," "Qué hermosos ojos tienes tú Rahel," and
"Decidle a la morena" sung by Música Judeo-Española de Madrid; "Sin com-
pasión" played by Santa (rock group); "Quintet for strings opus 163" by Schu-
bert
Cast: Fernando Fernán-Gómez (Angel), Laura del Sol (Teresa), Antonio Band-
eras (Alberto), Francisco Rabal (Manuel), Amparo Soto (Laura), Enrique Pérez
(Cobos), José Yepes (secretary), Adriana Ozores (Mercedes), Willy Montesinos
(Revuelta), Jesús Sastre (mayor), Elisa Molina, Rafael López, Javier Jiménez,
Ricardo Solanes, and Ramón García (stilts group), Charo Barragán, Elena Barragán, Virginia Ceruelo, Ana María Mengiano (children)
Premiere: October 15, 1984 (Madrid)
35mm, color
95 minutes

1986
EL AMOR BRUJO [Love, the Magician]
Emiliano Piedra P.C.
Producer: Emiliano Piedra
Director: **Saura**
Screenplay and Choreography: **Saura** and Antonio Gades (based on the bal-
let by Manuel de Falla)
Cinematography: Teo Escamilla

Production and Costume Design: Gerardo Vera
Editing: Pedro del Rey
Music: Manuel de Falla performed by Rocío Jurado and the National Orchestra of Spain directed by Jesús López Cobos
Cast: Antonio Gades (Carmelo), Cristina Hoyos (Candela), Laura del Sol (Lucía), Juan Antonio Jiménez (José), Emma Penella (Aunt Rosario, the sorceress), La Polaca (shepherdess), Gómez de Jerez (El Lobo), Enrique Ortega (José's father), Diego Pantoja (Candela's father), Giovana (Rocío), Candy Román (good-looker), Gómez de Jerez and Manolo Sevilla (singers), Antonio Solera, Manuel Rodríguez, and Juan Manuel Roldán (guitarists), Antonio Gades's dance company, "La Mosca," "Azúcar Moreno"
Premiere: March 23, 1986 (Madrid)
35mm, color
100 minutes

1987
EL DORADO
Iberoamericana (Madrid) Chrysalide (Paris)
Producer: Andrés Vicente Gómez
Director: **Saura**
Screenplay: **Saura**
Cinematography: Teo Escamilla
Production Design: Terry Pritchard
Editing: Pedro del Rey
Music: Alejandro Massó; based on sources from the Spanish Renaissance and on the following works: "Recercada sobre un madrigal italiana" by Diego Ortíz, "Orchésographie" by Thoinot Arbeau, "Hotus Conclusus" by Rodrigo Ceballos, "Duélate de mí, señora" by Miguel de Fuenllana, "Paseábase el rey moro" by Luis de Narvaez, arrangement for vihuela by Narvaez of Joaquín des Prez's "Mille Regretz," Prelude to act 3 of "Tristan und Isolde" by Richard Wagner, "No la debemos dormir" from the Canionero de Uppsala, "Tres morillas me enamoraron" from the Concionero de Palacio, and a Basque folk lullaby
Dedication: To Carmen Rico-Godoy
Cast: Omero Antoniutti (Aguirre), Lambert Wislon (Ursúa), Eusebio Poncela (Guzmán), Gabriela Roel (Inés), Inés Sastre (Elvira), José Sancho (La Bandera), Patxi Bisquet (Pedrarias), Francisco Algora (Llamoso), Feodor Atkine (Mon-

toya), Abel Vitón (Henao), Paco Merino (Alonso de Esteban), Mariano González (Zalduendo), Gladys Catania (Juana), David González (Munguía), Alfredo Catania (Vargas), Luis Fernando Gómez (García de Arce), Rodolfo Cisneros (Duarte), Gerardo Arce (Valcázar), Manuel Ruiz (Juna Corzo), Adrián Díaz (Miranda), José Solano (surgeon), Gustavo Rojas (Carrión), Aidée de Lev (Spanish woman), Franklin Huezo (guitarist), Rubén Pagura (minstrel), Wilson Morera (Uracuru)
Premiere: April 20, 1988 (Madrid)
35mm, color
149 minutes

1989
LA NOCHE OSCURA [The Dark Night]
Iberoamericana (Madrid) and La général d'images (Paris)
Producer: Andrés Vicente Gómez
Director: **Saura**
Screenplay: **Saura**
Cinematography: Teo Escamilla
Production Design: Gerardo Vera
Editing: Pedro del Rey
Music: Johann Sebastian Bach
Cast: Juan Diego (Saint John of the Cross), Julie Delpy (Ana de Jesús/the Virgin), Fernando Guillén (jailer), Manuel de Blas (prior), Fermín Reixach (Brother Jerónimo Tostado), Adolfo Thous (Brother María), Abel Vitón (Brother Jacinto), Francisco Casares (Brother José), Marielena Flores (mother superior)
Premiere: February 23, 1989 (Madrid)
35mm, color
93 minutes

1990
¡AY, CARMELA!
Iberoamericana (Madrid) and Ellepi (Rome) with the participation of TVE
Producer: Andrés Vicente Gómez
Director: **Saura**
Screenplay: **Saura** and Rafael Azcona (Based on the play by José Sanchís Sinisterra)

Cinematography: José Luis Alcaine
Production Design: Rafael Palmero
Editing: Pablo G. del Amo
Music: Alejandro Massó
Cast: Carmen Maura (Carmela), Andrés Pajares (Paulino), Gabino Diego
(Gustavete), Maurizio di Razza(Lieutenant Ripamonte), Miguel A. Rellán
(deputy treasurer), Edward Zentara (Polish official), Mario de Candia (Bruno),
José Sancho (artillery captain), Antonio Fuentes (artillery second lieutenant),
Mario Martín (political boss), Chema Marzo (mayor), Silvia Casanova and
Alfonso Guirao (prisoners), Felipe Vélez (doctor)
Premiere: March 16, 1990 (Madrid and Barcelona)
35mm, color
102 minutes

1990
LOS CUENTOS DE BORGES: EL SUR [The Borges Tales: The South]
Aries Cinematográfica Argentina S.A.
Producer: Víctor Albarrán
Director: **Saura**
Screenplay: **Saura** (Based on a short story by Jorge Luis Borges)
Cinematography: José Luis Alcaine
Artistic Director: Emilio Basaldua
Cast: Oscar Martínez (Juan Dalhmann), Nini Gambier (Doña Rosario Flores),
Alexandra Davel (Sara Dalhmann), Gerardo Romano (Carlos Manchón/assas-
sin), Juan Leyrado (Sergio), Arturo Bonin (Casiano), Villanueva Cosse (Don
Alejandro), Jorge Marrale (Guillermo Brige), Carlos Thiel (Santiago Fischb-
ein), Luis Tasca (doctor/owner), Guillermo Sosa (Matías/doorman), Olga
Bruno (Manuela), Cástor Durán (Bertini), Alejandro Colunga (Celia), Nilda
Raggi (Anita), Ana Beltrán (elderly woman in the cemetery), Adolfo Guiraldes
(old gaucho), Patricio Gago, Lorenzo Guiraldes
35mm, color
55 minutes

1991
SEVILLANAS
Juan Lebrón Producciones (Sevilla)
Producer: Juan Lebrón

Director: **Saura**
Screenplay: **Saura**
Cinematography: José Luis Alcaine
Production Design: Rafael Palmero
Editing: Pablo G. del Amo
Music: Manolo Sanlúcar
Cast: Manolo Sanlúcar, Paco de Lucía, Rocío Jurado, Lola Flores, Camarón de la Isla, Manuel Pareja Obregón, Paco Toronjo, Los Romeros de la Isla, Salmarina, Las Corraleras, Merche Esmeralda, Manuela Carrasco, Matilde Coral, Rafael "El Negro," Carlos Vilán
Premiere: April 27, 1992 (Seville)
35mm, color
52 minutes

1992
MARATÓN [Marathon], documentary, official film of the Barcelona Olympics
Ibergroup Producciones Cinematográficas
Producer: Andrés Vicente Gómez
Director: **Saura**
Cinematography: Javier Aguirresarobe, Miguel Icaza, Carles Cabecerán, Alfredo Mayo, Josep María Civit, José Luis López-Linares
Editing: Pablo G. del Amo
Music: Alejandro Massó and Ryuchi Sakamoto
35mm, color
120 minutes

1993
DISPARA [Shoot] (known in English subtitled or dubbed versions as *Outrage*)
Arco Films (Madrid), 5 Films (Valencia), Metro Films (Rome)
Producers: Jaime Comas and Galliano Juso
Director: **Saura**
Screenplay: **Saura** and Enzo Monteleone (based on the story by Giorgio Scerbanenco)
Cinematography: Javier Aguirresarobe
Production Design: Rafael Palmero
Editing: Juan Ignacio San Mateo

Music: Alberto Iglesias
Cast: Francesca Neri (Ana), Antonio Banderas (Marcos), Walter Vidarte (Manuel), Eulalia Ramón (mother), Coque Malla (Juan), Chema Mazo (father), Concha Leza (doctor), Achero Mañas, Rodrigo Valverde, Daniel Poza
Premiere: October 1, 1993 (Madrid)
35mm, color
100 minutes

1995
FLAMENCO
Juan Lebrón Producciones (Sevilla)
Producer: Juan Lebrón
Director: **Saura**
Screenplay: **Saura**
Cinematography: Vittorio Storaro
Production Design: Rafael Palmero
Editing: Pablo G. del Amo
Music: Isidro Muñoz
Cast (listed by musical number):1. Isidro Muñoz; 2. Moralito Chico, Antonio Jero, La Paquera, Fernando de la Morena; 3. Merche Esmeralda, José A. Rodríguez, El Portugués, Pepe de Lucía; 4. Diego Carrasco, Manolo Sanlúcar, Juan C. Romero; 5. Joaquín Cortés, Juan P. Muñoz, Fernando Anguita, Pedro Antón; 6. C. Moneo, Mario Maya, Antonio Vargas, Israel Galván; 7. Antonio Toscano, José A. Rodríguez, Juan C. Romero; 8. Fernanda de Utrera, Paco del Castor; 9. José Menese, María Pagés, José A. Rodríguez; 10. Enrique Morente, Juan Manuel Cañizares; 11. Manuela Carrasco, José Mercé; 12. Farruco Farruquito, Chocolate, R. Amador; 13. Carmen Linares, Rafael Riqueni; 14. Juan la del Revuelto, Remedios Amaya, Aurora Vargas, Quique Paredes, Martín Chico; 15. La Macanita, Juan Parrilla, Niño Jero; 16. Lole, Manuel; 17. Matilde Copral and her school, Rancapino, Chano Lobato, Paco Jarana; 18. Paco de Lucía, Ramón de Algeciras, Pepe de Lucía, Carlos Benavent, Jorge Pardo, Rubén Danta, El Grilo; 19. Polito, Duquende, Tomatito, El Cirilo, Belén Maya; 20. Manzanita, Antonio Carmona, Juan J. Carmona, José Miguel Carmona, Carlos Ruiz, Javier Benegas.
Premiere: June 15, 1995 (Madrid)
35mm, color
102 minutes

1996
TAXI
Filmart (Madrid)
Producers: Javier Castro and Concha Díaz
Director: **Saura**
Screenplay: Santiago Tabernero
Cinematography: Vittorio Storaro
Production Design: Juan Botella
Editing: Julia Juániz
Music: Manu Chao; "Pena penita" and "Un amor" by the Gypsy Kings; "El cachorro me dijo"; "Get It Up"; "Tus labios"
Cast: Carlos Fuentes (Dani), Ingrid Rubio (Paz), Agata Lys (Reme), Angel de Andrés López (Velasco), Eusebio Lázaro (Calero), Francisco Maestre ("Niño"), Maite Blasco (Paz's mother), Francisco Boira (Francis)
Premiere: October 11, 1996 (Madrid)
35mm, color
108 minutes

1997
PAJARICO [Little Bird]
Filmart (Madrid)
Producers: Javier Castro and Concha Díaz
Director: **Saura**
Screenplay: **Saura**
Cinematography: José Luis López-Linares
Production Design: Rafael Palmero
Editing: Julia Juániz
Music: Alejandro Massó
Dedication: To Lali and Anna
Cast: Alejandro Martínez (Manu), Dafne Fernández (Fuensanta), Francisco Rabal (grandfather), Manuel Bandera (Uncle Juan), Eusebio Lázaro (Uncle Fernando), Juan Luís Galiardo (Uncle Emilio), María Luisa San José (Aunt Beatriz), Violeta Cela (Aunt Lola), Eulalia Ramón (Aunt Margarita), Paulina Gálvez (Aunt Marisa), Eva Murciel (Loli), Israel Rodríguez (Emilín), Rebeca Fernández (Amalia), Andrea Granero (Sofía), Iker Ibañez (Loli's boyfriend), Borja Elgea (Toni), Rafael Alvarez, "El Brujo" (tramp), Alfredo Zamora (stout man), Cristina Espinosa (Martita), Laura Inclán (Celia), Sonia Castilla (Rocío), Beatriz Sánchez (Maruja), María Esther Fernández (employee)

Premiere: October 16, 1997 (Murcia)
35mm, color
104 minutes

1998
TANGO
Argentina Sono Film, Alma Ata International Pictures (Madrid), and Astro-labio Producciones (Madrid)
Producers: José María Calleja de la Fuente, Alejandro Bellaba, Luis A. Scalella, Carlos L. Mentasti, and Juan C. Codazzi
Director: **Saura**
Screenplay: **Saura**
Cinematography: Vittorio Storaro
Production Design: Emilio Basaldúa
Editing: Julia Juániz
Music: Lalo Schifrin
Choreography: Juan Carlos Copes, Carlos Rivarola, Ana María Stekelman
Cast: Miguel Angel Solá (Mario Suárez), Cecilia Narova (Laura Fuentes), Mía Maestro (Elena Flores), Juan Carlos Copes (Carlos Nebbia), Carlos Rivarola (Ernesto Landi), Sandra Ballesteros (María Elman), Juan Luis Galiardo (Angelo Larroca), Julio Bocca (himself), Enrique Pinti (Sergio Lieman), Oscar Cardozo Ocampo (Daniel Stein)
Premiere: September 25, 1998 (Madrid)
35mm, color
115 minutes

1999
GOYA EN BURDEOS [Goya in Bordeaux]
Lolafilms (Madrid) and Italian International Film
Producer: Andrés Vicente Gómez and Fulvio Lucisano
Director: **Saura**
Screenplay: **Saura**
Cinematography: Vittorio Storaro
Production Design: Pierre-Louis Thèvenet
Editing: Julia Juániz
Music: Roque Baños; "Nocturne" for cello and orchestra by Piotr Illich Tchaikovsky; "Les Tambourins" by François Couperin; music by Luigi Boccherini

including "Fandango" from Quintet G 341 Opus 40 no. 2 (mistakenly cited as Opus 37 in the film credits) and Minuetto" from String Quintet G 275 Opus 13 no. 5; "No hay que decirle el primor"
Dedication: To my brother Antonio
Cast: Francisco Rabal (Francisco de Goya), José Coronado (young Goya), Dafne Fernández (Rosario), Maribel Verdú (Duchess of Alba), Eulalia Ramón (Leocadia Zorrilla de Weiss), Joaquín Climent (Moratín), Cristina Espinosa (Pepita Tudó), Paco Catalá (Asensio), Mario de Candia (Bayeu), José María Pou (Godoy), Saturnino García (priest/Saint Anthony), Franco di Francescantonio (doctor); José Antonio (dancer), Carlos Hipólito (Juan Valdés), Emilio Gutiérrez Caba (José de la Cruz), Manuel de Blas (Salcedo), Pedro Azorín (Braulio Poc), Joan Valles (Novales), La Fura dels Baus group performing the disasters of war sequence
Premiere: November 12, 1999 (Madrid)
35mm, color
104 minutes

2001
BUÑUEL Y LA MESA DEL REY SALOMÓN [Buñuel and King Solomon's Table]
Rioja Films, Centre Promotor de la Imatge (CPI), Castelao Productions (Filmax), Road Movies (Germany), Altavista Films (Mexico)
Producer: José Antonio Romero
Director: **Saura**
Screenplay: **Saura** and Agustín Sánchez Vidal
Cinematography: José Luis López-Linares
Production Design: José Hernández
Editing: Julia Juániz
Music: Roque Baños
Cast: Gran Wyoming (old Luis Buñuel), Pere Arquillué (young Luis Buñuel), Ernesto Alterio (Salvador Dalí), Adriá Collado (Federico García Lorca), Amira Casar (Carmen/Fátima), Valeria Marini (Ana María de Zayas), Jean Claude Carrière (Producer Goldman), Armaando De Razza (Bishop Avendaño), Juan Luis Galiardo (critic)
Premiere: September 29, 2001 (San Sebastián)
35mm, color
105 minutes

CARLOS SAURA

INTERVIEWS

From Black Spain to Silver Bears: Part One

AUGUSTO M. TORRES AND
VICENTE MOLINA-FOIX / 1968

NUESTRO CINE: *You left the I.I.E.C (Instituto de Investigaciones y Experiencias Cinematográficas/National Film School) in 1957 and as your final school project you made a short film named* Tarde de domingo *[Sunday Afternoon], which to me is reminiscent of the famous scene in* Umberto D *where the maid spends a long time in the kitchen doing her chores. Are you familiar with* Umberto D? *To what extent did it influence you?*

CARLOS SAURA: I had seen it, but many years before. It was very important for me to do this project, although I didn't feel very close to its subject matter. I was pretty lost. I came from the world of photography—I was a photographer—and I had a very aesthetic and very Eisensteinian view of film, which came from the unfortunate instruction given at the I.I.E.C. at that time, where all they told you about were Pudovkin, Dovjenko, Eisenstein—people I admire a great deal, but in a different way. I remember that I had imagined making something very different, a film based on a narrative by William Irish, something a bit Hitchcockian, which I really wanted to do at the time and which I would have done well because I would have worked out its mechanics; but Eduardo Ducay, who then was a critic for various magazines, convinced me that there was a closer world, that I should look around me. He did me a great favor because if I hadn't done *Tarde de domingo*, I would have done something other than *Los golfos* [Hooligans]. It's very basic, very clumsy. I haven't seen it again, nor do I have the desire to do so.

From *Nuestro cine* 88 (1969): 27–34. Translated from Spanish by Linda M. Willem.

NC: *At the same time, on your own, you made* Cuenca, *which in a way is the beginning of the series of documentaries that were made during those years about Spanish towns. What do you think of it now?*

CS: Now, I don't know because time passes very fast, but at the time it could have meant something in Spain because it was, really, the extremely honest vision of a man—me—who didn't know anything about film and who traveled around the province of Cuenca for a year with a camera in his hand gathering whatever seemed to be the most significant. It was a backlash against the kind of documentary that was being made at the time— architectural documentaries speaking of the grandeur of Spain—although it does have rocks, monuments, and that type of thing in it too. What I was interested in was, first, showing what life was like for the people of the province at different levels of labor, and then, to criticize this type of documentary about stones. It was to say, "It's 1957 and Spain doesn't have anything to do with those documentaries about the greatness of Spain, the Empire, and all that." In a small way it was part of the destruction of that myth of the Spanish Empire, which we still are living with.

NC: *In 1959 you made* Los golfos *with a group of people who had just left the I.I.E.C. and who soon afterwards went their separate ways. At that time, what importance did that group have?*

CS: It was a tremendous time when a group of young people, primarily from the I.I.E.C., got together entirely out of enthusiasm. The whole group was formed before the meeting with Pedro Portabella, the producer, which was completely fortuitous because he came from Barcelona and had nothing to do with us. The vicissitudes were tremendous because the script—that Mario Camus, Daniel Sueiro, and I wrote and which at the time seemed like something monstrous—was banned four times and was nearly impossible to do. Finally, tired of our insisting so much, they told us, "Do whatever you want, and then we'll do the cutting." We did it out of enthusiasm, with very little money, with a camera in hand, and lots of improvising.

NC: *In the years immediately following the making of* Los golfos, *this film was talked about in terms of Italian cinema, of neorealism. That's how we saw it then, but now that surprises me a lot because, apart from it still seeming very lively to me, rather than being neorealistic, it reminds me—to a certain extent and imported to Spain—of* A bout de souffle *[Breathless], from the same year, and of that whole style that came from Renoir's realism.*

C S : It doesn't have anything to do with Italian neorealism. I feel that many critics got that wrong. It started with some vaguely neorealistic suppositions, because it's a movement that left its mark on all of us in Spanish cinema today, in one way or another. I didn't want to make a neorealistic film. If anything, in a way it's a romantic film. When I went to Paris to do the subtitling, *A bout de souffle* had just premiered. I already had my film finished for some time, and it left me quite surprised. I can assure you, although it's silly to say so, that many of the things that Godard had done in the editing were things I had thought about but hadn't dared to do. I have an article by Sadoul that compares *A bout de souffle* with *Los golfos* and says that the way that the sequences are cut is absolutely deliberate—to have them left in the air, without being resolved or explained—and that *Los golfos* was even more advanced than *A bout de souffle*. I don't think so. Karel Reisz, who saw it in Mar del Plata, wrote me a terrific letter saying that it was one of the few films he had seen in his whole life whose editing had captured his attention. Many things were done through intuition, and others because I wanted a very loose film. It's not a neorealistic film because it's too subjective to be so—I like to make things subjective—it isn't an objective treatment of reality.

N C : *In commercial terms* Los golfos *was a failure, and in addition, the* Viridiana *incident occurred soon afterwards, so for a year you found yourself in a very difficult environment where you could not work. What did you do at that time?*

C S : I wrote two scripts, one called *La boda* [The Wedding], which in some ways became the basis for *Peppermint frappé* even though it doesn't have anything to do with it, and the other, *El regreso* [The Return]. This script, which is an adaptation I did with Mario Camus of a novel named *Estos son tus hermanos* [These Are Your Brothers] by Daniel Sueiro, was a story that seemed wonderful to me at the time but which was foolish to try to make. It was about an exiled man who returned to Spain in those years.

N C : *At that time did you begin to give classes at the I.I.E.C.?*

C S : No, I began right away. No sooner did I end my studies than I was named an adjunct professor of acting, and after about two years I was a professor of directing.

N C :   *They say that as a professor you were very severe, that you didn't pass any-*
one. Is that true or just a myth?
C S :   It's a myth. It could be that I was very strict, although I don't think so,
because I always have taught what I know and at that time I didn't know
much about technical things. All I did was to try to orient the students. If I
was a little hard, it was because I was choosing among them. At that time
many people were entering the program, and the majority—then not now—
had a completely fantastic and idiotic idea about cinema. For them cinema
meant sleeping with the stars and that sort of thing.

N C :   Los golfos *was presented at Cannes, and there you met Buñuel, who was
presenting* La joven *[The Young One]. What did this mean for you?*
C S :   I became familiar with Buñuel's cinema at a kind of gathering held in
1957 in Montpellier that was called "First Meeting of Hispanic Film." I met
Sadoul, Pierre Billard, Thirard, and Marcel Oms—there, a great French
group—and I also saw *El* [This Strange Passion] and *Tierra sin pan* [Land
Without Bread] there. *El* impressed me a great deal; it seemed marvelous to
me. Since Buñuel is Aragonese and I'm Aragonese and the families more or
less know each other—I have distant family ties with Buñuel and friends had
always spoken of Buñuel as something incredible—when I saw him at
Cannes I took advantage of the situation to talk to him, and we have been
good friends ever since. It was there—with Pedro Portabella I think—that we
convinced him to come back. I don't know if we were being presumptious or
not. Despite his enormous desire to return to Spain, he would not have come
back to make *Viridiana* because he had certain reservations. We convinced
him by saying that it was extremely important for him to come back because
we really needed him. At that time he personally got along with us very well.
He realized that there was the possibility of a dialogue and that there was a
group of people who knew him and respected him.

N C :   *How did you end up doing* Llanto por un bandido *[Lament for a Bandit],
which is so different from* Los golfos *both thematically and financially?*
C S :   I was out of work for three or four years due to *Viridiana*. They banned
those two scripts, including *La boda*, which was being made ready to film,
practically with the promise of the D.G.C. (Dirección general de Cinemato-
grafía/Chief Administration of Film) that we could do it. But a week before,
even with the actors under contract, they said no. I found myself in the

position of not being able to do anything. I was researching a great many possibilities and topics, but since at that time it was impossible to deal with contemporary Spanish reality, Mario Camus and I hit upon the idea of transferring to it to another era, to another format that the censors could not ban, to make something about the bandit life of the 19th-century. We proposed it to a few producers who said no, and then Dibildos became interested and mounted it.

N C : *How did it occur to you to have Buñuel play the part of the hangman?*
C S : It was a very amusing idea, and it wasn't just that Buñuel was the hangman but also that the seven executioners were Bardem, Berlanga, Sastre. . . . The sequence was cut—just a few brief fragments remain—something that in my opinion was a catastrophe because the film began with a climate of violence, which it doesn't have now, and which justified the brutal and monstrous reaction of the character named "El Lutos" (Lino Ventura). With the disappearance of this sequence—which was marvelous—the justification of the character "El Tempranillo" (Francisco Rabal) and the presence of the bandits also disappeared.

N C : *Don't you think that the main flaw was the script, which was constructed so poorly that the ending was incomprehensible?*
C S : I think that it is a very difficult film. Sometimes I think that someday I'll make another film about bandits and about that Spanish era, because I feel passionate about it. There is a lot that could be said about the film. I'm not saying that the script was good, but I believe that in spite of it, the film could have been better. There were disputes concerning the production, above all with the Italians who, despite my resistance, made us put in a battle that had no reason being there and which wasn't well planned, and there were other last minute changes that they filmed against my will. There wasn't a big enough crew to make a film of such scope. We didn't have either the mechanical or economic means. Everything was made with an Arriflex and a five-meter dolly. Another thing was my inexperience. I, at least, wasn't prepared to stage battles and things like that and, besides, I wasn't at all interested in them. I had something lovely in mind—a static film, with immobile extreme long shots and an enormous clarity of definition—which would have given it something very different than what was done, I think.

But that all collapsed, first due to the CinemaScope and then with the lack of light and because of the battles, until in the end it was a disaster.

NC: *But it had some scenes—the night of the wedding, for example—that I remember were excellent.*

CS: Yes, I did achieve what I wanted to in the intimate scenes because there weren't any problems there, although I did have to fight to the death with the Italian editor in order to remove the extra shots that they made me do as part of the international co-production. I took all the shots that I could from a distance in order to view the characters moving in a very normal way out-side, and I didn't go to close-ups because I was thinking of doing it in almost immobile extreme long shots, with small corrections of the camera. And the last battle—which was only a skirmish due to our lack of resources—we filmed the way I wanted to, in a sequence-shot taken from a distance and composed of small actions. But it turned out badly because we would have needed a week of preparation and unfortunately that couldn't be done.

NC: *Up until that moment you had always collaborated with people from the initial small group from the I.I.E.C., but after this film you went your separate ways. Many of them moved to commercial cinema and you kept on doing what interested you. Was there some specific reason for this?*

CS: The trauma began when *Llanto por un bandido* wasn't going well. Dibil-dos was having problems in France with the co-production of another one of his films and he couldn't get French distribution. It still hasn't been screened for legal reasons. Then I had realized that I had made a film that wasn't of any use to me at all. It wasn't as if I could do it all over again. Films with horses and wars are done with lots of money or they aren't done at all. Then it occurred to me to do the complete opposite: to make something very basic. The beginnings of the idea about *La caza* [The Hunt] came to me on one of the sets of *Llanto por un bandido*. It was a set from the Civil War where there were some trenches. It was a hunting ground. I thought that I could stage a kind of hunt there among men who had gone to hunt rabbits. At that time it had more parallels with the Civil War, including a split between those who had gone to hunt: two in one camp and three in the other. Very basic. I spoke with Angelino Fons and he began to think about the possibility of making *La caza*, a very inexpensive film with very few characters. We began to write the script, we contacted Elías Querejeta, and we made *La caza* at a time when I truly didn't think I would make any more films in my life. I was on the verge of going into commercials or returning to photography because I couldn't take it anymore.

N C : *In the time between* Llanto por un bandito *and* La caza *the structural changes of 1962 occurred, through which José-Maria García Escudero was named General Director of Cinematography and Theater, which among other things caused the conversion of the I.I.E.C. into the E.O.C. (Escuela Oficial de Cinematografía/Official School of Cinematography), and you stopped giving classes. What exactly happened?*

C S : Truth be told, I was on the verge of resigning several times. The I.I.E.C. wasn't going where it should have. It wasn't interesting to me, but I put up with it both out of a weakness on my part and because the students asked me to stay. Then some opposition candidates for the professorships came forward. I completed the requirements that were asked of me, I presented myself, and as expected, I simply wasn't elected.

N C : *But they didn't elect either you, or Patino, or Picazo.*

C S : It didn't surprise me in the least. Really, I think that the election of professorships at that time was a perfect formula to lighten up the I.I.E.C. I know that some people who decided whom the professors would be said, "No, because Carlos Saura is the one to blame for the pessimism in young Spanish cinema." That was one of the reasons.

N C : *Would it have been possible to make* La caza *without the structural changes that brought about García Escudero's appearance?*

C S : It wouldn't have been made because we wouldn't have been able to propose such an idea to the previous Chief Director of Cinematography. You know that in a conversation with Miguel Picazo and me, when we were talking about our wanting them to let us do things, he said, "If you do it that way, we will be shooting each other in the streets again." I think that García Escudero has done more than anyone after the war for Spanish cinema. Yes, if the Spanish cinema ever makes something of itself historically or not, an analysis of the García Escudero period will show that without him nothing could have been done. At that time it was very risky to change Spanish cinema, and he did it. His faults and defects? Everyone has them.

N C : *Do you view his actions as a type of personal contribution or do you think that they were just convenient within the political situation of the time?*

C S : Yes, of course, things aren't only one way. If they named him, it was because they thought that he would be different from what was there before and that he would bring a different program. It could be that politics brought García Escudero to the position of Chief Director of Cinematography, but there is no doubt that he was personally disposed to do that much earlier. So, if he accepted a political post, he was ready to engage in politics. But since I believe that world cinema is unfortunately administered by people beyond our control, one hopes that they are intelligent, understanding and have good judgment. It's hard to ask for anything more.

N C : *Don't you think that the symbolic part of* La caza, *rooted in the Civil War, remains over and above the specifics?*

C S : No. We took out the allusions to the Spanish Civil War, and there had not been more than one or two in the script. We just left the word "war" because at the time we made *La caza* we didn't want to make a film about the Spanish Civil War. The basic idea had evolved quite a bit. Of course, there was the Spanish Civil War, but we wanted a broader meaning. I believe that we did it right because it was an enormous success, for example in the United States, where the allusions to the Spanish Civil War were much more remote, although some critic spoke a lot about it. I have talked with people who told me that the same thing could have happened if the hunters had gone through the Vietnam War. Naturally, it was made in Spain, it has Spanish characteristics, its characters are Spanish, and what I know about is Spain. But we deliberately took out direct allusions because that seemed to easy to us.

N C : *The film opens abruptly. It seems like you wanted to present the characters right away, making it very clear from the beginning who they are, in order to get on to more important things.*

C S : That's true, but there is a very simple explanation. Starting with *La caza* I decided to do something that I always felt like doing: to film in the order of the script, beginning with the first scene and ending with the last one. This has its advantages and its drawbacks. One of the disadvantages is that without any previous experience in the mechanics of narrative, you put too many things in the first scenes because you don't know if you'll be able to include them later. You are somewhat obliged, like in *La caza*, to explain the life of these men in a few words, so that they are very clear in the first four shots. Soon you realize that it is very easy to explain things little by little, in small doses. For me, the advantages are enormous because you can keep on developing the film while you are shooting it, and you can solve the problem of the actors. Let's not fool ourselves. Some Spanish actors are very good, but they lack experience. I'm always afraid to describe a character: "Julian is forty years old, is bald, and has big or small ears, eyeglasses, and a firm or cruel mouth, or whatever." That's what I hate more each day, but you do it because you have to present the script to the censor and the producer, and then you don't find the character in real life because it's a fabrication. You invented him and he doesn't exist. Then you say, "Who is going to be this character?" So and so. But if you do the film in script order, this gets lost right away. You have a man, who is also an actor, who is a certain type, who has a way of thinking, being, moving, and you can take advantage of it completely. You end up integrating into the character what the actor is in reality, or what he sees in the character. This seems perfectly valid to me because it is a way of getting an effective result from the actors while I'm following a path that is of interest to me.

N C : *In* La caza *a series of traits appear that were not in your previous films: burlesque elements and a type of indirect eroticism, still in their initial stages, which in* Peppermint frappé *become developed and serve as the film's foundation. Was* Peppermint frappé *the film that freed you from some things and one which you made by ignoring a series of constraints within the atmosphere of the middle class?*

C S : Although I never found myself guided by a definite orientation in this world, from *La caza* onwards, I found a series of elements that have worked well for me to this day. I could have made proletariat cinema. It has often concerned me. But I don't know that world. How could I go to a mine, for example, to make a film? It seemed very pretentious for me to spend a year in a mine, studying the problem carefully, and then deciding whether I should make it or not. On the other hand, since I am part of the bourgeois structure, I have a bourgeois family, I know the Spanish bourgeoisie. Why should I kill myself when with much less effort I can make films about the Spanish bourgeoisie, which in addition will be more valid? After *La caza* that became very clear to me. I realized that the Spanish bourgeoisie—and by

extension that of the world, and including the middle class—has a series of
fixed images: a medieval notion, concerning feelings, primarily held by men
towards women. It is that notion of woman as object, which fashion magazines show in a very clear way. "Elle," "marie claire," "Jour de France" and
"Vogue" sell more and more all the time. The veneration of modern things
is evident in consumerism: how objects begin to flood our lives. They dominate us to a certain degree, and we can't do without them. Each day we are
more and more surrounded by machines, and by objects. In this way, modern life is becoming a frightening chaos. These elements are of interest to me
because it is very clear that the technocrats—those men that dominate their
profession—have had or have inherited a more or less religious upbringing
in their personal lives. A series of moral taboos remain with them, as well as
an absurd notion about friendship or altruism, instilled in them by a traditional religious education: things are done to receive a reward. This is where
the idea of the French students, and of the whole world, comes from,
although it's only in its initial stages, that everything is bad in the times that
we are living. I don't know where it starts: morality that's individual, collective, or work-based. The behavior of man today is completely without right
or wrong. This is something that I see clearer every day, and which I began
to see a little in *La caza*, where the criticism is focused on those men from
the bourgeoisie who had made the war, and also I see it a bit in the objects.
In *Peppermint frappé* it's somewhat clearer because it contains the myth of the
women-object held by the traditional man with his religious notions and his
particular education. He can be a terrific doctor, but it doesn't let him get
away from this concept of the woman-object. And it's in *Stress es tres, tres*
[Stress Is Three, Three], which is more modern in this aspect because the
protagonists are young people: two thirty-year old guys and Geraldine—a
young married couple with a daughter and their friend. They are technocrats: one is an architect and the other is an industrialist. The same thing
happens to them both. They are incapable of resolving their petty emotional
conflicts and they are filled with unresolved friction that leads them to a
type of self-destruction. When the bourgeoisie, from Spain or anywhere, seriously wants to resolve these problems, it always ends in destruction, because
the solution, which is very difficult, would be to leave there or go to a completely opposite place, which almost no one ever does.

N C :   *Apart from this self-awareness about your possibilities concerning film, is there also a realization that the vocabularly you have used up until now is not in accord with the reality of the Spanish public that is going to see the films? Have you been using a postwar vocabulary that has been transcended, and are you trying to find a more current one?*

CS: Unfortunately, when I make a film, I can't think about the Spanish audience, because if I were to do so, I would make a type of cinema that perhaps would be much less mine. This may seem pretentious, or a form of vanity, but I believe that the director capable of speaking to the general public in Spain would be one who had a type of mystery in terms of popular vocabulary. But what a film director or a writer or a painter can't do is to try to get close to something, because if this involves a betrayal of his world, then the work turns out to be a hybrid and the director isn't going to be very satisfied with what he did. I think that Chaplin had this popular streak. He was born of the people and reached nearly everyone. If in addition he has an intellectual resonance, that's another matter entirely. I set up my cinema in a different way. I ask myself, "What problems can I show, do I know, and are of interest to me?" I only do films that interest me.

NC: *In your latest films, do you still use storyboarding, in the manner of Hitchcock or Losey, that you always used in the past?*

CS: I did it for the last time in *La caza*, although I didn't actually use it. That's something that normally is done when you're bored or when there's a particularly difficult scene that's in your head and you begin to sketch it in order to remember it. I have a very bad memory, but a terrific visual memory, so if I make sketches, I remember. At times I do it simply as a mental exercise. I think that it's a good thing to do at the beginning until you become secure in the mechanics and with yourself. I've always said how lovely it would be to make a script like that: to make a sketch and then write some dialogue, in a way that it could then be shot.

NC: *How can you explain that* Peppermint frappé *has been so successful in Spain, given the fact that it is your least clear film and one in which your presentation is more sophisticated?*

CS: I don't know. It could be because of Geraldine, or because of José-Luis López Vázquez, although basically what I think is happening is that there are many people like Julian, the protagonist. When I say that I make my own cinema, it isn't completely true because, logically, the things that are of concern to me also concern many people. We all know Julian. He is a subjectified character who is traumatized by a horrible religious and sexual upbringing. We are all familiar with this problem in Spain.

N C :   *Is the distant origin of* Peppermint frappé *in Unamuno's* Abel Sanchez?
C S :   Yes, there is a distant kinship. That script that I talked about earlier, *La boda*, is the beginning of *Peppermint frappé*, and it is based on *Abel Sanchez*.

N C :   *Don't you think that there is some relationship between* Vertigo *and* Peppermint frappé?
C S :   I showed the film to the guys at *Cahiers*, who liked it a lot I think, and they were all in agreement when they told me that it didn't have anything of Buñuel in it, but rather it was the direct descendent of Hitchcock. It was the first time I was told that. One of those guys, all of whom are very clever, I think it was Comolli, who had seen *Vertigo* some forty times, explained to me that there were two entire sequences, shot by shot, which were identical. I sincerely like Hitchcock very much. I had seen *Vertigo* many years before and I only remember a few individual things. It didn't bowl me over. I liked it, but I liked *Psycho* more. If there is any influence, it is on the subconscious level.

N C :   *Although it is an overly broad subject, what do you think about the current state of Spanish cinema?*
C S :   It continues to be terrifying. It's a very complex problem. I do think that there are directors, but many lack the decisiveness to make a personal work, so they stay in the middle of the road. There are exceptions, though, like Basilio M. Patino and Angelino Fons. But on the other hand, nothing changes: there are no producers, censorship doesn't evolve—another of Berlanga's scripts was just banned. All this has a monstrous effect. We require our directors to make a marvelous first film, when in Spain it is impossible to do so because there isn't any cultural preparation, no movement like the one that exists in France or England. I think that we will have to wait a long time for things to work out with Spanish film, if it ever does. We will calmly wait to see what happens, wait for more people to emerge, and wait for those who have made one or two interesting films to either reaffirm their personalities or go to the devil, something that could happen to any of us.

N C : *Don't you think that the only thing that's been achieved with the economic aid is that there are a series of films, directly financed by the state, which are exactly what it wants them to be?*

C S : Obviously, all state protections in all countries are a form of control. Now, between the possibility of getting financial subvention that permits one to make a film, or not having it, I don't know which one is right. If the state eliminates the subvention, the only solution would be for there to be complete freedom of expression, so that films would generate income for the producer and director. Without that compensation, I think that it is better that protection does exist because that way something can be done. The ideal would be for them not to exist, and also for there not to exist the kind of paternalism concerning what you can do, and since this is a capitalist country, for capitalist terms to be established, which I may not be in agreement with. If we are going to play around with this, let's do it in a competitive way, like everyone else in the world. Let's have the same freedom as in France or England. Let's be able to touch on political, religious, economic, and sexual problems.

N C : *And why don't you try to break away from this system?*

C S : That would be lovely to do within a strong movie industry, like the French one for example. Personally I'm willing to do it, but if five of us in Spain don't work as a protest, nothing at all will happen to Spanish cinema.

N C : *What about doing what the "Barcelona School" is timidly beginning to do: making productions without presenting the scripts to the censors or shooting them without authorization, like Jacinto Esteva did with* Después del diluvio *[After the Deluge], for example. If at some time it turns out that the films which the festivals ask for are not authorized, wouldn't that lead to a possible solution?*

C S : We need to move toward a solution, be it this one or another one, and we need to get greater freedom, or at least for things to be easier, so that we don't make films just for ourselves. But how can we do that? For me, that is the problem. At a personal level I can say, "I won't make films," but does that solve anything? I don't think so. What we should do is all agree on a series of things and present a program, but right now I don't see that as a possibility because the ideal thing would be to find a practical solution, like the French do, and not go to extremes, like we always do here. But the solutions that they give me never are any good; they are always infuriating. They tell me, "We have to move toward proletariat cinema; we need to give cameras to the workers; we need to make 16mm films; we need to get rid of the movie industry." And then I say, "That's monstrous." Ideally, a breaking away from taboos is good, but practically speaking, it can't be done. What is the solution? I think it could be found—although many professional people wouldn't like it—by saying, "Let's see why we have to depend on censorship and on state aid. Why can't we distribute our own films in another way?" But then we enter into a national problem, not just in terms of cinema, and that is where our solution would be linked to a collective national solution.

N C :   *But suppose, for example, that the script that you are now writing with Azcona is banned by the censors or is cut by 10 or 15 pages. Wouldn't it be better to confront the problem with the script completely filmed?*
C S :   But what would that solve?

N C :   *There is a big difference between presenting a script to the censors, or presenting a film directed by you, with all your fame, and which might also have won a prize at a festival.*
C S :   But let's begin at the beginning. No festival in the world is going to accept a film that isn't officially presented by its country. It's a very slippery and delicate problem. One time we tried it. A script was banned and we were all going to get together to form a protest, but there wasn't any way to do it. Right now I make the films that I want, within certain limits. I go to one festival or another. I may win a prize, or not, which really is very difficult, whatever happens. In Berlin, Orson Welles and Godard were there. It is very difficult to go to a festival and win a prize. They say, "What is happening is that they are using you to say that in Spain some people are making great films." Yes, I agree. This is a game that I can accept up to a point. Speaking selfishly, what is happening is that I can make my cinema. Then if, for example, they ban this script, I have two choices: bow my head and write another one, or say, "Good-bye, have a good day," and go to make it in England. Just today I received a call from Paramount to make this script in England.

New Interview with Carlos Saura on *La prima Angélica* [Cousin Angelica]

ENRIQUE BRASÓ / 1974

ENRIQUE BRASÓ : *How was* La prima Angélica *conceived? What exactly was its point of departure?*

CARLOS SAURA: The initial idea for *La prima Angélica* came from a specific reference to a "Cousin Angélica," in a scene from *Ana y los lobos* [Ana and the Wolves], and refers to the childhood of one of the characters. Let's say that this was the point of departure. For some time, I've been haunted by a series of images, scattered images, which little by little took the shape of a film. Some refer to sensations, to memories of events I personally experienced. Others are made up, and reflect my own preferences and choices.

EB: *How do these two types of images in the film operate in relation to each other? What is, in your opinion, the significance of this ongoing oscillation between two moments in Hispanic life, 1939 and 1973?*

CS: While reading Valle-Inclán, I came upon a phrase which became the key to the development of a structuring principle. It said: "Things are not as we see them, but as we remember them." This sentence resonated in me and gave the film its structure. Everything was possible. The possibilities of integrating those two types of images I mentioned above were immense: personal images in the form of war memories and invented images, projections of my consciousness and my dreams. The problem was to know how to integrate the two in a coherent narrative, that of a specific character who will move

From *Positif* 162 (1974): 32–34. Reprinted by permission. Translated from French by Paula Willoquet-Maricondi.

continuously and seamlessly from one period of time to another, without a mediating device, without resorting to the habitual "flashback," but rather showing a past which is constantly being recaptured and lived as a present. This speaks to the idea that events correspond more to the memory which we have of them than to the ways in which we experienced them.

E B :   *What role did Rafael Azcona play at this stage in the development of the script?*
C S :   Azcona and I've been working together for several years. We have made a number of films together, so there is a perfect understanding between us.

We grew up in similar worlds, in a way, and in relation to *La prima Angélica*, a film that is very representative of our generation—of those in their forties and fifties—it so happens that we have had similar experiences. Any Spaniard of our age group, from the middle class, who has had a strong religious upbringing and remembers all this well, will relate to these experiences.

E B :   *In* La prima Angélica, *one feels that 1936, the year of the Spanish Civil War, weighs on the year 1973. Is this weight the sign that something has endured, that the very image of the character in the film is anchored in the past?*
C S :   The war had a decisive influence, not only on those who lived through it—like us, who were children at the time (I was four when the war started)—but also on future generations, on those who were born after the war and who suffered its consequences, even though they did not experience it first hand. I'm talking not only about the consequences of an entire political system, an entire educational system which is repressive, but also of personal conflicts, of losses in the family (those who were executed, died in the war, or were sent into exile). There is no doubt that the Civil War has had an impact on today's generation, and that it still has an impact on their behavior and lifestyle, if nothing else because it marked their parents so terribly.

I think that Luis, the main character in my film, is someone who was profoundly touched by the Civil War. Personally, I never agreed with the widespread idea that childhood years are the golden years of one's life—maybe because of my own experience. On the contrary, it seems to me that childhood is a particularly uncertain period because, among other reasons, one's childhood is lived almost entirely in an in-between world, and unfolds in a world of great fears and great needs of all kinds. And all of that leaves

profound, indelible scars, particularly when one has to live in a hostile environment, like the main character in the film.

E B : *In a way, isn't the main character trying to find the past, to reconstruct this
past which has shaped his being, and at the same time trying to escape from it?*
C S : Certainly. My point of departure is that Luis is a character in crisis from
the beginning, which means he is open to any "possibility." When he
returns to the town to bury his mother who died twenty years earlier, there
is no doubt that consciously or not he returns to this place because he could
not have done otherwise. He comes to a point in his life when, after having
escaped his past, he is compelled to find himself in this past. He has to confront a portion of his life which, until then, he had tried to forget. So, on the
one hand, there is a slight denial of this past—at least, he makes no effort to
incorporate himself into the past. But, in the course of the film, the past will
increasingly impose itself on him, until he is fully dominated by it. The film's
narrative trajectory is such that while the present dominates in the first half,
Luis is consumed by his past at the end. The power of these ghosts, of these
figures from the past, of these events, and particularly of these visions and
memories is such that they end up devouring the character. There is even a
point when Luis tries to escape, to leave the city. But he can't.
    A doubling takes place, and this other image from the past, of himself in
the past, contains the key to his identity. So he comes back a second time in
order to discover it, take possession of it, and confront it.

E B : *There is something strange in* La prima Angélica, *which is that in spite of
the turbulent nature of this past, with all the sadness and bitterness of 1936, one
can feel that even at the stylistic level there is a greater fascination with this period
of time than with the present, 1973.*
C S : This was not planned; it happened unconsciously. But it makes sense
that, given the circumstances in which the film is set, the encounter with
the past is of greater significance for the hero than the present, the insignifi-
cant present of the countryside and of bland characters who have no interest
for him. Maybe it's because he has control over the present and he can
observe the familial setting from a certain distance, with a certain detach-
ment. On the other hand, it's the opposite in relation to his childhood: since
the events are beyond him, he cannot control them. He is completely domi-

nated. That's why he behaves in a way that is either more fearful or more passionate, as if under a spell.

E B :   *What censorship problems did you encounter in relation to your treatment of the Spanish Civil War from a 1973 perspective?*
C S :   I can truly say that with *La prima Angélica* I did what I wanted to do. Of course, I don't know what I could have done if there had been no censorship at all in Spain. Nonetheless, given that there is censorship in Spain and a whole set of limitations, it seems to me that the way I dealt with the war reflects my intentions: to evoke it from a child's perspective, according to his own understanding of the war. I remember being in Barcelona at the end of the war. Barcelona was a Republican zone. When Franco's troops arrived, I was very confused because the "good guys" became the "bad guys," and the "bad guys" were now the "good guys." I did not understand at all what was happening nor why. And this is what I've tried to show in the scene of July 18, the first day of the war, in the house in Segovia. I really didn't know what to make of it; I didn't understand what was happening.

E B :   *What about the underlying eroticism that begins to surface in the relationship between Luis the child and Angélica the mother?*
C S :   There is a doubling of the characters in the film: each character, except for Luis, has a double. First, the relationship between Luis the child and Angélica the child is clearly colored with eroticism, a nascent eroticism between two children—a nine and an eleven year old—which is free from exterior influences. But, since at the same time there is a relationship between the two adults, Luis and Angélica, things become complicated. That is, the eroticism between Luis, the adult, and Angélica, the child, refer more to the past (his memory) than to the present. On the other hand, relative to Angélica, the woman, Luis takes on a paternalistic attitude, never clearly erotic. Since no encounter with the present-day Angélica is possible, she becomes simply the means to recover the other Angélica, the Angélica child from the past who, in a sense, appears in the shape of the Angélica child of the present.

E B :   *To conclude, would you say a few words about the final scene? It departs from the way you customarily end your films, and in some ways it summarizes and explains the behavior of the four characters in relation to one another.*

C S :   The last scene was not scripted. I thought of it while shooting. Basically, it is one image; for a long time I had been haunted by the image of a mother and daughter. This was an idea I had in mind and that one day became a scene in a film. I'm fascinated by this image; it seemed really exciting to me to try to capture in film the extent to which a character is doubled. In fact, it is the image of the doubling of Angélica—the mother and the daughter of '36, who at the same time represent the mother and the daughter of the present, where the child of 1936 and the mother of 1973 are one and the same person. It's the fusion of two images that are present all through the film, and that are brought together in this final moment. This also shows the extent to which an event (Luis's punishment) can weigh on a child (in this case Angélica) and how incapable an adult can be of understanding the significance of this. I also wanted to show how isolated a child can be in relation to adults who can only offer a cruel absence and a total indifference.

Interview with Carlos Saura

JUAN CARLOS RENTERO / 1976

JUAN CARLOS RENTERO: *To what extent did your experience as a photographer influence you in becoming a film director?*

CARLOS SAURA: I can't say with any certainty what exactly has influenced my later stage as a filmmaker. What I do know, though, is that it did facilitate my entrance into the world of cinema and it awakened my passion because at first I didn't think about specializing in it.

JCR: *What did you learn in film school? Are you in favor of going through its program in order to become a director?*

CS: When I began film school, it functioned as the I.I.C.E. At that time it was the only place to learn. The bad thing is that, on the graduate level, it didn't count as a director's degree. Really it was a meeting place for a group of individuals who wanted to make films. Instead of being scattered all over, we would get together at school. We found ourselves influenced by the French New Wave and by the *Cahiers* critiques, which seem to me to be the very best things to have been done so far. Then I was a professor for six years, which was the best way to see how the future directors were evolving. It was a place where neither censorship nor red tape existed. When they became active, the Administration realized that it was an ideological weapon that needed to be controlled.

JCR: *For those of us currently studying camera work at the School of Sciences and*

From *Dirigido por* 31 (1976): 12–17. Reprinted by permission of *Dirigido por*. Translated from Spanish by Linda M. Willem.

Information, Juan Julio Baena is a controversial figure. You worked with him on Los golfos *[Hooligans] and* Llanto por un bandido *[Lament for a Bandit]. What opinion do you have of him?*

C S :   In general I don't have any opinion because I really don't know him. I can tell you that as a cameraman he is a real professional, absolutely beyond reproach, but that's all since I didn't get to deal with him sufficiently as a person. I also know that he was giving classes at the Film School where Cuadrado and other great cameramen of the Spanish cinema came from. Currently I don't know if he is still at the school or what he's doing, but I insist that as a professional he seemed to me to be very good.

J C R :   *In 1959 you debuted your first full-length film,* Los golfos. *It was the year of* L'avventura *(Antonioni) and* A bout de souffle *[Breathless] (Godard), both revolutionary, the first one thematically and the second one in terms of technique. Neorealism as a genre had died and we saw the arrival of "critical realism," headed up by young people. Nevertheless,* Los golfos *is talked about in terms of neorealistic cinema.*

C S :   I don't exactly know why. *Los golfos*, like all of my films, is a consequence of the one before. I endeavored to make something that was similar to a documentary, a documentary entertainment. At any rate, I don't think that it has anything to do with neorealism. Besides, I know two types of realism. On the one hand, the films of Rossellini, and especially the first part of *Roma città aperta* [Rome, Open City] which is purely a documentary about a specific situation, made precisely out of reality itself; and the other, a type of neorealism that De Sica and Zavattini make, which sometimes falls into sentimentalism and which are normal stories. Neorealism wasn't so much the capturing of reality as the narrating of a story. Of course all of us who were making films at that time were attracted to the movement, like in the case of Berlanga, for example, but that doesn't mean that we were making that kind of cinema. Look, I'd even say that we found ourselves closer to the New Wave, and I in particular to the cinema of Buñuel. But, finally, with *Los golfos*, rather than neorealism and its influence, one can talk in terms of a search for Spanish reality and its formation.

J C R :   *The first part of* Llanto por un bandido *was really interesting, but then it weakens somewhat as you focus more on Tempranillo's personality. Besides, I think you had lots of censorship problems.*

C S : Well, what happened was that the opening scenes of the execution were really massacred by the censors, to the extent that they indicated where we had to put the credits in order to cover things up. It was something incredible. To top it off, we had to take out a great many things: the appearance by Buñuel and by Buero Vallejo reading the names. Really, in a way, the film was a homage to censorship.

J C R : *A few years ago the film was shown on television in a homage to Spanish cinema. Was it the cut copy? That is, was it the same one that was exhibited commercially?*
C S : Yes, yes, of course. The fact is that no other copy exists. The censors went to such an extreme that they burned the negative, with the implicit intention that it couldn't be seen in the foreign market either.

J C R : *Llanto por un bandido was a Spanish-French-Italian production with José Luis Debildos, and it seems to me that your experience with him wasn't very good.*
C S : I made the film somewhat to get out of an impasse because my scripts were banned by the censors. But don't think that my collaboration with Debildos was bad. What happened was that the filming of *Llanto por un bandido* coincided with the making of *La Tulipe Noir* [The Black Tulip], a film by Alain Delon that Debildos was also involved in, and for that reason many things that I needed to use couldn't be given to me. But I think that those who really manipulated the film were the coproducers. At first I wanted to make a more contemplative film with the footage, and in the editing they ended up creating a dynamic rhythm. There are things that I like in the film, and others I don't. But I don't know, that frequently happens.

J C R : *La caza [The Hunt] of course involved contact with Querejeta and, what is even more important, with his crew which, beginning with this film, became yours. How did you get in contact with Querejeta?*
C S : I presented the *La caza* script to various production companies and no one wanted to do it. I remember that they told me to go see Querejeta. I already knew him from when they made *Viridiana*, from the time of Eceiza, Patino, etc. It was proposed and accepted. In addition, I knew that he had a complete crew of collaborators.

J C R : *La caza seems to me to be a vital work in your career. Besides, there is an explicit violence that wasn't—nor will be—a constant in your films.*

CS: I agree with you. *La caza* is a straightforward film. It's very important to me because I show a terrible violence, an essential violence that I wanted to expose. With respect to my work, it seems to me to be distant from *El jardín de las delicias* [The Garden of Delights] and closer to *Ana y los lobos* [Ana and the Wolves].

JCR: *When you say that it is closer to* Ana y los lobos, *are you referring to the fact that, in a way, they are hyperexplicit in contrast to the rest of your films?*
CS: No, no, not at all. Also, it's curious that *Ana y los lobos* seems hyperexplicit to you because the majority of the criticism said that it was a very difficult film. There even was someone who found it boring for that reason. What I was referring to was that *La caza* and *Ana y los lobos* are linked together more stylistically than with *El jardín de las delicias*, possibly because they both deal with similar themes.

JCR: *In a certain way* Peppermint frappé, Stress es tres, tres *[Stress Is Three, Three], and* La madriguera *[The Burrow] form a trilogy in your work.*
CS: Well, the truth is that I never set it up on that level, to make a trilogy, besides they don't have too many points in common. In principle what I did want to make a trilogy of was the Spanish War, but I also abandoned that idea.

JCR: *I think that a real unity exists among the three films which, in addition, I find as homages to Geraldine.*
CS: There is absolutely no homage to her in these films. What I indeed can say is that, for me, she is essential in the film because in a way I consider her indispensable.

JCR: *Beginning with these films you have been reproached for making constant use of symbolism and for claustrophobically enclosing your protagonist.*
CS: The issue of symbolism seems to me to be a very relative thing. It's just a question of asking yourself where, when, and how, as soon as you begin looking at film after film for specific things. Keep in mind, for example that the *Quijote* is a symbolic work. Besides, it seems to me that *Peppermint* doesn't use any symbolism at all. It's a film that lacks it completely, the same as *Stress*, which was a film made very quickly, in a straightforward manner. However, in *La madriguera*, yes, I do make frequent use of symbols. In terms

of enclosed spaces, I'm also in complete agreement since they didn't exist in my previous films, like *Los golfos*, *Llanto por un bandido*, and *La caza*. At any rate they don't seem to me exaggerated enough to be called claustrophobic.

J C R : *On the other hand, in* La madriguera *there also is an attempt to criticize the bourgeoisie.*

C S : It wasn't my intention to directly criticize the bourgeoisie. Nevertheless, when one disagrees with the society in which one lives, it's obvious that it has to be noted. But no, I really don't think that I'm interested in studying human relationships at the level of the destruction of the social class. Keep in mind that each of my films arises as a consequence of the one before, that's primary, and then each arises from things that I feel or that in a way are weighing on society. So a critique of the bourgeoisie can be seen in *La madriguera*, but it certainly is true that it wasn't directly instigated by me.

J C R : *On* La madriguera *Geraldine, Azcona, and you worked on the final form of the script. You haven't done that ever again. Were there problems working together?*
C S : No, what happened was that Geraldine's participation was only at the level of that film. In *La madriguera* the woman's problem was essential, and we tried to work on it the best way possible.

J C R : *In all of your films there's a constant return to the past. This considerably complicates your films by constantly playing with reality/fiction, and although it's present in an absolute form in* La prima *Angélica [Cousin Angelica], in* Cría cuervos *[Raise Ravens] it's pure paroxysm, sometimes confusing them both.*
C S : Really, it's that it excites me to play with the idea of time and its cinematographic coordinates. On the other hand, this is not gratuitous or accidental, as nothing is in my films, but rather it is a consequence of the passion that I feel in one way or another for the past. Yes, because I believe that the past is essential within people and that, in a way, they are currently the way they are because they have had a past. In this sense I would say that my characters behave as they do, react as they do, and express themselves as they do because they have lived through very specific conditions. On the other hand, I'm also excited by fiction. For that reason it's present in many of my films, although not all of them. What is indeed certain is that beginning with *La madriguera* the use of the coordinates of space/time and reality/fiction are an absolute constant.

JCR: *Also, your films have been faulted for being ambiguous, cold, stereotyped. Do you agree?*

CS: Let's take these one at a time. I understand ambiguity to be the providing of several paths that don't lead anywhere in particular. So I think that in my films the ambiguity doesn't go beyond my own ambiguity. The truth is that this can seem complicated. Montesquieu once said that you can't explain confusion by using confusion precisely because you fall into a greater confusion. In terms of the coldness, I must confess that I'm delighted that they say it, that I'm cold, cerebral. As for stereotyped, I don't know. I don't think that my cinema is exactly stereotyped. But that part about being cold is curious because I've already told you that I like them to say that, but the thing is that in foreign countries everybody says that I'm passionate, something which, frankly, I resist believing. Every film is a necessity for me. Also, in conclusion, I'm against labels and I think that there's a great proliferation of people who devote themselves to labeling everything, calling each thing what they like.

JCR: *In El jardín de las delicias [The Garden of Delights] Antonio Cano suffers a car accident that makes him lose his memory and leaves him in a wheelchair. His family is beginning to cure him little by little, and when they accomplish it, Antonio Cano goes back to being intransigent. Is this attitude due to his preferring his former life of unconsciousness more than the real life that they offered him?*

CS: Well, I never planned it that way, but naturally I accept it from you. Really my intention was to create a tyrannical character, an absolute dictator within the personality of Antonio Cano. When he revives, in a way he is limited to being himself, that is, to being like he was before the accident. At any rate, I never noticed if Antonio Cano behaved in the way that he did because he preferred his former life, but it seems like a good interpretation to me.

JCR: *There was a moment when you said that the character returns to life or revives. Do you really think that he revives again? Because he already had a way of behaving before the accident which, according to your intentions, he begins to recuperate with his memory.*

CS: Well of course he revives again. Antonio Cano isn't anything, he doesn't exist, he lacks consciousness. Then there are a series of individuals who make him see the past so that he can feel the present. It's a little like

Kaspar Hauser. He had to be taught how to walk and also how to talk. He had to know in a way who he was or where he came from.

J C R : *Listen, now that you are comparing* El jardín *with* Kaspar Hauser *for me, I realize that they are pretty close, although I hadn't noticed it. I'm very enthusiastic about Herzog's film.*

C S : Yes, me too, and I insist that there are many points in common. Look at just one: both Kaspar Hauser and Antonio Cano were restored to health by individuals who belonged to a society that automatically rejected them.

J C R : *What surprised me most about your film was the great job done by López Vázquez, who adapted himself perfectly to the role despite being a normal person. When I say that about a normal person, I'm referring to the fact that Herzog's* Kaspar Hauser *was played by Bruno S, who had led a very hard life.*

C S : I've always thought that José-Luis López Vásquez was an extraordinary actor, and you have the proof in the films we've done together, which turned out very well, because otherwise I wouldn't have worked with him any more. What happened was that I was very interested in the cases of people who had lost their memory. I was in various sanitariums. I really knew how my character had to react. Perhaps he's the richest of all the ones I've created in my films, and also the most finely wrought. At any rate I think that none of this would have been any good if López Vásquez hadn't seen the essence. But as you have confirmed, he adapted himself completely to the character and made him revive exactly as I wanted him to. Even when he doesn't speak, as you pointed out, one notices what he's feeling, what he's trying to communicate. And this feels absolutely normal. I think that López Vázquez is one of the finest actors in Spain, and outside of it.

J C R : *Antonio Cano could react that way because there had been the Spanish War.*

C S : Obviously this conditioned him, as in a certain way it conditions all of my characters, but really it's due to his own nature, which was also marked by the Spanish War. At any rate, the film offers various interpretations, as you can see.

J C R : *In* Ana y los lobos *you generalize much more than in all your previous films, alluding to the taboos that afflict us. I don't think that you like this film very much, perhaps because you don't consider it to be that personal, despite the fact that I like it a lot; it may be the one that I like the most of all that you've made so far.*

CS: No, on the contrary. You're wrong. I also like it a lot. It may be the one that I also prefer of all that I've made so far. I also don't think that part about it being impersonal is right. Think about how the taboos that I present in *Ana y los lobos* are also taboos that afflict me directly, how I have felt them in some way throughout my entire life, since being a Spaniard persistently reverberates in me. In addition, remember that all of the films that I make operate out of something that's very much mine, and of course that everything in *Ana y los lobos* is part of me or of the taboos that I've felt at specific moments.

JCR: *Do you believe that religion, sex, and the army are the three great taboos of Spanish society?*

CS: Well, I don't know. I suppose that Spanish society has many more because, logically, it's normal for it to be that way. What you can be completely sure of is that they are the most important ones, or at least that ones that I think are more important, and at this point I'll confess that they are considered to be the essential conditioning elements of my life. I repeat that I don't know if they are the most important—for me they are—but they are important, which is sufficient, although obviously many more exist.

JCR: *To what extent does the female character influence or is important in your films?*

CS: She is essential. Keep in mind that in many cases the majority of the things that happen have the woman as the nucleus, for example in *La madriguera* and *Ana y los lobos*. Besides, Geraldine is very important in all my films because in a certain way she helps me just with her presence in the performance. Actually, I've worked with her in all my films from *Peppermint* through *Cría cuervos*, with the only exception being *La prima Angélica*.

JCR: *When you began the filming of* La prima Angélica *you hadn't yet received the censor's O.K. for* Ana y los lobos. *At any time did you think of incorporating some themes from* Ana *in* La prima?

CS: You say that when I began *La prima Angélica*, *Ana y los lobos* had not yet been approved, however, I don't remember if it was still banned or not. In terms of if I incorporated some of the themes from *Ana* in my next film, I can clearly say no because when I film something, I completely forget the previous one. That is to say, consciously I didn't include anything from *Ana* in *La prima*, although I can't deny the fact that all my films have reminiscences from the previous one, which on the other hand is completely logical since an *auteur* who expresses himself in a way through his films has to have many points in common in all of his films. But, finally, I didn't voluntarily transfer anything from one to the other because the first one was banned.

J C R :   *Is the character that López Vázquez embodies in* La prima Angélica *autobiographical?*
C S :   I suppose that you're asking me that because of the parallels it has to me. Well no, truly. None of the characters in my films is autobiographical; they have points in common, more or less, with my personality, but they never reach the point of being me, not only due to an excess of narcissism, but because I sincerely have never set it up that way. Luis is a man who remembers his past with fear and nostalgia within the context of the Spanish War. I insist I won't deny a certain proximity to my personality, but from there to being autobiographical is a big difference.

J C R :   *The soldier that Fernando Delgado portrays in* La prima Angélica, *who walks around with the arm in a sling—that doesn't seem accidental to me.*
C S :   You can be sure that, as I've told you before, nothing in my films is accidental. The smallest details have a meaning.

J C R :   *Then, what was the meaning of the soldier with his arm in the position of a salute?*
C S :   I think that it was a very coherent sequence within the film. Unfortunately—or fortunately—it was publicized in an unexpected way to an incredible extent. This also served to create a certain advertisement for the film, which also is important. At any rate, it went very well, it worked wonderfully.

J C R :   *The Cannes award also influenced this.*
C S :   I'm going to tell you something very important. At Cannes they didn't give us a major prize because there was amazing pressure from within Spain itself. I remember that when we took the film to the censors, they wrote to us saying that it wasn't right, that we were sacrilegious, that we were attack-

ing the state and the fundamental laws of the government and the principles of the National Uprising.

JCR: *Nevertheless, the film passed without being cut.*
CS: Yes, like *Ana y los lobos*. There was a moment when they suggested we cut it, and we flatly refused.

JCR: *Where is* Cría cuervos *with respect to your earlier work?*
CS: I don't know. I haven't worked it out it for myself. I also don't know if I'll continue with this line of childhood, which I really wouldn't call a line. The only thing I can say is that I will now do other things, make other films, but I haven't thought about what. When I do something, as I've told you before, I don't think about what I'll do afterwards, and I forget completely about my previous films, although there's no doubt that each one arises as a function of the one before. *Cría cuervos* with respect to the one before? I don't know, maybe my next film will clarify it.

JCR: *Are you getting something ready now?*
CS: Yes, I'm working on something but I can't give you any advance notice about it. I'll write the script myself, that's all I can say.

Carlos Saura: An Individualist in Conversation

VICÉN CAMPOS / 1976

VICÉN CAMPOS: *Many people have reproached you for not being in touch with the Spanish reality of your own times and for reflecting on the Spanish War without bearing witness to an era. In principle, that seems wrong-headed to me because I think that your films travel back to the past as a substantiation of the present, having them virtually complementing each other.*

CARLOS SAURA: This is a reproach that I don't understand. The Spanish War has been, and still is, weighing on us. It pertains to an immediate past that can be separated from our present only with difficulty. It also has been said that I'm obsessed with my childhood. It's not true. It's one thing for me to be preoccupied with my infancy and to take an interest in it, but it's another thing for me to be solely preoccupied with it.

VC: *Fine. What I was referring to was that without having lived through the war, you reconstruct it as part of a past that you don't know.*

CS: Excuse me, but I believe you are mistaken. When you say that I haven't lived through the war, you're wrong. I lived through it, and I lived through it dramatically at times, and in a way I have suffered its consequences, as have many Spaniards. What I didn't do was fight because I was four years old when the war began. But I lived through the war and I have violent and dramatic memories of it. There is no doubt at all that those years have left a profound mark on me and have taught the terrible lesson that there is nothing more horrible than a civil war. But I insist that I don't think that my

Cinema 2002 14 (1976): 34–37. Translated from Spanish by Linda M. Willem.

films can be interpreted as a function of my childhood. Of course an *auteur* who tries to explain a series of things to himself, as happens to me, has to resort to personal experiences, but not just to his childhood experiences but to any type of experiences. My films are not deliberately autobiographical. I mean that there is no authorial intention to be revealed in them. My films, I think, are transpositions of my own or assimilated experiences, the product of readings, of images, of this or that thing. One of the problems that worries me the most is the lack of clarity there is in getting to a profound understanding of things. It worries me how the impressions, the memories, the facts that I now need vanish away. What I try to do through my films is simply to put a series of thoughts and images into an order.

v c : *I think that a great parallelism exists between two eras in your films: the era of the war, and the present one.*
c s : Well, I'm sorry, but I don't think it's like that. The war appears in some of my films, and perhaps it's present in a way in them all, but there is no intent to establish immediate comparisons. At least not in all my films. Obviously in *El jardín de las delicias* [The Garden of Delights] and in *La prima Angélica* [Cousin Angelica] the war and its consequences are talked about from two different observation points. In *La prima Angélica* the disasters of a civil war are observed through someone who feels himself to be a loser of that war. *La caza* [The Hunt] is something else. In *La caza* I tried to say how easy it was for a civil war to break out when tensions, intransigence, and violence are unleashed. In *Cría cuervos* [Raise Ravens] there is hardly any allusion to the Spanish Civil War, and that is in order to stress that for the new generation it's already something distant. One of the children asks: "Listen, Rosa, when was the Spanish War?" And not even Rosa, the maid, knows. She has to think a few moments to remember that it began in 1936.

v c : *I distinguish between two stages in your cinema: the first goes from* Los golfos *[Hooligans] to* Llanto por un bandido *[Lament for a Bandit], which were attempts to break into the industry; and the second, begins with* Ana y los lobos *[Ana and the Wolves] or rather with* La caza, *where a hypothetical war is spoken about, and concludes with* La prima Angélica. *Is* Cría cuervos *the beginning of another stage?*
c s : First of all I'd like to clarify something: *Los golfos* and *Llanto por un bandido* were not attempts to break into the industry. *Los golfos* entailed a mar-

velous experience in which a group of people who at the time were associated with the Film School worked together. My idea was to make, for the first time in Spain, a film cut like a documentary, a straightforward film, direct and immediate, done in natural settings and taking advantage of my experience in photography and documentary cinema. We couldn't believe it when it was picked for Cannes. We went to the festival and there we got the news that the censors had cut almost ten minutes of the film. In brief, *Llanto por un bandido* is something else. It was done when, after the *Viridiana* ban, there was no possibility of making anything at all. Besides, I don't believe too much in that whole thing about stages, or cycles, etc. What is indeed the truth is that after *Llanto por un bandido*, where I saw myself swamped by the film's financial situation and by the enormous difficulties that I had to solve without having either the means or the experience necessary to do so, I resolved to make a cinema that I could control one hundred percent.

v c : *I think that there is indeed a unity.*
c s : Well, I don't know. What I do think is that as of *La caza* my work has a coherence within its incoherence because I've decided to work with elements that I know to the core, to work with characters and settings I've lived with.

v c : *Then when you get to* Cría cuervos *everything changes, because* La prima Angélica *entails the end of this second stage.*
c s : The end of what stage? I'm not the one to say so, but in any case, *Cría cuervos* could be the conclusion of a series of things, and the beginning of a series of other things. But I think that all my films have done that. At any rate, I've already been taught a bit by experience about this mania to codify everything, this telling you that you are already finished, and that you have nothing to say, and how you're not renewing yourself. For the most part this is the advice of those who feel themselves to be in possession of the truth and who adopt a paternal tone with the child who isn't doing what they want him to do. It's very interesting to see that many times what critics—the ones who interview you—want is for you to say what they want you to say. At any rate, dead or alive, what I want is to continue to make movies, and for as long as I can.

v c : *What I wanted to find out is if* Cría cuervos *is a new stage for you?*

c s : I don't know. It can be the basis of a future work. I never think about a project until having completely finished the one before. For that reason I think that, in a way, my films express me and that each one responds—for better or worse, but that's another matter—to my way of being, to what I'm thinking at those times. For me the experience of *Cría cuervos* especially entails a search into areas that up until now have remained hidden. Perhaps the possibility of a more intimate cinema. But I don't know for sure.

v c : *Within your cinema the Spanish War is a constant, a means, or both at the same time.*
c s : I've already told you that the Civil War has weighed on my life and surely still weighs on it, and that for that reason it's normal for it to be one of the themes that appear in my films. Now you can talk about the war, it's even very possible that in a little while there will be a proliferation of films on the subject, but when I made *La caza* you couldn't even mention the words civil war or Spanish War or the War of '36, even to the point where they prohibited any allusion to Spain or to '36. That's why in *La caza* they speak about a war, although of course everyone knew which war we were referring to. In *El jardín de las delicias* and especially in *La prima Angélica* the subject was already talked about specifically. But I insist that I'm not impassioned or obsessed with the subject. It simply seems to me that it continues to be a topic of conversation and remembrance at the present time, and is an instructive example for the future.

v c : *Currently people are going out into the streets asking for democracy, amnesty, and freedom. I think that, as a creator and in possession of such a defined craft as is the cinema, your obligation in a certain way is to show the reality of the present time, because I think that everyone who witnesses history necessarily has to grab a hold of what's happening daily in his society. I don't know if you understand me.*
c s : Yes, yes, of course I understand you. I understand you but I only halfway share what you are telling me. I think that there are immense possibilities to express oneself and that no one should say, "That is what should or shouldn't be done." It seems to me that everyone should do what he likes best and is interested in. No one has the right to impose this or that subject matter, this or that way of doing things. To make political films is very good for someone who wants to do that. That doesn't interest me very much. Neither am I interested in making didactic films for the time being. It seems

a tragedy to me that we continue with the same singular obsession of shaking off the weight of the giant boot that has been pressing down on us to the point of exasperation. I think that by now the time has come that if we forget about this still omnipresent threat, we can express other problems that viscerally affect us. To propose that we all should make political films "of the first degree" seems nonsense to me. I advocate the existence of this political cinema, as long as it can coexist with whatever other type in which the politics are secondary.

When I began to make films I was reproached for not making a "realist" cinema that was more in accord with reality. With what reality? With yours, with mine, or with that guy's? When people spoke about realism at that time and said that Berlanga was an opportunist because he made "escapist" films—a term that was in vogue during the 50's and 60's—they would confuse "realism" with a cinema that claimed to be about the proletariat. Why, instead of *Peppermint frappé* didn't I make a film about the miner's situation in Asturias? And I usually said that it seemed to me a very good thing for a film—or for forty films—to be made about the miners in Asturias, about Alto Hornos, or about Puertollano, but that I wasn't the most appropriate one to make them for various reasons: because I don't know the topic sufficiently well, because there are people better prepared on those topics than I am, and finally, because other topics excite me. Your reproaches right now remind me of those reproaches. Besides, I'm not at all interested in providing historical testimony. I limit myself to giving my opinion about certain subjects that interest me.

Of course the matter becomes exasperating because in Spain it has been impossible to speak about a great many things—almost everything—to express yourself freely, to show things as they are, to give opinions, etc. Many times people talk about "politically engaged cinema" without knowing what it is. I remember when we were showing *Peppermint* at Cannes. It was precisely at the time of the "French May" in 1968. We were the first to withdraw a film from the exhibition, at grave risk to our good standing. We were at the point of not returning to Spain under the threat of reprisals. What had been sought in the "French May" was very exciting. But the first thing they asked for was freedom and respect. They asked for creativity in all things. They were looking for the commonality in all forms of labor. Of course there were fanatics who only accepted a cinema of struggle, a political cinema, to be used as a political weapon. But they were in the minority.

Godard, Truffaut, Malle, and so many others, what they were asking for was to make it easier for whomever wants to express himself in film to be able to do so.

What I would like to see is for a certain dogmatism to disappear, the dogmatism that says that what you have to do is this and not that, the dogmatism of having to think this way and if you don't think this way, you are an enemy that has to be destroyed. Finally, what I am against is any type of totalitarianism. If we have, hopefully, gotten out of one kind, we don't want to enter into another kind. At least I don't want to. The changes that are being brought about in this country—within my consubstantial pessimism—have to allow a greater freedom of expression, and because of that, the possibility to confront subjects that have thus far been taboo. The opportunistic shifting from one group to another openly shows how quickly things are forgotten. Many will point to this cinematographic opportunism of now speaking about what up until now couldn't be spoken about, but there will be few who will go on to a work where what truly is in play is the existence itself of being an individual who is trying to express himself freely, who is fighting tooth and nail to gain some clarity for himself, and, in passing, to bring clarity to those who identify with him: his doubts, his hesitations. I think that during these years many writers, painters, film directors have seen their hopes frustrated. Many of us who have managed to survive did so against a widespread opinion that said that since what should be done couldn't be done, it was better not to do anything. What I have always refused is to do anything that wasn't in agreement with what I wanted to do, but always within the possibility of doing it.

I'm annoyed by trendy terminology, and for that reason, since people are speaking a lot about "possibilism," I don't like it at all that they are saying that I have been and am a "possibilist," although there is some truth in it, but the term gives the impression of a pact, a commitment to somebody that one doesn't agree with. No, what I've tried is to do what I wanted to do. Certainly more than once it's been necessary to take a roundabout way, to skirt the issue a little, or a lot, instead of going straight to the subject. But to me it seemed fine to do so. After all, in times of repression people always have had to find a way to say things indirectly. Our great writers of the Golden Age are examples of what I'm saying, from Gracián to Quevedo, including Calderón and Cervantes. That is to say, what I've always declined is "collaborationism." I think that these days there are going to be many opportunists, and that's normal. I don't want to be an opportunist and so I'm not going to do what they want me to. I'll do what I want to do, as I've continued to do up until now, and if you'll permit me some levity, I'd say that I'm ready to do what I have the most fun doing, which is making films.

I think that in Spain it's necessary to make films or television programs that are realistic "of the first degree," that is, ones that straightforwardly reflect reality, that show us what they are thinking, that portray any man or woman in any job and on any day. I think that this type of work can be made with imagination and intelligence and it can be given a dimension that goes beyond a simple documentary. I think that an investigation, an examination, can be transformed into something else. I think films that apparently are grounded in an exploration of the different members of a family can become magnificent films. *El desencanto* [Disenchanted], which Jaime Chávarri just shot, is an extraordinary example of what I'm saying: a film which straddles between a documentary inquiry and something else that I wouldn't know how to define very well, which makes *El desencanto* simultaneously function as a fiction and as a documentary, makes it a testimony, and opens up multiple suggestions in other directions. It seems to me the commitment that one develops toward others, toward society, is very big, but for me, the commitment I have toward myself is more important. I'm a great individualist, I've always said so, and I'm ready to defend my turf because I think that it's only through the individual that anyone can understand other things. It seems to me that it's essential for a man to be able to fulfill himself as an individual, as a person, because that way it will be much easier for him to fulfill himself within society. After all, the basic problems are the same or very similar for all men.

v c : *Focusing on* Cría cuervos, *there are those who have repeatedly stressed the absence of Rafael Azcona in the writing of the script. What was this due to?*
c s : Rafael Azcona and I have worked together for a long time and this has been enriching for me. Azcona is a demanding, hard working, and sensitive man and his collaboration has been essential in terms of my films, but we are quite different people and little by little we have come to realize that these differences can sully our collaboration. Rafael himself suggested that I write my own scripts, and the truth is that although more than once I had written a script on my own, I never had dared to make the decision of being totally responsible for it. The experience has been positive and fascinating. I

needed to take this step to search deeper into dark areas that only I could get to the bottom of. The results are yet to be seen, but I should say that I've thought deeply about the decision to work alone and in no way is it an indication of vanity, but rather, of good faith toward myself.

v c : *Many people have linked your film with* El espíritu de la colmena *[Spirit of the Beehive] by Víctor Erice, and I've heard that you like the film a lot. What do you think about how they relate to each other?*

c s : I don't see any approximation at all between *Cría cuervos* and *El espíritu de la colmena*, at least not in the malevolent sense that some critics have used to pass judgment on *Cría cuervos*. But it's possible that I never would have made *Cría cuervos* if I had not seen Víctor Erice's film, among other reasons because *Cría cuervos* without Ana Torrent wouldn't have made any sense to me. I think that there is a real flippancy about opinions at the time they are given, and judgments are made with a surprising lightheartedness. Already in Cannes, during the year of *La prima Angélica*, some French critics said that *El espíritu de la colmena* resembled a film of mine. What nonsense! At any rate, I'm used to it. It's determined by the time period: I've been told that I was a second Buñuel, that I copied Losey, Fellini, Antonioni, Bergman, and even Bresson. *El espíritu de la colmena* is a marvelous film. It has nothing to do with *Cría cuervos*.

v c : *In* Cría cuervos *Ana is a witness to her mother being deceived, and she suffers due to that. Later she sees her aunt with another soldier, and she doesn't seem to like that either.*

c s : There isn't any hasty moralizing, or in any case, I don't think that the fact that the father is an adulterer should be considered the primary negative aspect that influences the girl's behavior. In any case, what it would be is a function of the repercussions that this adultery has on the one truly involved—on the mother—and for that reason, a function of her rejection that influences Ana as a child. One must not forget that in a way Ana the mother, Ana the child, and Ana twenty years later could be considered to be a single character, broken down into component parts.

v c : *There are a couple of scenes where the American flag is displayed. Does that mean anything?*

c s : No, absolutely not. That scene was done on a day that it rained and
there was terrible traffic. It was necessary to do it that day, specifically that
day, due to a problem with the actors or something like that; I don't remember what it was. The American flags had been placed on María de Molina.
Naturally we never would have done such a thing on purpose. It all was
accidental. Besides, I think that remains fairly clear in the film itself because
later, when we had to shoot Ana's flying scene, we did it on another day
under other circumstances and the flags were no longer there, and time and
space are practically continuous.

v c : *I have the impression that* Cría cuervos *lends itself to different interpretations if it is viewed globally.*
c s : I hope that's so. I've been surprised to read some criticism which shows
a total failure to perceive my intentions. I recognize that I will be judged in
this way or that way, and naturally everyone has a perfect right to say if my
film seems good, bad, or just fair, but the flippancy and lack of thought that
stand out in some of these critiques seems inexcusable to me. I believe that I
have some right to protest these frivolous remarks. My films are complicated
perhaps, but I believe that they are within the reach of anyone. There is a
lamentable fact, and it is the laziness of a certain type of viewer who goes to
the movies with the sole idea of being swept along by the action or by the
spectacle. I'm incapable of explaining what I do. Besides, it seems pointless
to me. A film like the one I present is a unique, nontransferable work. It's a
totality that includes an experience or many experiences. It's a summary of
readings, of trips, of conversations, and of thoughts. For that reason I reject
a flippant and hurried judgment. *Cría cuervos* is, or can be, understood this
way: as a meditation that a thirty year old woman makes within the immediate future, and a meditation that is intended to put into order some scattered
memories, the majority of which belong to the year 1975, the date in which
the film was shot. I've always been fascinated by the idea of seeing the present as if it were the past. They say that the present is life and the past is
death. I think that death is omnipresent in *Cría cuervos*. One day when I was
obliged to give a definition of my film, I said that *Cría cuervos* is a film about
a girl obsessed with death. I don't know if that's true. I think it's that and
many other things, like, for example, a girl whose life develops within a hostile environment. It could be said that more than a film about death, it's

about the incongruity of a system of education and cohabitation; that *Cría cuervos* simply is an imaginative film about a sensitive and imaginative girl. But all of this—what difference does it make? I've already said that my lack of clarity at the time of judging things concerns me. *Cría cuervos* is, finally, an attempt in search of this clarity.

Interview with Carlos Saura on *Cría cuervos* [Raise Ravens] and *Elisa, vida mía* [Elisa, My Life]

ENRIQUE BRASÓ / 1977

ENRIQUE BRASÓ : *Since you began making films,* Cría cuervos—*and then* Elisa, vida mía—*is the first film based on a script which you wrote alone. Does this constitute a change in your cinema? Why have you stopped collaborating with Rafael Azcona?*

CARLOS SAURA: The decision to work alone has come at some cost and, honestly, at first I had the feeling of having made a mistake. Not having an interlocutor with whom to discuss this or that scene, not being able to rely on another person in some cases and, most of all, my own laziness about writing were the main reasons why I delayed this experience. The collaboration with Rafael Azcona was fundamental to me and we worked for years in perfect symbiosis. But, as sometimes happens in the best of collaborations, this rapport began deteriorating, our perspectives on certain issues began to differ, and the decision to end our collaboration was mutual. Which is not to say that we will never take it up again. Now I'm happy to have taken this step; in some ways I feel more confident, and working alone gives me a sense of having greater control. I'm putting to use a working system which had been in effect for some time but which, now that I'm my own script writer, gives me more freedom; this has to do with approaching the script as a process which begins the moment you write the first word and ends when the first cut comes out of the lab. In any case, for some time now I've had the feeling of working alone, perfecting something which I cannot fully define

From *Positif* 194 (1977): 3–8. Reprinted by permission. Translated from French by Paula Willoquet-Maricondi.

or identify. I would simply like to say that now what I like most is having control over the different elements that constitute my films; I would like to control everything, for it all to "belong" to me. I already know that that's impossible in cinema, but it is increasingly possible to simplify things so as to have a better handle on them. Now, for the first time in my life, I feel like I have the power to make a film anywhere, with two actors, and whether we shoot it on Super 8 or 16 or on video is all the same to me because, in the final analysis, these systems and techniques amount to the same thing. What makes a difference is that you have to know basic things, such as the fact that 35mm has greater resolution than Super 8, so when you want a character to appear lost in an all-powerful landscape, you'd better give up that idea if you have to shoot in Super 8, at least for now.

EB: *From a narrative standpoint,* Cría cuervos *is structured as a reflection on time: the adult Ana remembers the child Ana, who in turn remembers certain fragments of an earlier time. Is this reflection on time designed to drive* Cría cuervos, *or is this idea due to other factors?*

CS: It's possible. From a narrative standpoint, one could say that this reflection represents the perspective of a child; in other words, the intention is to enter the world of a child, the workings of the mind of a child. Based on that, the events in this story unfold according to the desires and inclinations of Ana, the child, until we begin doubting the veracity of what we are being told—since she is a very imaginative child. But, superimposed on this outlook, as if floating above it, there is another evocation, that of Ana as an adult. These two narrative planes overlap and form the bases on which the film is structured. The fact that the story is told by Ana as an adult woman, twenty years later, suggests that the story is told from a future perspective. This was not a gratuitous choice, but the only way I found to approach the present with the eyes of the past. As for the driving force, I think the idea which motivated me to make this film is simply that of the identification between a little girl and her mother, and the extent to which this child, like so many children, is immersed in what we call a child's world, a world which is, in fact, much more the doing of adults, a repressive world in which children are no more than the reflection or the projection of adults. I don't know how we can feel proud of the fact that children imitate us; in this respect, they are merely perpetuating our errors. I think children would have to kill the adults in order to be able to be themselves. Ana, the young protagonist in *Cría cuervos*, unconsciously understands this. But of course, she doesn't buy the stories of a childhood paradise, nor of childhood innocence, nor all the stupidities that we adults happily recite.

E B :   *It's interesting that* Cría cuervos, *while centered around childhood and focusing on a child's world, is also a film about death: the film begins with the father's death, and Ana's rebellion is first evident in her refusal to kiss the body; the death of the hamster as well as that of her mother are both moments of catharsis that mark her profoundly; Ana's conscious desire is of death, of killing. . . . How did this convergence of childhood and death arise for you?*

C S :   I think children view death differently from adults. For an adult, death is the end of a process of decay and depletion. For a child, death is identified with disappearance, without the sense of tragedy; beings, animals, things die, disappear, and once it happens there is no point dwelling on the subject. For Ana, the child, her mother's death means her disappearance, which means that at any point she may reappear, and so she can bring her back whenever she feels the need. I think children are incapable of creating clear distinctions between the real and the unreal, the gap between the real and the imagined can be bridged without conflict. Unlike adults, the child doesn't need to go through a process of rationalization to bridge that gap.

Ana, the child, is not so much preoccupied with the theme of death as she is imbued with the feeling of having the power to kill, the power to make anyone she pleases disappear, and also the power to bring them back. For example, she is capable of making her mother be part of her life by strongly desiring her presence.

E B :   *The idea of death is also important in* Elisa, vida mía, *with the agony and the death of the father, the dead woman along the road with whom Elisa seems to identify, the decaying corpse of her husband's mistress. . . .*

C S :   It seems to me there is no point in trying to forget that death is always around us and that, like the illness which precedes it, death is the quintessential tragic element, the final event in life. Aside from its visceral aspect, death is in part the product of our thinking and our knowledge, and that's why death cannot mean the same thing for a child and for an adult; that is, our understanding of the "fact" of death is tied to the process of understanding and maturing. But death gives meaning to life, that is, life would have no meaning without the idea of death. In *Cría cuervos*, when Ana's mother, during a moment of lucidity toward her terrible illness, is reflecting on having been betrayed and says, "It doesn't matter . . . they betrayed me . . . it doesn't matter," she is discarding a whole way of life, the one in which she was brought up, where rewards and punishments are superimposed over the fact of death, and dictate that you have to resign yourself to accepting the sanctions that life presents to you because your reward will come after death.

In *Elisa, vida mía*, the characters have a more fatalistic conception of death and they see it as something inevitable and permanent. In a way, the death of Luis, Elisa's father, represents her own birth. We built our own personalities on the ruins of our ancestors. So, Elisa comes into being out of an experience that predates her, that of her father, and through it she organizes and solidifies her identity. But, there are imagined and real deaths in Elisa's life. We'll never know, for example, if Elisa's account of her friend's suicide is real or imagined, just as we'll never know if the story of passion that ends in the crime her father recounts in such details really happened.

E B : *Did the great success of* Cría cuervos *have special significance for you? How do you feel about it? Did it influence* Elisa, vida mía *in any way?*

c s : It's wonderful to see that there are people who really take an interest in what you do. I don't quite understand how it happens, so when this kind of communication takes place I'm a bit perplexed; it feels like a miracle and I have difficulty believing in it. I have the feeling that it doesn't depend on me, but on external factors, one of which, of course, is the quality of the product. I would really like to know the secret—if there is one—to "communicating" with a large number of people, but since I don't know this secret, I have to content myself with telling stories that interest me, in the hopes—sometimes I'm not very optimistic—that others will like or be interested in the same things that appeal to me. In any event, my role is to echo what happens around me. I attribute the "success" of my recent films to the fact that I've worked continuously and that, while fluctuations are inevitable, I've been slowly discovering a better system of communication or one that is better suited to a certain segment of the public and critics. I prefer to stay at the margins of this process and to continue exploring what seems to be a very attractive personal adventure. One of the advantages of the commercial success of my previous films is that I'm able to launch myself into the next project with more tranquility and without the usual worries. In this respect, *Elisa, vida mía*, which is a very modest film, was made with more ease; in particular, I had plenty of time to shoot it and I even had the luxury of shooting scenes which I knew would maybe never make it into the final product—something I had never dared do until then. Keep in mind that my collaboration with my producer, Elías Querejeta, dates back to 1965 when we made *La caza* [The Hunt] and that I always had the freedom I needed, within the limits imposed by the difficulties of making films in Spain under the Franco regime and the need to stay within a limited budget. Within those limits, however, I always felt free to do what I wanted and Elías was never a producer in the strict sense of the term, but rather a friend and a collaborator.

EB: *What is the origin of* Elisa, vida mía? *Was this film born of your earlier film, as is often the case, or rather of the last image of* La prima Angélica *[Cousin Angelica], a mother and a daughter slightly changed?*
CS: One can say that *Elisa, vida mía* grows out of *Cría cuervos*, given that with my method of working, each film grows out of the previous film. As for its origins . . . I think *Elisa* grows out of a series of disparate elements: a childhood picture which Oona, Geraldine's mother, gave me (you could see two little girls in the woods and one of them full of emotions, ghost-like); a forgotten poem by Garcilaso de la Vega; the desire to do something about the difficulty of sharing a life with someone; the desire to explore the theme of solitude which occupies my thoughts a lot; an interest in showing the differences and difficulties involved in literary and visual adaptations. Deep down, who knows, *Elisa* may be nothing more than a film about our inability to do something, which ends up leading us to do something else: like a novel, a film, a written page, I don't know what else . . . I think there are a number of themes in *Elisa*, all put together inside a story that is very simple, almost banal.

EB: *What is the origin of the title*, Elisa, vida mía?
CS: The title comes from a fragment of an eclogue by Garcilaso de la Vega, a 16th century Spanish poet: "Who would have told me, Elisa my life / when across this valley swept by a sweet breeze / we walked picking tender flowers, that I would see, with a long separation / come the sad and lonely day / that would put a bitter end to my love?"

I read this poem for the first time when I was studying Spanish literature for my baccalaureat. About two years ago, while re-reading Garcilaso, I once again came across this eclogue which had mysterious qualities for me: I was fascinated, held by its beauty, by the mystery that surrounds these words, by the pain of an unrequited passion. Out of all this came the first impetus to write the script.

E B : *Would you explain the process through which the transformation (recurrent in your cinema in general) occurs from the microcosm of the family in* Cría cuervos *to the individualized characters in* Elisa, vida mía? *By what process does the displacement of the familial structure occur from* Cría cuervos *to* Elisa, vida mía?

C S : In a way, I've always addressed intimate problems, particularly those that relate to couples, to the relationship between men and women: I tried to do that in *Peppermint frappé, Stress es tres, tres* [Stress Is Three, Three], *La madriguera* [The Burrow]. . . . For me, *Elisa* was like another encounter with myself, an encounter which began with *La prima Angélica* and which continued with *Cría cuervos.* There has always been in Spanish cinema a kind of fear of showing one's sensitivity. One reason for this is that a false image of us has been created; outside of Spain, people think that to be Spanish means to be brutal, rudimentary, violent, when in fact you can easily see the sensitivity of a number of our writers, painters.

I now feel liberated from a number of moral obligations, of certain social responsibilities, let's say. Since Franco's death, I've felt free of these obligations and I decided to focus on other aspects of my life which seemed essential to me.

There is a quote by Baltasar Gracián where he says: "Open your eyes first, I mean your inner eyes. And to know where you are going, look." So, I'd like to open my inner eyes, to look at myself as I am and to see why I do certain things. Let's just say that in this respect I've followed a path which has led me from the general to the particular.

E B : *As to your characters, there is increasingly in your work a chain of exchanges, of displacements of personality (like Aunt Paulina in* Cría cuervos, *an authoritative figure standing for the absent father, a dear figure standing for the absent mother) and, at the same time, a chain of identifications (Ana and her mother in* Cría cuervos, *but especially and fundamentally in* Elisa, vida mía, *in the relationship Elisa/Father where they in turn identify and "disidentify" with each other). Is this in any way an exploration of the theme of the "double"?*

C S : I've been working on this question for years, since *Peppermint,* which I made in 1967. There's a large body of literature in Spain where the theme of the double personality appears, from Cervantes, to Lope de Vega, to Calderón, etc. Of course, long before that there was Narcissus. We are ourselves and our reflection, that is, we are both, etc. It must be said that the replacement of another personality is fundamental to our work as directors in cinema, and that the actors are working on this very representationality. I've always found representations fascinating because they contain this doubling, this catharsis, where you say what you cannot say directly, through secondary, terciary, or quaternary characters. In *Cría cuervos*, layers of time are interwoven, although theoretically they are clearly marked—there is a present, a past, a future. When I write a script, I think about these layers of time, although in my own life I'm sometimes incapable of establishing these distinctions; and everybody knows that when you least expect it, an image, a memory—from the past or from your imagination—will surface, and nobody understands how these mysterious mechanisms occur. I have a lot of difficulty coordinating ideas, I don't have a good memory, I feel like I live immersed in chaos. I try to bring this chaos to the surface in my films, and to find a certain coherence inside my own incoherence and confusion.

E B : *Is this linked to the theme of the previous question, because the notions of "representation," of theater, of masque are always present: Ana and her sisters dress in disguise in* Cría cuervos, *there is the staging of* El gran teatro del mundo [The Great Theater of the World] *in* Elisa, vida mía?
C S : In life, we always play a part. We've inherited a system, an upbringing—which we pass on, impose on our children—based in part on appearances and in which "accessories" play an important role: clothing, uniforms, the decor of the places where we live, external signs. . . .

We use these very same subliminal elements in cinema and in the theater: representation on top of representation. We must not forget the ludic side of all this, of course, the playfulness. As for the *El gran teatro del mundo* of Calderon, at first I thought it was very dangerous to try to introduce this into a film because it might give it a didactic tone. The truth is that if the film refers to this work, it's because I find it truly marvelous. I always tend to use things in my films which I find pleasing without worrying too much about whether they are necessary or appropriate.

E B : *Your latest films tend to be structured around unique settings which seem to imprint their own characteristics on the people who occupy these spaces. A specific example is the house in* Elisa, vida mía; *does this mysterious, isolated place predate the genesis of the film? And if not, if it was conceived later, does it change the original nature of the characters?*

C S : There are two practical reasons why I tend to work with these unique kinds of settings: first, in order to have greater control over the elements I have at my disposal; second, and perhaps most importantly, since *La caza* I decided to follow the chronology of the script and this forced me to structure things in such as way as not to burden the production team too much. What at first was simply a necessity has now become a working method which I cannot escape; I realize now that what I wanted and want to do is to continue reducing as much as possible the elements I work with, always looking for greater intimacy and greater concentration.

The house you see in *Elisa* doesn't match the one described in the script, which was a windmill surrounded by rich vegetation. We looked for the right windmill for a while without finding one that offered all the desired characteristics. One day, I realized that I was on the wrong track and that it was not a windmill I needed but a house in the country. There was a beautiful area in the province of Segovia which attracted me but we didn't find the right house there. Then, one day, we finally found the house. The house you see in the film is the house as it really was: we didn't change the layout of the rooms, nor the colors of the walls, and we furnished the interior with objects from that region. I could have lived a portion of my life in this house. The most intriguing part of the shoot was to see how quickly Fernando Rey and Geraldine took to the setting, to the point that after a few days of shooting, I felt like an intruder in this house.

E B : *In some ways,* Elisa, vida mía *is your film that contains the most allusions and at the same time it is the most ambiguous. One could say that it is a film about ambiguity. An ambiguity that colors the entire film since the first and the last shot are identical, as if the film had not taken place. On the other hand, there is a constant ambiguity surrounding the events, the chronology, the characters, the reality, the imagination, the dream, etc. How do you see your last film in relation to this issue? What is your position in relation to this ambiguity? Or is it for you something transparent?*

C S : *Elisa, vida mía* was made by piecing together the various elements that come into play, and in a way the intention was to make something that one can never really make. If you accept the notion that everything one does in life is somewhat autobiographical, without falling into the trap of unveiling oneself to the public, then *Elisa* is the closest I've come to expressing my own thoughts in film. The fact that one feels very close to one's characters— and in the case of Elisa, I really do—doesn't mean at all that their behavior reflects one's own at all times; let's not forget that the cinema, the novel, the theater are representations and the stories we tell are more imagined than actual. In fact, it's hard to escape the temptation to represent oneself. One feels more confident recounting familiar events, and it's easier to imagine those things one has dreamed, or remembers, or wants passionately. What I mean to say by this digression is simply that, if there is ambiguity in the film, it's because it corresponds to my own ambiguity. The first thing that comes to mind when I try to explain the film is that I'm facing a wall that separates the images from the words and there is no adequate way to translate one system into the other when they each use such different vocabularies. Unexplainable films always appeal to me more; they have an underlying mystery and their appeal and magic come at the time of projection. I'm not a very good spectator and I regretfully acknowledge that I'm getting worse, maybe because I'd like for that rare and mysterious underground communication between author and audience to happen more often. I would be happy if I could bridge this gap in one of my films.

E B : *To be more specific, and drawing from the previous question, how do you personally see the erotic scene between Elisa and her father (from a realistic, imaginary, or poetic point of view)?*
C S : You can't take this scene out of the context of the rest of the film because it would not make any sense. But I suppose this scene can be interpreted in a number of ways; in relation to the characters, the woman could be Elisa or her mother. In the case of the former, the relationship would be incestuous. As for when it takes place, it could be in the past and referring to Elisa's mother; or it could be in the future, in which case it would certainly be an incestuous relationship; or it could simply have been imagined. By whom? Of course, now we are approaching a question which brings together all the central themes in the film: is this Luis' story (Elisa's father) or Elisa's? Does the story belong to a character who is double, half Luis, half Elisa, which in the final analysis would be me, the filmmaker?

In a way, Luis is a witness to his daughter's conjugal drama and he imagines an erotic situation which is actual, or one which is yet to come, because either scenario is possible.

EB: *For me,* Elisa, vía mía *is a film of unparalleled poetry, and at the same time it displays an astonishing control over the various levels of reality, imagination, fantasy, over the very question of time. How do you feel about its poetic nature? How are the planes of reality, imagination, and fantasy fused together?*
CS: I don't know how to explain this. I think this fusion is part of my very being; I think we all live on several distinct temporal planes simultaneously, that we are not conscious of our own existence, that our lucid moments—if we even have them—are sporadic. The poetic has, for me, an imaginative and inexplicable dimension; in any case, it's what makes you vibrate without your knowing exactly why. In fact, the only things that I try to show in *Elisa, vida mía* are my own preoccupations, and I do so by means of my sensibility and intelligence.

EB: *To conclude, what are your views on contemporary Spanish cinema, those films made in recent years as well as those of the 60s?*
CS: Cinematically speaking, the most important event for me in the last few years is that the Spanish audience is now coming to see our films; what I mean to say is that they have redirected their attention away from the overtly commercial products and toward a cinema that is more mature, more refined. And what is more astonishing is that, for the first time in years, this public is taking an interest in Spanish films, which is to say that they are interested in what is happening in Spain, which was unimaginable two or three years ago.

What is also interesting to note is that since Franco's death, Spanish cinema no longer carries the label "Francoist" abroad. This kind of simplistic thinking made it common outside Spain to label all Spanish-made films Francoist. Until very recently, Spain was one of the worst places in Europe to make films; things have changed now and there is a growing interest in our cinema. I think, however, that it is somewhat premature to speak of a Spanish film renaissance, even though it's not hard to find four or five films every year that are truly amazing. I think these are the result of individual efforts rather than part of a coherent film movement.

Interview with Carlos Saura

ANTONIO CASTRO / 1979

ANTONIO CASTRO: *The first question is obligatory. Why go back six years later to the same characters you used in* Ana y los lobos *[Ana and the Wolves]?*
CARLOS SAURA: You know that this was an idea that I had for a long time. I suspect that it is an idea that all authors have: to return to certain characters from the past to see what they are doing now. I felt that the characters hadn't concluded their life cycle in *Ana y los lobos*, but rather, to me, they were still alive. It was a matter of seeing what they were doing now, if they lived in the same house, etc. That was the pretext, let's say, but what attracted me more was not having to explain the past of some characters. When you write a novel or a script, even though you say you don't do it, you have no choice but to write a kind of *curriculum vitae* for the characters: where they were born, what they have done, etc. Or if you don't write it, you have it in your head, so as to be able to develop the action of the story.

In this case, the marvelous advantage was that this *curriculum* was already given in my other film, and at the same time there was visual material—I'm a man of images and the literary world is a bit off to the side for me—that was already done about the past of these characters, so I was able to dispense with the legwork I almost always do, looking for photographs or new settings.

On the other hand, I have the impression—although this is something that you will have to tell me—that *Mamá cumple cien años* [Mama Turns One

From *Dirigido por* 69 (1979): 44–50. Reprinted by permission of *Dirigido por*. Translated from Spanish by Linda M. Willem.

Hundred] doesn't have anything to do with *Ana y los lobos*. My idea was to pick up the characters, but not the story. That is, to make something else entirely, coming from my present state of mind at the time, which was very different from that in *Ana y los lobos*.

A C : *By proposing a continuation of the characters with Ana alive, you modify to some degree the ending of* Ana y los lobos *because the ambiguity of whether it really occurred or if it was just the materialization of the dreams of the three brothers disappears with the presence of Ana.*

C S : Well, it can be interpreted that way, or it could be the opposite. It can also be interpreted that the ending was real and that the story has nothing to do with *Ana y los lobos*. I have always said that the end of *Ana* was imaginary, but I now want to add that even if Ana had really been raped and killed in *Ana y los lobos* that wouldn't have been a reason for stopping her from appearing in *Mamá cumple cien años*, because I never had the intention of establishing a continuity in the story between both films. It's as if I'm doing the life of Luis, the father in *Elisa, vida mía* [Elisa, My Life], with the same characters, in the same house, and I move forward without worrying about Luis in *Elisa, vida mía*.

A C : *What I would say is that in* Ana y los lobos *you leave the possibility of both a real ending and an imaginary one, while in* Mamá cumple cien años *the first possibility is practically excluded.*

C S : In this case, yes. I've always thought that *Ana y los lobos* was more like a short story. Better yet, a fable. The characters are clearly archetypes. There are good ones, bad ones, etc.

A C : *You made* Ana y los lobos *in 1972, still under the Franco regime, and the film is more clearly symbolic than your others. You regularly have been accused of impenetrability. How has the change in the political circumstances, the death of Franco, influenced your way of expressing yourself?*

C S : You present a problem that has tortured me since I began to make films. For a long time what was in style were films that existed on the surface level, those that said that "people live on the screen," which is a very debatable point and one which doesn't interest me in the least. Fortunately, what then came into style was a more elaborate type of film which more closely approaches what I do.

I'm totally against the model of American movies coming back into style, where one must tell linear stories. Cinema is fiction and it always has told lies. Cinema is one big lie. The characters don't represent anything; they interpret the stories that are invented by the scriptwriters and directors. I'm delighted by those who say that my cinema is symbolic or cryptic. Since I've never done this on a conscious level, it comes as a surprise to me. It always has been linked to my need to find a personal voice of my own, and to the possibility of expressing myself the way I want to. They think that I am a very wise person who has dispassionately worked out an entire program about how to make films, but that's not true. I—as an *auteur*—don't have the sensation that I am making a cryptic film. The only thing is that instead of telling a story linearly, I take a roundabout way, like what is so often done in literature. But in movies this is very often rejected, because different forms of artistic expression are not understood.

I'm totally against limiting cinema to a simplistic way of telling a story that is easily understandable, with a beginning and an end, that has clearly defined characters, and is easily identifiable with everyday reality. I don't know why cinema has to have rules which are totally different than in literature, for example.

A C : *Well, I guess it's because it's taken for granted that the viewer of films is less sophisticated and makes less of an effort than the reader of a book, which leads to the praising of linear plotlines and obvious presentations. Fortunately, it seems that this is gradually being abandoned.*
C S : You have perfectly clarified what I wanted to say. I don't want to make, nor do I think that everyone should have to make, the same simple, linear, and obvious story. Something must be left at the margins, to be more complex, since human beings are tremendously complex. What I like is to tell stories at various levels. I am attracted by investigations of time and space, and the interplay between them. Now when you ask me how I've changed the way I express myself since Franco's death, I can only say that I keep accommodating myself to circumstances, because it's circumstances that keep pointing out and forcing you to choose a path, even though I don't want to. Now I feel freer and better deep down. I'm much more optimistic as a person now and I see more possibilities. But I never figured that after Franco's death I'd be another person and I'd make a different kind of cinema. That idea never occurred to me, apart from the fact that I always thought

that Franco was dead before he died. For me Franco's death has been much slower. Before Franco died there already had been a process. . . .

AC: *Of decomposition. . . .*
CS: That's it. I don't feel anything different except feeling freer as a person.

AC: *In* Ana y los lobos *Ana was the character who functions as a catalyst for the obsessions and lifestyles of the others, whereas in this film Ana is more integrated; she is almost an extension of the family.*
CS: That could be. She is more integrated. Perhaps she's now closer to this family in its current state. That relates to the fact that the feelings of the English, French or Swiss middle class are very similar to those of the Spanish middle class. Geraldine and I saw this character—and we worked on this a lot—as very common, much less attractive than in *Ana y los lobos* where she was 18 years old and had a freshness that she now lacks. This Ana is a married woman, very much of the middle class, common, and not interesting in the least.

AC: *Almost like Geraldine's character in Altman's films, but less of a caricature.*
CS: Maybe, I don't know. Altman always makes an exaggerated caricature of Geraldine, but there is a bit of caricature here too. The model was that of an English girl from the provinces, with a certain amount of bad taste in clothes, but not as exaggerated as what Altman does.

AC: *The theatricality, the feel of a movie farce, is reinforced by the* pasodoble *that begins and ends the film. It's as if we were going to attend a performance, and the camera's movement at the end, leaving the house, reinforces the feeling of it being the end of a performance.*
CS: Well, not deliberately, since the ending was improvised. That is, I filmed something different than I had written. I found it a day before finishing the film. Immediately people looked for intentions in it that were not clear to me at the time. I don't think that it was so obvious that the family stayed locked up in the house. I had presented the final shot as more of a chorale. I wasn't all that conscious of the interpretation given to it in France: that everything is continuing the same, that nothing has changed. Up to that point I can agree, but then things continued to the point where they both-

ered me—that there was a symbolism about Spain, and so forth—which was absolutely false and which I never put forth.

AC: *Well, a possible use for criticism is to explain, to show things that are done instinctively, to look for the reasons why choices are made that many times, over the course of shooting the film, are not done consciously.*
CS: That seems all fine and good to me, but the bad thing is that generally that's not the case. Frequently it is the protagonist who claims to be the critic. But why are we talking about this?

AC: *I feel it must be talked about. If someone wants to do work that is more or less serious and useful to others, the first thing is to analyze the possible contradictions within criticism, what methodology is used, and what is being looked for.*
CS: I'm very concerned about film criticism, for selfish reasons. I'm one of those who believes that criticism should serve as a vehicle between the work that is made and the audience, and that what should be done is to present it in an almost didactic fashion. I believe very little in creative criticism, if it isn't done right, with the seriousness and rigor that isn't possible in two pages and which can't be done on a daily basis. It has to be done by grasping onto the work of a person and analyzing it thoroughly. But, more than a critique, that is a critical study, and in that I really do believe. But what interests me is criticism that stimulates the interest of the viewer to see a film that has some real value. That's why I'm against negative criticism. I'm in favor of critiquing only those things that are worthwhile, a little like the way it is done in literature, where negative criticism is rare. In literature, no one attacks a writer because his latest work is slightly inferior to the one before. I don't remember having read anything like "this book is a piece of shit and this man is a fool."

AC: *Well, but 25,000 books a year are edited and not all are critiqued, whereas 400 films are premiered and all get reviewed.*
CS: Yes, but I think that the most constructive labor, for the author and the public, is to speak about something worthwhile. You orient the audience. Of course I'm speaking of daily or weekly criticism, which is what I think influences people to go to see a movie or not. I think that there is fantastic work to do and that it has a lot to do with the ethics of being a critic. If someone

is a critic to show off his knowledge, his wisdom, or his subjectivism, it's better for him to devote himself to writing or making films.

A C : *Returning to what we were talking about earlier, the use of music in your film is very curious, including the mixture of music.*
C S : You know that for a while I stopped using any kind of music. I choose the music myself, and I choose what like. In *Mamá cumple cien años* there is a military march by Chueca that I like a lot. It really is more of a two-step that I already used in *Ana y los lobos* and which serves as a link to the other film, and it is called *El dos de mayo* [The Second of May]. The truth is that all of this mixture contributes to the feeling of farce, very much our own, a hodgepodge of oriental, military marches, and refined music, which corresponds quite well with what I believe we are, or at least with what I am.

A C : *Lately "criticism" has said that many influences, other than just those of Buñuel, are detectable in your films.*
C S : Well, that could be true. I'm a receptive person. I never shield myself against this type of thing because it seems very positive to me. We are all influenced by what happens around us. There is a continuous process of saturation in life and it's impossible to stay on the margins. Besides I don't want to stay on the margins. But this saturation isn't only from cinematic material, which in my case is probably the smallest amount. I'm saturated more with what I read, with the visual material I use, and of course, with life, friends, conversations. What I argue about more—although I don't think it's worth arguing about—is when they say: "You are like Bergman." Well, no sir, I am not like Bergman; I will never be like Bergman; nor do I have any interest in being like Bergman. Actually, Bergman does interest me a lot—he seems like a fantastic person—the way I like Fellini or Buñuel or Wajda or John Huston. What I refuse to accept are these simplistic identifications. Generally they come from a critic's inability to delve into the depths of a personal work. The clearest case is that of Buñuel, and above all in France, because in Spain—curiously—almost no one has found me similar to Buñuel. But everyone in foreign countries does. And not just me, but also Borau and Victor Erice, whom they say in France is a disciple of mine because I was a professor when he was in school, when Víctor's cinema is not at all like mine. These are simplifications.

A C : *And a lack of understanding.*

C S : And a lack of understanding. What happens is that, out of necessity, there are things in common between Buñuel and me, and with Borau, naturally. When you travel through the world you realize that there is an absolute lack of familiarity with our culture. Today, the dominant culture is Anglo-Saxon, and even more so in the world of cinema. I just came back from Harvard, and it makes you realize how much curiosity and lack of knowledge there is about us. For example, the imaginative process in Latin countries has nothing to do with the imaginative form in the Anglo-Saxon world.

A C : *Exactly, the treatment of time and space—especially time—is fundamental in your work and it is connected to the imaginative process you were talking about.*

C S : It's true. One of the things that surprised me the most was that they were doing a study about the relationship between the cinema of Resnais and Carlos Saura in terms of space and time. I never thought that I had any type of specific relationship with Resnais, although I am a great admirer of his. But the truth is that I then realized that there could be something there, since I had a script—which I hadn't made—that was very similar to *Providence.*

A C : *It seems to me that there is a very clear similarity from the outset. You both are interested in mental processes which break down traditional conceptions of time and space. But beyond that you take entirely different paths.*

C S : I think you are right. But I'm much less cold than Resnais. He is much more capable of distancing himself than I am, and, in addition, I still like to tell a story.

A C : *In* Ana y los lobos, *the main character was Geraldine. In* Mamá cumple cien años *it is Rafaela Aparicio, and this difference is even reflected in the title.*

C S : Ana y los lobos is a film told through only one character. I don't think there is even one scene—well, in reality there are one or two scenes—which Ana is not in. It's only when the girls find the doll that Ana isn't there. On the other hand, *Mamá cumple cien años* is a multifaceted film. But indeed it is the mother who stands out above them all.

A C : *And besides, you make her able to see and hear everything from her bed. You endow her with omnipresence. Why?*

cs: Indeed, the mother is the great protagonist because even if she isn't there, she is present. But I hadn't thought much about it beforehand. That wasn't my point of departure. In terms of endowing her with omnipresence, it seemed like a very fascinating and very lovely idea, but I wouldn't be able to give you an exact reason why. I simply liked it a lot.

AC: *And the presence of the ray of light when she talks to Ana in the grotto.*
cs: Well, there exists an iconography throughout the film, a theatrical iconography that I like a lot. Since my childhood I have been very influenced by a theater director named Rambal. This man should have been very important, not only in Spain, because I remember that Orson Welles said in a very old interview that a Spaniard named Rambal was one of the great men of world theater. Rambal would stage great big novels—*Michael Strogoff*, by Jules Verne, for example, *20,000 Leagues Under the Sea*—in the theater, and he would do it with fantastic inventiveness. There appeared grottoes, mysterious lights, oceans with waves that moved, but done in a way that I, who was little, really believed. I've always been obsessed with this, and in *El jardín de las delicias* [The Garden of Delights], for example, I already tried something similar, as if it were a theatrical play within a film. But I cannot give you a specific reason. To me, I enjoy being able to do it and to escape from a realistic way of presenting things. I saw that image with the grotto with that miracle like something from Saint John of the Cross, whom I like so much. A great miracle, a little like the miracle of the mother at the end who dies but doesn't die, which also is very Rambal, very much like theater with big effects, like voice, wind, and storms.

Previously, during Holy Week, they used to do scenes of Christ's passion in all the towns, and I remember that Rambal once did something really beautiful in Huesca. You know, the figures were completely still, but the effects—lightning, thunder, wind, etc.—were marvelous. So for that reason there is a little bit of everything: Rambal and memories from my youth. Many times you don't think too much about their possible meaning because then you might not put them in. Or maybe you would, who knows?

AC: *When* Ana y los lobos *premiered, many people tried to find some symbolism in the mother. They even went so far as to say that she was a representation of Spain. Do you think that this opinion has any merit?*

cs: It does have some merit, but it is way too simple. I think that a Spanish family—like a French or English one—represents rather faithfully the country in which it lives. In that sense this family—which is exaggerated but has a very real foundation because elements from my own family and from any Spanish family are included—can represent a certain part of Spain. But it ends there. It is absurd to say that it represents Imperial Spain, or whatever. Because I don't really know what Spain is. It's just a word.

I can talk to you about the origin of *Ana y los lobos*. I made this film because when I was young and wanted to talk about the political problems or about sex or about religion, my mother always said that we didn't talk about those things at home, which is the same thing that Spanish censorship told me later: "Everything you want except sex, politics, and religion."

AC: *But it still is curious that the restrictive practices and taboos of the administration exactly reproduce those of the family itself.*
cs: Yes, but that would be more acceptable—due to being more evident—in *Ana y los lobos* than in *Mamá cumple cien años*. At any rate, the problem of the film's interpretation is your problem. If I were to do it, it would be like betraying myself.

AC: *Fernando's character seems the least successful to me, despite having some points of interest. And I didn't end up seeing very clearly his progression from mysticism to wanting to fly.*
cs: That's very curious, because yesterday my brother brought me the latest *Cahiers*, where there is a critique of *Mamá cumple cien años* that says he is the most interesting character in the film. To begin with, I think that you have to forget the Fernando from *Ana y los lobos*. He is a different character that doesn't have anything to do with the other one. He is a man who is trying to fly, and why not? According to the guys at Delta who helped me, there are quite a few elderly people who try to fly, because it really doesn't take all that much physical strength. This desire to fly, I have it. That dream—which according to Freud has a very clear interpretation and therefore I don't think so—we all have it. On the other hand, he wants to fly to attract Ana's attention, and the most tragic thing is that he never flies.

Fernando, like many of us, is a paranoid with a fixed idea. I sometimes think that I'm a bit paranoid about cinema, but not cinema in general, but rather, the cinema that I make, my work. I believe that deep down this is fortunate because we can concentrate on something that completely fulfills us. I'm very close to this type of person who does something enthusiastically. He seems wonderful. I believe a lot in the character.

AC: *In all of your films there exists a certain transformation: old clothes found in trunks, people who dress in the clothes of others, etc.*
CS: It's true. I couldn't explain why since I myself don't know. I have a strong sense of play. I believe a lot in the ludic aspect of life. It really fascinates me that we are all ourselves and many other people too. I'm attracted to the duplicitous doubling of faces, of forms—the transformation. But I'm not capable of explaining it. Just like the theater attracts me a lot. But what I mean is theater in the cinema, because theater on a stage doesn't interest me at all. In the actor, there exists this duplicitous doubling I was talking to you about. He is always himself, and at the same time he's playing the part of someone.

Besides, the transformation reacts to old images from infancy. That's why I like attics so much, those enormous attics filled with mysteries that were in the houses from the provinces and the towns. In attics, I see the possibility of finding things—notebooks, books—something that I did for example in *La prima Angélica* [Cousin Angelica]. It fascinates me a lot, but I don't know how to explain it any further to you.

Also, one must keep in mind the multifaceted nature of women, who are always richer to analyze as characters than men are. Women exchange dresses, hairstyles. They take delight in the game of transformation, and I like to be a spectator at this transformation.

AC: *In the entire final part of the film, there exists a persistent threat of the spring trap as soon as the house is abandoned.*
CS: This is another image that has been stressed since the period of *El jardín de las delicias*. I always think that the more like paradise a garden is, the easier it is to imagine dreadful things. I tried to bring this to the film in *El jardín de las delicias*. In this house, something similar happens. This is a marvelous place, but in return it can be much more dangerous than it seems. On the other hand, these traps exist. I didn't invent them.

AC: *You already used them in* La caza *[The Hunt].*

CS: I'm a bit repetitive, but where we filmed *La caza*, they were there. The spring trap is a terrible weapon. On that same property there had been spring traps which were used not to hunt animals but to capture fugitives, to hunt people, which is even more terrible.

AC: *This appearance of paradise that hides a terrible danger is present in all your work. One could talk about the deceptiveness of appearances not only in terms of landscape but also of people.*

CS: Actually, appearances hide the profound truth about a character. You can't trust appearances. That's why I don't like linear films, where everything is appearance. Reality is much more complex. How and why do those images appear in your head? And why that disorder, which is an ordered disorder? I don't see such a difference between what is called everyday life and memories, desires, dreams. In Huelva now—I just got back from a tribute they gave me—one of the participants of the round table on film and literature—I think it was Cela—was speaking about how film lacks the capacity for introspection. I completely disagree. The foregrounding of a face, with an already established context and ambiance, can be as expressive, as profound, as tremendous, and as dramatic as five pages of literature explaining the frame of mind of that man. But the problem—and I am very worried and frightened by it—is the absolute ignorance of cinema on the part of most people well-versed in literature. It deeply irritates me to see intelligent people saying astoundingly stupid things about cinema.

AC: *Curiously, you never have made a film that was an adaptation of something else: a novel, theatrical work. . . .*

CS: I hope I will hold out without having to do it. The only reason is that if someone is a man of the cinema and wants to be an *auteur*—and I want to be one—the least he can do is to take the material from his own experience. I think that there is a type of ethical obligation in this area. That doesn't keep me from respecting some films based on adaptations, and finding them marvelous.

AC: *In particular, this is a clear difference between Buñuel and you. Buñuel has made many adaptations, and you none. Buñuel—like all the Europeans of his age—has a literary rather than cinematic grounding, and this is very noticeable, while in your case it is the opposite.*

CS: Well, now that you mention it, I think you're right. The strength of Buñuel's films is in their content, not in their images. And besides, he has said things that I have never understood and are in the same vein. He says that he enjoys doing the script, and I don't at all. For me the script is preliminary work for making the film.

AC: *In addition, he has confessed to being a frustrated writer. For him the script is a thing in itself, and for you it is a tool.*

CS: Yes, and he keeps reading a lot, and on the other hand, he never goes to the movies. His referential system is always literary and not cinematographic, that's true.

AC: *Now that it is becoming fashionable—there are studies about Eisenstein and Buñuel from this point of view—have you read any psychoanalytical interpretations of your work that seem interesting to you?*

CS: Well, I've read some things that were published in, I think *Cinema 2002,* but I don't agree with them at all because I don't find myself there. It seems very clever and very attractive. I find it interesting to read, but I don't see myself in those terms. On the other hand, I somewhat avoid this type of thing. It bothers me that they explain the movies to me, and I don't believe very much in the type of psychiatry that uses a novel to say that someone is like this or that. It is not easy to interpret the author through his work. A part of the author is there, but we don't know what part. Perhaps what one wants to give. . . .

AC: *Using the work on the screen.*

CS: Obviously. As you know, Antonio, it is very cathartic, freeing us of the aggression we carry within us. I have made my most aggressive films—*La caza* and *Ana y los lobos*—at times when my personal aggressiveness had reached its peak, when the solution was either to explode or make a film.

My infancy and things like that come to light in almost all of my films, but I don't think that is very difficult. But what has happened is that my films—specifically *Peppermint frappé* and *El jardín de las delicias*—are presented at medical conferences in order to study them from a medical point of view.

AC: *In terms of* Mamá cumple cien años, *the influence of Fellini has been men-*

tioned, above all for the mother's descent, which is similar to a scene in Giulietta
[Juliet of the Spirits].

CS: I don't think it's at all similar to Fellini. I like Fellini a great deal, but I
didn't like *Giulietta* at all. There is an immediate and very Spanish reference,
which is the mystery of Elche, whose music I have used on many occasions—
Peppermint frappé, etc.—where there is an angel that descends from the sky.
Also in the theater of Rambal. What happens is that the world of Fellini is a
parallel world. We Spaniards have lived many of the things that are in
Amarcord.

AC: *As a way of ending with the similarities: Rafaela Aparicio's jumbling together
of the prayers is reminiscent of* Simón del desierto *[Simon of the Desert] when
Simón mixes up the prayers.*

CS: Above all, it was a game between brothers, and the song of Saint
Anthony was one that my father used to sing. They are intermixed prayers,
and I didn't think about Buñuel when I did it. I don't think that Buñuel is
present in that scene. He may be present in other cases, but not in this one.
But on the other hand, I do feel that, just like films are made based on novels
or plays, they should be made based on films. I'm so pigheaded about this
that I even said it once to Buñuel as a joke. There was a time when Buñuel
and I had a very close relationship.

I never liked *Simón del desierto* very much. It always seemed to me like the
outline for a film. Buñuel offered to let me continue it, passing all the docu-
mentation on to me, but I didn't accept. One of the things that really
touched me most emotionally was that when making *La vía láctea* [The Milky
Way] because of insurance problems due to his age, Buñuel had to sign a
document, and he empowered me alone to be able to continue the film. This
gesture moved me greatly.

Interview with Carlos Saura

ENRIQUE ALBERICH / 1981

ENRIQUE ALBERICH: *Given the fact that* Mamá cumple cien años *[Mama Turns One Hundred] makes use of characters that were already present in* Ana y los lobos *[Ana and the Wolves] and now with* Deprisa, deprisa *[Hurry, Hurry] there's a recurrence in the treatment of a topic that you had previously undertaken in* Los golfos *[Hooligans], would you say that these are cases of premeditation, ongoing preoccupations, or simply chance?*

CARLOS SAURA: To start with I have to confess that I don't believe in chance. Nevertheless, it's clear that I didn't make *Deprisa* thinking of *Los golfos*, which is a film that I consider to be very different, but without which it's possible that I wouldn't have returned to this topic. Also, there is my old experience as a photographer, as a documentary maker. There are a series of influences. But what basically happens is that I have the good fortune to be able to make whatever I like—because it certainly is quite difficult to succeed in cinema in this country—and as you well know, when one can do what he likes, he has the tendency to deal with subjects that interest him, and so frequently there are topics that repeat. At any rate, there's no fixed pattern.

EA: *What motivated you to make a film about this topic?*

CS: It wasn't anything sudden, not at all. All my life I've cut out newspaper notices and information on these matters. It's something that has always interested me. I've been keeping this material until certain things coincided

From *Dirigido por* 83 (1981): 20–23. Reprinted by permission of *Dirigido por*. Translated from Spanish by Linda M. Willem.

that led me to make the film. Those of us who make films, and who some-what consider ourselves to be *auteurs*, we are interested in all of these burning questions because they are things that in a way affect us all, and in that regard I think that *Deprisa* resembles *Los ojos vendados* [Blindfolded Eyes] a lot, to give one example.

E A : *I imagine that the preparatory work was very laborious.*
c s : The most interesting thing is that the original script is more theoretical than anything, that it was completely subject to modifications, to actions that the actors or other circumstances could bring about. Over the course of months we visited different places, neighborhoods, looking for actors. I wanted to pick some guys that knew each other, who lived in the same area, in the same environment. With them we extensively revised the script and we worked it out on video, because it seemed fundamental to me to capture their language. Actually there are very few words in the film that are from the original script. What is from the previous script is the general idea of the film, that is, a love story together with escalating violence.

E A : *It is precisely this escalating violence that is seen in the different ways that the film's three robberies are staged: you don't show the first one, instead showing Angela on look-out; the second still retains a certain coolness to it; but the third one is already more spectacular and is carried out through shots that are from closer up, more impressionistic.*
c s : Yes, I agree. This escalating violence is totally premeditated. Note that if the short prologue of the car robbery is taken out of the film, it really begins with the sequence of Angela and Pablo's meeting in the bar. The whole film operates through Angela, who participates more and more in the group and who acquires greater responsibility. It is she who carries the story.

E A : *Which contributes toward confirming that the film, above all, is a love story.*
c s : Yes, a story of love and of friendship (because characters other than the two protagonists do intervene). I think that in a certain way in all of my films there is a love story. After all it is something fundamental in life and also very common. It's something that is there, and by necessity, it must be shown.

E A : *Despite its title,* Deprisa, deprisa *has an unhurried, very contemplative tone.*

CS: Well yes, but that doesn't entail any contradiction. Those who live in a hurry are the characters, not me. I've brought about an approximation of their world and I've used the tempo that seemed most appropriate to me. These characters, who in specific moments exert a brutal tension where violence dominates, in their normal lives end up being very calm, and I've noticed that they usually spend hours and hours without doing anything.

EA: *Speaking of that, in the film there's a lot of dead time, scenes where "nothing happens." The pond sequence, for example, isn't justified in terms of the plotline.*
CS: In the first place my principal aim was not to tell a story. Here, the plot is a bit secondary. I don't see why all of the scenes in the film have to be justified. In addition, the pond is there, it's in Villaverde, in the neighborhood where we filmed, and it's like a tradition there. It's true that stories are told about catching lots of fish there and about there being a house at the bottom, although I don't know if there is. But what is there is its idyllic, mythic side in which the weight of the past contrasts with the present, and all of that interests me.

EA: *Although you state your avoidance of any kind of moralism, there is a certain sympathy shown toward the kids.*
CS: They are very simple, naive characters. At no point do I say that they are bad; they are just looking for their freedom. Certainly the theme of freedom came from them. It's a freedom that I don't exactly know how to define, but it exists: the desire not to be controlled, to be left alone.

EA: *The aspirations of those kids are very mundane, even a bit ordinary: to have a car, buy an apartment, etc.*
CS: I've already told you that they're not at all complicated kids, they're extraordinarily simple. There's no contradiction in this attitude either, it's just that they never do without the things society offers them: an apartment, a refrigerator, etc. What for me is somewhat tragic is that, by necessity, things had to turn out badly for these kids in one way or another. The escalating violence couldn't take them anywhere else. The destruction was inevitable. It was too difficult to survive.

EA: *Meca's passion for burning cars is a very "Saurian" detail.*

C S :   It's possible. If you like, it's a "movie element," but I do think that things like that happen in real life.

E A :   *I think that one of the principal characteristics of the film is its ambiguity, and in this respect the film straddles between being a documentary and a fiction.*
C S :   Perhaps that's so, although I think that it's primarily a fiction film. The truth is that I can't scientifically determine where one thing ends and the other begins. I don't think that anything I've ever seen on film is pure documentary, and maybe not even what I've seen in my life. When you manipulate the material, it stops being a documentary. The filming of the recent attempt on Reagan's life, for example, is a documentary. But if you want to reproduce it, in a way you are falsifying it, it's no longer the same thing, you've given it your personal point of view. Inventiveness always enters into the game, if not in the facts, then in how they're handled.

E A :   *There are some characters that I don't see very clearly. The doctor, for example, acts rashly and without the probability of success.*
C S :   I've studied this problem in depth. The reason for his way of acting is very simple: the girl calls a clinic and asks for a doctor—nobody thinks twice about this—the address is confirmed as usual, and the doctor comes. He sees the situation, takes advantage of the opportunity, and takes off with the million. I had my doubts about the sequence being credible, but keep in mind that a doctor did advise us and confirmed that a shot in the liver like the one Pablo had in the film is a mortal wound, incurable even when operated on immediately. The doctor sees this and his choice is simple. He has lots of reasons for wanting to get out of there as soon as possible.

E A :   *There also seems to be a premeditated intention to place blame on the doctor who, ethically speaking, doesn't make a good impression.*
C S :   No, ethically he doesn't make a good impression because not all doctors are impeccably moral. A medical degree doesn't guarantee perfect conduct, and actually there are many doctors who would act that way. Should the kids be attacked because of their conduct? Well, they aren't the only ones who can be reproached.

E A :   *For what purpose did you choose the music you used?*

CS: I really like this music, and besides, it's the type of music that these kids listen to. In the film the different musical tempos are planned out, and there's a great respect for the special atmosphere that music creates. I also shoot with it. I'm interested in doing it that way because I think that music always contributes toward creating a distinct, special atmosphere.

EA: *There is a lot of music; at times it seems to be excessive.*
CS: It's just that I wanted it to be consistent, for the music to modify and fit the environment, which is something that happens in reality, and for it to become dominant. These kids are constantly listening to this type of music. It's something inherent in them.

EA: *Is it true that in France the film was at the point of being classified X?*
CS: Yes, that's right. The French Censorship Commission was just a step away from giving it an X rating, but it didn't end up that way. The curious thing about this is that they cited as a reason that the film's "great artistic qualities" contributed towards making it more morally dangerous.

EA: *Well, let's move on to talk about* Bodas de sangre *[Blood Wedding], your latest work. The first thing that's surprising about it is that you had accepted to make a commissioned film.*
CS: Yes, it's the first time I've done it, but it's just that a series of rather strange things coincided. It all began when I attended a rehearsal of Gades's ballet and was very enthusiastic about his version. Then Emiliano Piedra came to me and proposed that I make a film, and I accepted. But if I hadn't attended the rehearsal, and if it hadn't interested me so much, I wouldn't have done it.

I've already been a ballet photographer and I've always been fascinated by rehearsals. It fascinates me to observe the physical effort of the dancers, to see how they execute the movements with an authentic passion, killing themselves to do it well.

EA: *How was the collaboration with Gades? Did he influence you in your directorial duties?*
CS: No, not at all. There was no influence, otherwise I would not have accepted it. But in all other aspects the collaboration has been very close, it's been like dealing with a brother.

E A : *Seeing the film, it gives the impression that the editing was complicated.*
C S : Well, no, on the contrary, it was very simple because we edited while filming. More and more I tend to work in this way, with the editing mentally already done. Likewise, you have to keep in mind that I work with an editor who I'm thoroughly in sync with, and that facilitates things greatly. On the other hand, on this occasion it started out from a previous work, from a choreography that had to be followed. The editing was a product of being subordinate to this work.

I filmed with just one camera, and I tried to make the camera function as if it were my own eyes, as if it reflected my own sight. For that reason, I never once used a crane, and except for the obligatory ground level shots of the dancer's feet, I've retained the point of view of one's sight.

E A : *The filming of the dance between four walls, one of which was a mirror—didn't that pose any problems either?*
C S : No, there was no special difficulty with the filming, and in terms of the mirror, that didn't entail any problem. Remember that the set was mobile and that a wall could be removed and put back.

E A : *Do you consider* Bodas de sangre *to be an* auteur *film?*
C S : Well, I don't know. I haven't posed that question to myself. I suppose so, from the moment that I portrayed the ballet from my particular point of view, which surely would be different from the version that you would have been able to do, for example. I already sensed that if it were given my personal vision, the ballet would become something else. Although I respected Antonio's work, I gave it a personal vision. But nevertheless, I do have to recognize that this previous work existed, it's something different from anything that had been done before. Gades and his ballet are fundamental.

E A : *I'm of the opinion that one of the major achievements of the film resides in the cinematic treatment of the performance, in having avoided a simple filmed drama or ballet.*
C S : As I've already told you, above all I tried to give a personal vision. The ballet itself didn't interest me.

E A : *Does the story that Lorca's drama tells interest you?*

CS: What most interested me was the version that Gades had made, which I consider wonderful, very sincere, in contrast to some Spanish films (I don't want to mention names) that seek to be poetic but in reality are not; they're not sincere.

I think that in Gades's version there is a certain non-intellectual populism, and in this sense there is more of Gades than of Lorca.

Had I set out to film the story coldly, the truth is that I would have thought about it twice.

EA: *This time the script wasn't any problem.*
CS: In effect, it has been almost like taking to the extreme this obsession I have to film without a script. Certainly Gades still doesn't know that he appears in the credits as screenwriter, because he is in Argentina now.

EA: *Is* Bodas de sangre *going to end up at Cannes?*
CS: Yes, it's going to go, but I have to clarify that it won't be presented at a competition or at any official session. Rather it will be shown at a special session as a type of tribute to me, something which makes me very happy.

EA: *To conclude, can you give any advance notice about your next project?*
CS: It's going to be called *Dulces horas del ayer* [Sweet Hours of Yesterday], and it's going to be a story about a man whose present life doesn't excite him, and who feels nostalgia for a past that suited him better. Although some details remain to be cleared up, it's possible that we will begin shooting in June.

Antonieta, Carlos Saura Between the Past and the Present

VALERIA CIOMPI / 1982

VALERIA CIOMPI: *How did this project arise? How did you come in contact with Jean-Claude Carrière?*

CARLOS SAURA: I found myself in France at the end of last year, and Gaumont was apparently interested in talking to me about directing a film. I dined with the top executives at Gaumont and they then talked about three possibilities, and one of them was this *Antonieta* script, which was a film that was to be made in Mexico according to a script by Jean-Claude Carrière and which, in principle, seemed the closest to my world, the closest to me in a certain way, and I said that I'd like to read the script. Another one of the proposals they made me was a *Carmen*, and I had—and continue to have—a *Carmen* in the planning stages, so I said no. Besides, what they proposed was a *Carmen* in French and made in France, and the thing, in principle, didn't excite me too much. I think that Francesco Rosi is now going to do this project.

VC: *Then you set out on your first filming outside of Spain.*

CS: The truth is that on other occasions when I had received proposals to work outside of Spain, I always was a bit afraid, afraid of uprooting myself, of arriving in a country like the United States and beginning to work there. I don't think that can be done without knowing a country completely. It seemed to me to be a dangerous adventure, and a bit absurd. A film can't be made if one doesn't have a sufficient knowledge of the elements and have a

Papeles de Cine Casablanca 21 (1982): 31–37. Translated from Spanish by Linda M. Willem.

credibility with the objects, the people, and the language, which is so important.

On the other hand, upon reading Carrière's script—which I liked immensely—I realized that it was just a question of being a very accessible story for me, something very close and relatively comfortable and easy to make. Really it was a matter of it being a first draft that Carrière was willing to modify in whatever way was necessary, but before arriving at any firm agreement with Gaumont or with the other co-producers, Carrière and I went to Mexico and we worked on the script some fifteen or twenty days, adjusting some things about the terrain, speaking to people, etc., and that's when I really realized that the film could be made, and I accepted.

v c : *It was a co-production?*
c s : Yes, in principle it was a co-production between Spain and Mexico, but the Spanish participation was still up in the air. I pushed a bit for the Spanish participation to be more important. I didn't want to go alone so my only condition was being able to bring a minimal Spanish crew, but in a certain way that permitted me to have almost absolute control over the film. This crew consisted of Teo Escamilla, who sort of controlled the entire photography crew; Pablo del Amo for the editing; and Víctor Alvarrán as the first director's assistant. Víctor's work was very important since his tasks in a certain way exceeded those normally given a director's assistant. He's a very educated person who, at any given time, had to be ready to pick some of the actors, to plan the shooting locations, in short, his work somewhat straddled both directing and production. And who also came with us was Héctor Alterio, who had a small part in the film.

And with all of these elements already in our hands, the film was quickly mounted and done.

v c : *How long, approximately, was the shooting?*
c s : We began to shoot at the end of March, the filming lasted some ten or twelve weeks, because the most important part was done in Mexico, and then we were working two or three weeks in Paris.

v c : *Were changes to the script done during the filming?*
c s : No. Carrière is an excellent storyteller and the script was very well structured, but there were areas left very open since Carrière, as well as I, thought

that a script should never be finished, that it's something living. If he were not that way, I would not have been interested in making the film. I changed some scenes and I even added others, but this type of modification was done through a previous agreement with Carrière. What I indeed did try to do was follow the order of the script in the shooting, except for the part that takes place in Paris. At any rate, in the end, after examining my conscience, I believe that I was very faithful to the spirit of Carriére's story.

V C :   *On other occasions you have declared yourself against literary adaptations or scripts whose ideas were not your own. In this sense* Antonieta *is a completely new experience for you.*
C S :   Yes, in principle I'm against that, but with certain shadings because I don't like to be very dogmatic. I detest dogmatism of any kind. I think that when a literary work has found its own language and that is perfectly attained—in the case of a good novel for example—it seems to me that bringing it to the screen is a betrayal. Clearly there are many filmakers who have made magnificent films adapting literary works, even modifying them, but personally it seems too comfortable. It's really like the hardest part was given to you already done.

V C :   *Perhaps with certain minor literary works or decidedly bad ones, this sense of betrayal is not so strong.*
C S :   Yes, but this story of betrayal also is very subjective, as is the appraisal of good or bad novels. What happens is that there are novels that can't even be called novels, they don't have any literary value and they limit themselves to telling a story of no consequence whatsoever. In that case, yes, I do think it's much easier to adapt them. But for me it would be impossible to make the *Quijote* or any other literary work of value, like for example *Under the Volcano* by Lowry, because they already have an absolutely perfect literary structure.

Besides, and I've said this many times, what interests me is being an *auteur*. I've wanted to be one all my life and I have always refused to be an illustrator, to illustrate a novel or a theatrical work. I don't enjoy putting my talents into it—perhaps I should have started there. It's not that I have a problem of any significance with respect to the completed work, it's simply that I don't at all enjoy doing it. I've always considered myself to be an *auteur*, good or bad, but an *auteur*. So I've always tried to have the concepts come from me, to write the script myself or in collaboration with someone.

V C : *And* Antonieta*?*
C S : In this case, since the script was very close to me, Carrière did me an enormous favor of facilitating something that it would never have occurred to me to ever do. All of a sudden I found myself with a script I would have liked to have written, and that seemed fantastic because one of my dreams was to find a script for myself that I didn't need to write, because for me writing scripts is a tremendously boring job—although on occasion it can become exciting—and very, very laborious. I have to lock myself completely alone with my typewriter. It really is a matter of giving birth, and that's a disaster, above all when after finishing the script the other labor of shooting the film comes.

In this case the first childbirth was already done. I had to make small modifications, add some ingredients, but the story was already there and I liked it a lot.

V C : *When you entered into the project, was the cast already decided? Had they already been thinking about Isabelle Adjani and Hanna Schygulla?*
C S : I'd say that the film already was practically mounted by Gaumont and the Mexicans. They only needed the director. When I joined the project, they had already spoken to Isabelle Adjani, while the conversations with Schygulla were pretty much parallel to my coming on board, since the character of Hanna wasn't in the first script by Carrière.

V C : *Can you tell us a little about the film's plot?*
C S : Yes, it's curious because in this case I can indeed do so. I can talk about it a bit dispassionately because in a way I'm both inside and outside of the subject. I'm inside because it's a story that I'm very enthusiastic about and one that I could identify with as mine. And I'm outside because it's a matter of something that was already done. When I was given the script before deciding if I'd accept it or not, I didn't have to analyze the story.

If it were the question of an original plot of mine, I possibly would not have been able to do it. I don't like, nor does it interest me, to analyze what I'm doing or to talk about my films once they are done.

In this case the story develops somewhat on three different levels. In general, I don't like to make linear films. It doesn't excite me to follow a linear story from beginning to end. I don't know why, but it just doesn't interest me. In *Antonieta* on one hand we have the base-line story, that is, a Mexican woman, Antonieta Rivas Mercado, who was born with the century and who, at thirty years of age, fatally shot herself in Paris's Notre Dame Cathedral. That constitutes the core of the story and a little of the character to be encountered. Then we have another woman, Hanna Schygulla, who is putting together a project—it's not specified very well but the assumption is that it's a book—about suicides by women in this century. In her house she has photographs of Marilyn Monroe, Jean Seberg, Virginia Woolf, and over the course of the inquiries that she's making in Paris, the city where she lives, she comes across this case that begins to interest her. We could say that the pretext of the film is a little about Hanna Schygulla and her search for the character of Antonieta Rivas Mercado.

v c : *So there's a part of the story that develops in the present and another part in the past.*
c s : Exactly. And this investigation is what takes Hanna Schygulla to Mexico to speak with people who had known Antonieta and to investigate into this character. These are the two levels on which the film operates, and on the other hand, Carrière and I endeavored—and I thought this was very good and tried to do it as best I could—to explain a bit what the time period that Antonieta lived in was like, what historical events were happening at the time, keeping in mind that Mexico, from approximately the 1910's to the 1930's had gone through a tremendous upheaval with all of its sometimes bloody and violent events, to which the name Mexican Revolution has been given and in which it was Antonieta's lot to live, first as a child and then as an adolescent and woman. Antonieta, in addition, breaking with the norms of society at the time, abandoned her husband to become the lover, companion, and collaborator of Vasconcelos, a man who played a very interesting role in the political history of Mexico, and who even became a candidate for the presidency of the republic.

v c : *Is the idea for the script based on any book or biography?*
c s : Let's say that the plot of the film is largely based on material that has recently been published on this woman, who wasn't exactly unknown but there wasn't that much known about her in Mexico. Suddenly, due to a series

of circumstances, she started to become a figure of special interest as a victim of a specific society. This all seems a bit simplistic, but Antonieta was an extremely sensitive person, very fragile and with delicate feelings, who was incapable of withstanding a series of events that occurred in her life.

Some years ago a book entitled *87 cartas de amor, Antonieta Rivas Mercado* [87 Love Letters, Antonieta Rivas Mercado] was published, which was a compilation of letters that Antonieta addressed to the painter Manuel Rodrìguez Lozano. Some of these letters are very beautiful and textually appear in the film, all of which is based—with very little license—on historical events, and the majority of the texts that are used are ones written by Vasconcelos or Antonieta. The love letters also reflect aesthetic or moral concerns. Antonieta was a very cultured person who had translated many authors of the vanguard theater, and in a certain way she can be considered to be the founder of Mexico's Philharmonic Orchestra. She was very important to the development of Mexican cultural life. She found herself at the center of extremely important events, although she never became the protagonist. She had a great fortune and she used it almost exclusively helping the people who would gather around her, especially Vasconcelos. But she herself left almost nothing written except these letters.

These letters reflect the passionate platonic relationship that Antonieta lived with Lozano. She even reached the point of reproaching him for not wanting a sexual relationship with her, and the basic reason for this was that Lozano was a homosexual. Therefore, he never ended up rejecting her emotionally, in fact they had a very deep relationship on the level of sensibilities. But the tragedy for Antonieta was that she passionately loved this man and she found herself sexually rejected by him.

VC: *Can we talk a little about what it was like to work with Isabelle Adjani and Hanna Schygulla?*
CS: Well, about that I'd like to say that in addition to both of them being extraordinarily talented actresses, perhaps the most interesting thing about working with them was that they are two completely different women, as much in their real lives as in the film.

VC: *According to the film's plot one could say that Hanna Schygulla somewhat performs the role of the determined woman with a strong personality, and Adjani is perfectly identified with the image of fragility.*

CS: That's so, in a way, because things are never that clear. Hanna Schygulla is also a very sensitive woman, very delicate and enchanting, and really, working with them was perfect, there were absolutely no problems. They are such different women in their behavior and way of being that there was never any friction, which is quite common when there are two women working on the same film, especially if they are somewhat *prima donnas*. Rivalries always arise. What indeed is curious is that at a specific moment in the film these two women draw close to each other, they don't fuse into one, but a great understanding is indeed produced between them.

VC: *It's something that tends to happen almost always between the researcher and the subject researched.*
CS: Yes always, it's always like that. Besides I think, in any case, that a person who is writing a book about suicides has to have some special reason. And there always is a certain affinity between someone who seeks and what is sought.

VC: *That connects in a way with a topic that you touched on in another interview, which is the documentary side that exists in a certain way in all of your films.*
CS: Yes, although that's something I've never clarified completely. During the six years that I taught classes on film directing in the Film School, I never came to accept the division of cinema into genres. I must be a very odd person because this apparently is something that everyone is in agreement about, but I've never managed to believe in the separation that can exist between documentary and fiction, between a musical film and a detective one. Is a movie a musical just because there are musical numbers? I don't understand it. And the same thing happens with the documentary especially when it's in reference to my work. Where is the documentary part and where is the fiction? I wouldn't know how to explain it very well.

I have the sensation that at times I work more with everyday elements, more concrete ones, and I don't know if that can be defined as more or less documentary. There are certain cases like perhaps *Los golfos* [Hooligans] or *Deprisa, deprisa* [Hurry, Hurry] where this documentary aspect can be more present. I'm not interested in insisting too much on this point either, but there are examples in films of mine, like *Los ojos vendados* [Blindfolded Eyes], which is indeed a documentary in a certain sense because it responded to a very clear moment of mine, to some very specific personal experiences, and what I tried to do was to reproduce a series of things that I had thought about or had happened to me. In this sense it has a very strong documentary value. It reflects something that was happening in the country. It was much less imaginative than other things of mine. It was a real experience transferred to the screen.

Another example could be *Deprisa, deprisa*, where there is naturalistic dialogue and actors who respond in a way to the reality that they're portraying, or that is to say that a more immediate contact exists with the tangible reality we were talking about before.

In *Antonieta*, specifically, what I call documentary are the historical facts, which of course are manipulated, as *Deprisa, deprisa* also was manipulated. Everything is manipulated—dialogues, for example, and in summarized stories.

Taking this reasoning a bit further, I'd never speak in terms of documentary cinema, just in terms of fictional cinema. They say that the furthermost edge of documentary cinema can in a way be *cinéma-vérité*, but that's a lie. It doesn't exist. At any rate, the few times that it can exist is where the manipulation is less, that is, in a journalistic account. It's less, above all, if the person who makes it doesn't have any preconceived ideas and limits himself to filming what passes before his eyes. And that to me is closer to *cinéma-vérité*: not a documentary, but a document.

v c : *It's clear that a certain subjectivity always exists even in the most objective projects.*

c s : If you're a person who has a specific idea about something, this is going to end up being reflected in what you do. But this already is leading into the terrain of that word that I personally detest, namely "creation." It's too important of a word, and I don't believe in important words. What doubt can there possibly be that everyone takes the material for his works out of the things that happen in his life, from the books he reads or the films he sees and which influence him? The refusal to recognize or accept these influences seems foolish to me. One does things because one needs to do them, and there's no reason to try to find out why.

v c : *What is indeed curious is that this concept of "creation"—and that of auteurs to call it by another name—is acquiring more and more strength in a cin-*

ema that has remained to a certain extent distant from that idea, namely American cinema.

CS: Here we're entering a very controversial area. I am, and have always been, a bit against this extreme fascination for only American cinema. It doesn't seem fair either because—and I include myself in this—we aren't familiar with, for example, the cinema that is made in the Orient or we interpret it through the eyes of our own Western culture and we get it all wrong. You can have an extraordinary fascination for the cinema of Mizogouchi, you can be interested in his films, but if you are a person who is inside of the occidental world, you get very different things out of this same cinema.

We're ignoring and rejecting huge numbers of cultures and part of the responsibility for this also belongs to our theorists and our critics. Yes, I understand the fascination that exists for American cinema, but it seems nonsense to me to think that there's nothing else in the whole world and that we owe everything to American cinema.

I've always thought that it's unfortunate that American cinema is so strong. First, because it has imposed a narrative format, a way of planning and acting. That seems extremely serious to me because in a way it has impeded the birth, in many cases, of native cinematographies—which in the long run I don't know if they'd be better or worse, I don't want to get into that type of evaluation—with a narrative tempo that would correspond to the idiosyncrasies of each one of the countries or to the people who make that cinema, and which always would be much more interesting than the unification that is now seen in world cinema.

VC: *What for you would be the solution for this premature aging of cinema?*
CS: The only solution that I see is the one that exists for other modes of artistic expression. Whoever devotes himself to painting, writing, or making films has to marginalize himself a bit with respect to certain things and has to seek an individual path.

VC: *Returning to the discussion of American cinema, toward which you apparently have no special inclination: what type of cinema do you identify with the most or are interested in more as a viewer?*
CS: The truth is that things aren't just black and white with American cinema. There are some films within American cinema which have reached the very heights of what cinema is, and there are great *auteurs* in the United

States. But that dichotomy between American cinema and European cinema is very delicate. I remember that a couple of years ago I was in Hollywood because *Mamá cumple cien años* [Mama Turns One Hundred] had been selected for the Oscar along with other finalists. Then there was a dinner organized in the American Film Institute for the foreign directors who were there. At that dinner, which in a way was presided over by Cukor, were Mamoulian, Minnelli, Billy Wilder, William Wyler, Allan Dwan—in short, all of the great living directors of the glorious Hollywood era. Then Volker Schlondorff and I wanted to raise the issue of American cinema's colonization. It's a problem that was of very personal concern to us and we wanted to discuss it among colleagues, among professionals. We asked ourselves why there wasn't an equivalency, an equality in terms of screenings between American cinema and European cinema because, while American cinema in Europe easily represents sixty or seventy percent of all films that are shown, on American screens European cinema only represents something like five percent. What we were asking for was a certain parity in screenings, alluding also to a very simple reason, namely that American cinema at times doesn't have sufficient quality to give Europe that seventy percent of its films.

Then Billy Wilder—who is one of the quickest people I've ever seen at answering questions and also one of the most cunning and malevolent—said to us, "Look, I have a perfect solution for you." Then Volker asked him what that solution was, and Wilder answered, "That you come here to work, just like we came from Europe to work here." All of this is sort of to explain that the cinema that these men or people like Ford have made is somewhat the essence of all kinds of influences. The United States is the only country I know that has had that fantastic ability to absorb all of the people who have gone there.

The only tragedy is that we lost the American market at a time when European cinema, headed up by people like Fellini, Antonioni, Buñuel, Bergman, Resnais, had strongly entered the United States, and the loss of that market has somewhat caused the collapse of the entire European cinema industry, the almost complete disappearance of English cinema, the present situation in Italian cinema, etc.

V C :   *And French cinema?*
C S :   I think that French cinema now has an enormous advantage, which is the state protection and the extremely intelligent policy that is being carried

out now, and which makes one think that French cinema is going to come out ahead. It's also being marketed to a lot of well-educated young people. What surprised me most about the filming of *Antonieta* in France was the efficiency of the young French crews, an efficiency that contrasts a bit with the lightheartedness with which we tend to do things here.

V C : *Do you think that it's not so much a matter of lightheartedness as a lack of possibilities for young generations to be able to get an adequate apprenticeship in the industry?*

C S : Of course that is happening, but I also could reply there's a kind of generational void. There has not been an integration of younger people into the film crews. I don't know if what's happening is that young people are looking for young people to work with, which is something that has always happened. That's an historical reality that's hard to overcome, because I remember that when I started out, I had people like Bardem and Berlanga very close by, both of whom I admired and loved, but who belonged to another generation and didn't have anything to do with me. And I remember that the stories they told only half interested me because they didn't have anything to do with what I wanted to say. For me they were on another planet.

V C : *What projects do you have for the future?*

C S : I have a project to make an adaptation of *Carmen* with Emiliano Piedra, for which I'm counting on the indispensable collaboration of Antonio Gades. And after *Carmen*, which is a totally Spanish production, I'm going to make something in Brazil.

V C : *Did* Antonieta *respond in some way to a desire or need to stop working in Spain?*

C S : No, not at all, it was something purely coincidental. But the *Antonieta* experience has been very positive because it's made me see things in a different way, because I've always refused to shoot outside of Spain. And now, upon my return, I even see Spanish cinema in another way.

V C : *And how do you see it?*

C S : I don't know. I don't know. Here there are very talented and capable people but I have the impression that there is a destructive side. There exists a great lack of understanding that personally bores me a great deal. There's a very provincial attitude, in the pejorative sense of the word, a tendency to gossip and a tremendous frivolity and improvisation when it's time to do things. It's not that there have to be long-term plans, but one has to understand that making a film is a unique experience, and to try to continue working and making another film and then another one, and not to think that they are going to give you a Hollywood Oscar for the first thing you make and they are going to recognize you as a genius of all geniuses. And this happens because the director has been turned a bit into a star and many directors come to believe it. And for some that's fine, but others aren't able to carry the weight of the star.

v c : *Do* Antonieta *and your next* Carmen *project mean that you've broken off from Elías Querejeta?*
c s : No, absolutely not. What's happening is that lately I've been somewhat pushed along by events. Before I would have a project and it would be presented to Elías. Now things have a different rhythm which, on the other hand, I like a lot. I feel like working, I feel much more vital at this time. But Elías is fully aware of all this, and there even is a possibility that he will coproduce the Brazil project. And if that doesn't work out, we'll think of something else. At any rate, you have to understand that Elías and I have already overcome our "matrimonial" problems. We've gone through so many things together that it would be impossible for us not to remain friends.

Los zancos [The Stilts] by Carlos Saura: Interview

ESTEVE RIAMBAU / 1984

ESTEVE RIAMBAU: Carmen *has received great international acclaim. In* Los zancos *you use the same producer, Emiliano Piedra, the same actress, Laura del Sol, then substitute the presence of Antonio Gades with that of Fernando Fernán-Gómez. They seem two different directions coming from almost the same common place.*

CARLOS SAURA: Well, according to what you say, I'd always have to make the same film with the same people. If I'm thinking of making a ballet film, especially within the vein that we've already done together, I have to count on Antonio Gades because without him I can't do anything. It's a fantastic and marvelous collaboration but we need each other so much that the one can't do anything without the other. In the case of *Los zancos* it's not a matter of being a musical or ballet film. It's something else, and it's more like the other films I've made and which are not ballets. That's the reason I looked for Fernando Fernán Gómez who, if he's not the biggest actor, is one of the best actors that we have in Spain.

ER: *Besides being an actor, Fernando Fernán-Gómez also co-wrote the script for* Los zancos. *Did you agree completely in the choice of the subject matter and in the presentation of the character of the old retired university professor that he portrays? Is there some kind of personal identification with the process of this character's aging?*

From *Dirigido por* 119 (1984): 54–57. Reprinted by permission of *Dirigido por*. Translated from Spanish by Linda M. Willem.

CS: You see, I've had the idea for *Los zancos* in my head for some time now. I wanted to make a film which established a relationship between an elderly man, sixty or seventy years old, and a young girl. I had already decided that the girl had to be Laura del Sol and that the man, by necessity, had to be Fernando Fernán-Gómez. Then, moving from this phase to the collaboration with Fernando was relatively easy because I put myself in contact with him and I got him a bit more involved in doing the script together. We worked very harmoniously and with a great deal of freedom and friendship. It was a very pleasant job. By previous agreement, I had reserved the right to make the final decisions, because it's logical that the final word had to be mine, but the collaboration was valuable and I'd like to repeat it. Lately I'm in need of this collaboration with Antonio Gades or with Fernando Fernán-Gómez. I feel like I'm enhanced because different points of view sometimes enrich things.

ER: *At any rate, it's not the first time you've worked with Fernando Fernán-Gómez as an actor.*

CS: No, but it was very different because in *Ana y los lobos* [Ana and the Wolves] as well as in *Mamá cumple cien años* [Mama Turns One Hundred] Fernando fulfilled his obligation as an actor—he was very rigorous about his role—but our relationship didn't go beyond that. In the case of *Los zancos* it was completely the opposite because when we arrived at the acting phase, the character had already been well worked through and discussed. We wrote lots of pages together and drank lots of whiskeys together.

ER: *Despite the fact that, as you have said,* Los zancos *isn't a musical film like the ones that you've made with Gades, there is, on the other hand, a performance within the performance through the presence of a theatrical troupe, which the protagonist works in.*

CS: Yes, and that is something that, if it isn't in all of my films, it is indeed in many of them. I don't mean to say that this is a constant because that seems like a stupid and pretentious thing to say, but I really like performance and theater within cinema. I feel an enormous fascination for the world of theater, but within cinema. Not so much outside of it as within it. It's curious and it's something I can't explain because I don't know the reasons very well either. But that's where the side of dual personality, of parallel events, or of different planes of reality exists.

E R : *Along the same lines, you also introduce video into* Los zancos *for dramatic effect when at the same time it had aided you in your work on your latest films. However, I'd like to broaden the scope of the question by taking advantage of the setting of this Venice Film Festival where last year the future of film and of the image had already begun to be debated. How do you see film's prospects over the not-too-distant future?*

C S : All predictions of the future are susceptible to error, but I'm someone who loves video. Absolutely, to the point where I don't understand how there are other directors who don't use this medium. I understand the reluctance only in terms of the poor quality of the image that you get. There is one thing for certain, and that is that if someone dedicates a certain amount of time and work, then it's very sad to see it destroyed in a way on the small screen. We all know that this is strictly a technical problem and will be overcome in the future. But, on the other hand, the ease that video affords as a support, due to its immediacy, is extraordinary. It seems to be such a magical and marvelous work tool that it's going to revolutionize all of cinema. Film may disappear as a word but what won't disappear are the movies. And it seems fine to me for it to disappear. I think that up until now we have been in the prehistory and beginning with video we can talk about something else. That's how I definitely feel.

E R : *Godard asserted the same thing here last year during the press conference for* Prénom Carmen *[First Name Carmen].*

C S : I didn't know that but it doesn't surprise me because Godard is also a man who is attentive to the things that are happening. I'm someone who is very preoccupied with the technical side and I'm somewhat up to date on the latest things. If one wants to make films, one can't be at the margins in this aspect because everything is very interconnected.

E R : *I understand that* Los zancos *was filmed while taking advantage of the postponement of a project of major importance about Lope de Aguirre. Is this project still in the works?*

C S : There indeed has been a postponement of *Aguirre*. Unfortunately, I don't think this project is clear from the financial point of view since it seems very complicated to put together and I don't feel like concerning myself with that aspect. I don't know if it will be made or not. I hope that some day it can be made but I hope that it won't be too late because it's a film that requires a certain physical strength to cope with the climate and the Amazon jungle.

E R : *Nevertheless, I think that your next project is going to be connected with Gades.*

C S : Yes, we're going to make *El amor brujo* [Love, the Magician] with Falla's music, under the production of Emiliano Piedra, who is sort of a *factotum* and had pushed us to make the previous films. Perhaps he's the most enthusiastic of the three of us. With respect to the project, I'm now at the stage where I'm looking at some images, the mural that will serve as the set, etc. But I can't explain more than that, although it will be pretty free and we want to do it on the big film set at Bronston Studios, over a minimum of three months, even preserving the dilapidated state of that place. We're going to play with the lighting and the dance at the same time. That's the idea, but we don't know where it will end. One never knows, but in any case, it's a marvelous adventure.

The Flamenco Trilogy

PATRICK SCHUPP / 1986

PATRICK SCHUPP: *To begin with, Carlos Saura, I'd like to propose the follow-ing: I see this trilogy*—Bodas de sangre *[Blood Wedding]*, Carmen, *and* El amor brujo *[Love, the Magician] as in effect a three part entity: the world of flamenco, that is, the world of gypsies: first, seen from the theatrical perspective—the theater of Federico García Lorca; then, seen through the eyes of foreigners—Mérimée and Bizet; and, finally, seen through the work of the most authentic Andalusian musi-cian—Manuel de Falla. Do you agree?*

CARLOS SAURA: Your perception is very interesting, but I have to admit to you that, at first, we had none of that in mind. *Bodas* started out as a request from my producer and friend, Emiliano Piedra, who invited me to see the rehearsal of the ballet by Antonio Gades and his group. So, I made the film. And, since the reception was favorable, we decided to go further.

PS: *It's nonetheless remarkable that you were able to establish a continuity in the vision and the realization of these three films which, after all, were made sequen-tially but without any formalized connections.*

CS: I discovered the world of dance with *Bodas*, and it was after this first film that we began looking at other possibilities. For me, in effect, *El amor brujo* is a blending of the other two, and it's Spanish in essence, in terms of the music and the mood.

PS: *I felt that in* Bodas *the true star was the camera. In the second film, it was*

From *Sequences* 127 (1986): 37–42. Reprinted by permission. Translated from French by Paula Willoquet-Maricondi.

*the character Carmen. The entire film was structured around the character, the true
and the false, the dance and the operatic character. In the third film,* El amor
brujo, *it was the dance, purely and absolutely. What do you think?*
C S : In a way, you are absolutely right. *Bodas* is the gaze. The rehearsal which
I saw impressed me a great deal and, in making the film, I tried to translate
into images what I had felt at the time. So, the camera followed all the movements, without the necessary distancing you experience at a theatrical performance. For *Carmen,* what can I say? *Carmen* is Carmen. A fascinating
character, particularly in Mérimée's short story, which I like better than the
opera. Evidently, in the last film it's the music that counts, but what per-
suaded me to make the film was the character.

P S : *Next to this authentic gypsy character one also finds a very commercial atmosphere, with winks, curlicues, hair combs, mantillas, all the fixings one expects to
see in a postcard of a Spanish woman. Why?*
C S : But that is intended. I have tried, in a way, to exorcise the kind of ideas
that foreigners have of Spain, because this outlook is, in my opinion, the
product of their mentality.

P S : *So, it's really the world of gypsies—and by extension the Spanish world—but
seen by foreigners?*
C S : What is Carmen other than that?

P S : *How did you decide on the angles in* Carmen? *For example, did you select the
dance steps relative to an aesthetic imperative? Did Antonio Gades participate in
the elaboration of the scenes? Did he want to execute a particular step or movement
while you made decisions regarding the angle of the shot or the editing of a
sequence?*
C S : It varied. We collaborated constantly and completely. I took care of the
staging and the cinematography—it's my job—and all my suggestions
regarding the choreography were relative to the shots. I am sure you know
that the problem posed by the choreography in the cinema, as opposed to
the stage, is the changes in angles or positioning. For example, if the dancers
are moving in one direction and the camera is going in the opposite direction, that will by definition affect the choreography. So, you have to be very
careful about respecting the directions, the gestures, and the movements. It's
like in the theater, where you have two or three directions occurring simulta-

neously. Since many moves are impossible to reenact in film because of their diversity, you have to choose what will give you the best results.

P S :   *In that case, is the wide angle appropriate?*
C S :   I am not sure. What I do know is that I have to alter the rhythm—that is, the steps and the movements—in relation to the shot, and that's exactly what we did in *Bodas*. We had to reconstruct certain choreographic elements for the cinema specifically, and Antonio understood that very well.

P S :   *Can you say a few words about the theatrical staging of* Carmen, *after the film was made? You were directly involved as staging director and lighting technician, were you not?*
C S :   I have to admit that Antonio really did most of the work, given his exceptional experience of the stage. But it's true that the performance was a continuation of the film. I came up with some of the structures for the performance, made suggestions regarding the placements of props, but it was Antonio who made the final decisions. I learned a lot from him.

P S :   *What about the involvement of your brother, Antonio Saura?*
C S :   As a painter, he defined the space on stage, and he devised those immense areas of shadow and light which add so much to the performance. But, you see, these things vary from stage to stage, since no one stage is like the other. We had to adapt constantly. We staged the show in Paris, then we had to work within the parameters we were given.

P S :   *Antonio Gades is coming back to Montreal in January of 1987, once again at the invitation of the O.S.M, and he will put on the theatrical version of* Bodas. *Were you aware of this?*
C S :   Yes, he told me. And, as you can imagine, after the film was made he introduced certain changes in the choreography.

P S :   *I saw the original production in New York a few years ago; I had already noted significant differences in the film. Plus, in the film, we are shown the coming together of the troupe and a rehearsal scene. What really worked well in this film was taken up again in* Carmen, *but with less success. What do you think? Maurice Béjart brought this to the contemporary theater but, in general, rehearsals are a*

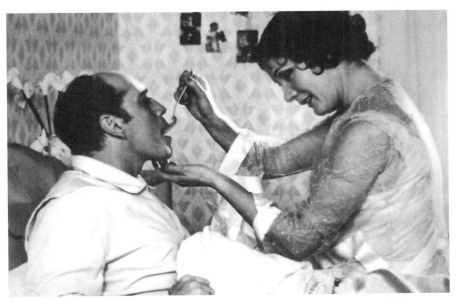

José Luis López Vázquez and Lina Canalejas, *El Jardín de las delicias* [The Garden of Delights], 1970

Standing: Geraldine Chaplin, Fernando Fernán-Gómez, José María Prada, José Vivó, and Charo Soriano; seated: Rafaela Aparicio, *Ana y los lobos* [Ana and the Wolves], 1972

José Luis López Vázquez and Lola Cardona, *La Prima Angélica* [Cousin Angelica], 1973

Geraldine Chaplin and Ana Torrent, *Cría cuervos* [Raise Ravens], 1975

Berta Socuéllamos Zarzo and José Antonio Valdelomar, *Deprisa, deprisa*
[Hurry, Hurry], 1980

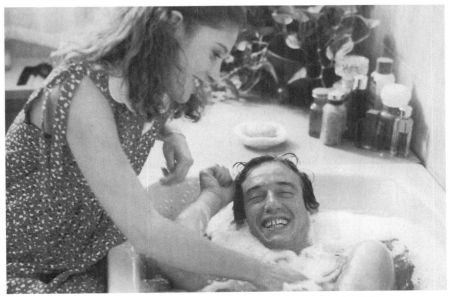

Assumpta Serna and Iñaki Aierra, *Dulces horas* [Sweet Hours], 1981

Isabelle Adjani and Hanna Schygulla, *Antonieta*, 1982

Antonio Gades and Laura del Sol, *Carmen*, 1983

Omero Antoniutti, *El Dorado*, 1987

Andrés Pajares and Carmen Maura, *¡Ay, Carmela!*, 1990

private affair, what you do to prepare for the public performance. It's like dressing to go out. We don't have our friends and acquaintances witness this, do we?
C S : You know, I am not a dance professional. However, there is something fascinating to me in the simple fact of rehearsing in order to perfect one's technique.

P S : *I guess that's why you were interested in* Bodas. *To bring up another matter, did Cristina Hoyos and Juan Ramón Jiménez contribute to the choreography or the shooting? Or is Antonio the only one responsible for these aspects?*
C S : Antonio is very clear on this matter. He is extremely knowledgeable in his field, but he also welcomed Cristina's and Juan's collaboration; they are the only ones whom he trusts fully.

P S : *Did you consciously choose to film in the Amor de Dios studio? It's one of the most respected flamenco schools in Madrid. Was it by chance that you included María Magdalena, the one who is teaching the class where Laura del Sol is discovered for the first time, and Ciro, the one who encounters Gades and Paco de Lucía when they arrive at the studio?*
C S : Antonio and I worked very hard before starting the film: we talked to people, we visited many schools, we met a number of dancers, and I felt that Amor de Dios offered the best conditions. Plus, it's very near my house.

P S : *Several of your films, as well as Rovira Beleta's* Los Tarantos *[The Tarantos], will be shown at the Spanish Cinema Festival which will soon take place here. I've seen Beleta's film and I remember well this Romeo and Juliet story set in the gypsy context, and starring a young Gades and the fabulous Carmen Amaya—this was one of her last professional appearances since she died of cancer four months later. What do you think of this film in relation to your trilogy?*
C S : It takes a totally different approach, one whose stylization appears intellectual. Rovira Beleta wanted to work with real sets, not constructed ones, but also with gentler ones, like his characters.

P S : *We now come to* El amor brujo, *which in a sense is also stylized, but the set is deliberately constructed. And, at the same time, you wanted to incorporate totally realistic elements in order to evoke the dance and to create the gypsy atmosphere. Why, then, didn't you include la Romera, a traditional wedding song, in the staging of the wedding which otherwise is very authentic?*

cs: Gades and I went to Granada where we spoke to gypsies from Sacromonte, and we decided to use the gypsy ritual from Granada, rather than the one from Barcelona. They differ in many respects, this being one.

ps: *At a certain point in the marriage scene, during the rumba, you showed two girls singing and evoking a very modern side of the flamenco. Was it deliberate?*
cs: Absolutely. I admire these two girls a lot—they are beautiful and talented—and this enabled me to get a little additional message across.

ps: *You wanted to illustrate the changing, modern nature of the flamenco with the sisters Azúcar Moreno, right?*
cs: Exactly. I like to bring things up to date. And these young ladies are good illustrations of the popular aspect of flamenco music and art.

ps: *The iron curtain at the beginning—what is its meaning? There are so many interpretations possible. I personally thought about the gypsy world, secretive, closed. One leaves the outer world and discovers the gypsy world which is closed, turned toward itself. Is this right?*
cs: Of course, I had that in mind. But there are many possible interpretations. I wanted to suggest a performance but also an artificial space which little by little becomes the reality.

ps: *That refers back to the play on mirrors in* Carmen, *does it not?*
cs: Isn't this juxtaposition of the real and the imaginary essentially cinematic? I wanted this to be particularly obvious in *El amor brujo.*

ps: *In most of your films (I've seen maybe 10 of them), there is always this chiaroscuro aesthetics, very delicate, which characterizes the world of flamenco, and which also seems to define your own artistic perception. You seem to take that very far in the trilogy.*
cs: In effect, I wanted to go in that direction with *Carmen.* But I thought the mirror was the audience. There is a mysterious relationship that is established when you look at yourself in the mirror. And in relation to dance, the mirror is also life.

ps: *The three-faced mirror is less visible in the film than in the stage performance where it's very much in evidence. Also, there is the scene with Hoyos and del Sol,*

who are facing the mirror, mimicking each other, as well as the one-way mirror,
through which Gades looks at the actors rehearsing, from behind which he asks
Cristina for help. I also tell my students that the flamenco is like a mirror which
reflects us back to ourselves as we really are, and we dance what we are.
C S : I think the very notion of mirror is something fantastic. Then, when
you multiply this notion by three, the magic is increased a hundred fold.

P S : *Critics worldwide have noted the importance of this play of mirrors which is*
designed to capture you. One can no longer separate the true from the false and
that's exactly what you wanted. Are we dealing here with Antonio the real life
choreographer or the dancer in the film? At the end, is Carmen killed or not? After
all, this is a story of obsession, like in El amor brujo, *is it not?*
C S : What enters the popular domain is not always controllable, so it can
take on excessive proportions. Passion is one of these elemental forces that
act on life, like love, death, murder, jealousy—everything we find in the
flamenco—beyond what the dance expresses. I wanted to create a synthesis
of all that in the trilogy.

P S : *There is something I noticed: the flamenco performance will not be authentic*
and real unless one has lived, has known suffering, misery, injustice. Isn't is also
surprising that Laura del Sol does not dance well? In Carmen, *Cristina Hoyos*
teaches her a move in all of its intensity, and in El amor brujo, *it's Gades who*
gives her a lesson in alegrías, after she has admitted to her inability to interpret the
dance as she would like.
C S : That's exactly what I wanted to achieve: the extent to which it's difficult to convey adequately the very essence of the flamenco with the gestures
that correspond to the feelings. Laura comes from a very different dance
school. She comes from the zarzuela tradition, from folklore, which she
knows well—and she is very talented—but that is external to the authentic
flamenco. Yes, in *Carmen* she makes an effort, but next to Cristina there is no
comparison. In addition to that, she wants to become an actress, which
seems to exclude dancing; I think that's unfortunate because if Antonio
worked with her for a while, she would soon be fantastic, given her vitality
and power. While Cristina has it in her bones, Laura does not. She is right
for the part.

P S : *The three films, when taken together, seem to contain a pretty complete reper-*

toire of flamenco styles, even going beyond that to more popular traditions such as the pasodoble, *do they not?*

C S :   In fact, all these things are related. But with the flamenco, one cannot cut it short. This mode of expression has its own demands, which will be more obvious to the professionals. A *cantaor* (flamenco singer) or a dancer should never have his expressiveness stifled because the deep human quality which has defined the flamenco would be threatened. It may seem easy, with time, to master a technique, but where will human truth be found?

P S :   *I think Gades found this profound truth, both human and traditional. His choreography seems simple, but it focuses on what is essential: the absolute purity of the line, the steps at once clear and precise, the gestures broad and appropriate.*

C S :   I would agree. That's why it's so fascinating to watch him work and rehearse. He knows exactly what he wants, and he achieves it because of his patience and his psychological acuity, stressing the proper movement in relation to its place within the larger choreography. Also, he always works in counterpoint to the rhythm, which adds power to what he does. And he is so demanding! Sometimes I tell him how much I like and admire what he does. I tell him how beautiful it is. And he protests, and says it's terrible. For him, the gesture is everything. So, he pushes himself (and others) to the edge of his ability in order to obtain the truth of the movements he selected.

P S :   *Maybe like the rehearsal sequence that expresses jealousy in* Carmen? *You conveyed that beautifully. This brings us to the* sequiriya *in* El amor brujo, *the dance that Gades and Hoyos perform together. Who thought of it and how was it developed? When he asks her to dance in the film, she says no with her mouth but yes with the dance. This scene is both striking and touching.*

C S :   What you are suggesting is very interesting and it takes a dancer and a well-versed person to discover and comment on this. Let me try to explain: first, they dance without music, *a palo seco*, we would say. In fact, the guitar is what starts it off, introduces it. Then it stops. The dance begins in silence. And finally, later on, the guitar music begins again, underscoring the intensity of the emotions. I don't think I ever saw this elsewhere. It seems to me it would be very difficult to dance to a kind of pure rhythm. But Gades can do this with Cristina because they know each other so well. They listen to their internal rhythms, and that's absolutely fascinating.

PS: *To sum up, do you plan to continue exploring flamenco dance in relation to cinema?*

CS: I don't know yet. I think I have said what needs to be said for the moment. But you can't predict the future.

Carlos Saura: The Culmination of a Dream

PEDRO CALLEJA / 1988

PEDRO CALLEJA: *You are famous for eluding reporters every chance you get. Why is it so hard to get an interview with you?*

CARLOS SAURA: Look, I live outside of Madrid, in the mountain range, very isolated, and I don't come down to the city much, so I'm not usually available to the press. Besides, look how troublesome all of you are! You all want me to give you an exclusive, to talk to you one by one, and to divulge my secrets to you. I don't understand it, but it annoys me. What I'd like is to be able to give huge press conferences, with all of the reporters questioning me at the same time, and that way I'd save myself a lot of time and trouble. Now look what happens to me. I have to come down to Madrid whenever they want to talk to me, and then they all ask me more or less the same thing. On the other hand, I like to talk very little, as little as possible. Now, I don't mind talking about a film of mine, because it's part of my job. I'm resigned to doing it. I have to do it, and I do it.

PC: *Is that the reason why you've required everyone who interviews you to have seen* El Dorado *first?*

CS: For heaven's sake! What I'm interested in talking about is my work, which is what I imagine is what also interests the interviewer. Isn't that so? We'll, it's better for him to have seen the film beforehand so that we can talk about it. If not, he wouldn't even know what to say.

From *Fotogramas* 1741 (1988): 54–58 and 86. Reprinted by permission. Translated from Spanish by Linda M. Willem.

PC: *Well, we'll talk about* El Dorado *then. Obligatory question: are you satisfied with your final result?*

CS: Well, this was a film that I wanted to make for a long time, and the fact of having made it satisfies me enormously. It's like completing something I had to do, like a ritual. . . . Whatever! On the other hand, I think that what one likes depends more or less on how each person focuses his work. I can't separate cinema from my life. The two things are interrelated and enrich or impoverish each other. I have my obsessions, my personal manias, and of course what I make always seems good to me. Now that doesn't mean that it really is good. It seems good to me because it's what I wanted to do. Specifically in the case of *El Dorado*, it's like the culmination of a dream: to make a film in Latin America, with ample resources at my disposal, with the actors I wanted, with total creative freedom. . . . It's in that sense I'm really very, very satisfied.

PC: *And the shooting, how did that suit you? There were rumors circulating about numerous production problems and about the bad conditions in the area.*

CS: Personally the shooting suited me well because I'm a bit of a tropical person. In general, I like Latin America very much, and I especially like the tropics. I'm the kind of guy who tolerates heat well and the difficulties that sometimes go with it. Much better than the cold. And there were days when one couldn't even breathe, sultry days with terrible humidity. It did indeed take us time to get used to this during the nine months of shooting and during the trips we had made beforehand. The film began to be shot on January 19th in Limón, Costa Rica. On the first day of shooting something both curious and dreadful happened to me: I felt out of practice, as if I had forgotten everything in the long time that had gone by between my last film and this one. I felt apathetic. I had no spark, responding mechanically to the environmental impulses. Then I had a quarrel with my first assistant because we couldn't manage to understand each other. And then there also was the mud, a mud that really isn't mud. It's a type of magma almost from the Tertiary Age. You don't know what could be below or where it will be found exactly. I think that the film reflects in one way or another all of these inconveniences. You can see that it was hard to pull it off. But, on the other hand, those locations have an amazing power. There are marvelous places. It's like returning to the prehistoric times, a type of beautiful dream that stands independent of time. Even now I continue to dream at night about those forests in Blancanieves and about that interminable, luxuriant growth.

PC: *What kinds of things did you rely on to solve these difficulties?*
CS: Well, I don't know. There were the coconuts, which are quite pleasant. You split them or make a little hole in them and you drink them. It's marvelous. I had about eighty a day. That's no exaggeration. And when it rained— and there it really would rain—I'd drink coffee to combat the depression that cloudy days inevitably produce in me. In the technical area, the arrival of the video, on the fourth or fifth day of shooting, calmed me down a lot. It's a device that helps you a great deal because you immediately have an approximate idea of what you just shot. What's bad is the appalling quality of the picture that those gadgets still have. And it's almost the year 2000!

PC: *Were there also rebellions during the filming of* El Dorado, *as there were during the Aguirre expedition?*
CS: It was just about at that point. If the shooting had lasted a few more weeks, we would have killed each other for sure! (laughter) No, seriously, I think it's just the opposite. Difficulties bring people together, especially in our case, which was so different than the real expedition by Lope de Aguirre. I usually kid around by saying that we really made two expeditions: the one we told in the film and our own private one. But there were profound differences. First of all, we had the enormous advantage of knowing where we were going, and second, we had a working deadline. We clearly knew that it would end on a certain day and then we all would return home to relax. In contrast, those poor men didn't know where they'd end up: they thought the river would end the next day; they imagined unknown cities, other landscapes, something. . . . And no. It was all a kind of tremendous trap.

PC: *Weren't you tempted to submerge yourself completely in the splendor of the surroundings and forget a little of the story you wanted to tell? Be honest.*
CS: Yes, there was a moment at first when the beauty of the surroundings dazzled me completely: the light, the shapes, the atemporal atmosphere, the wildness. And I thought "I have to try to retain this first impression in the film, try to transmit the intensity of seeing it for the first time." Then, quickly and unfortunately, I began to get used to it. Habit is what makes us lose little by little the fascination that always comes from the unknown and

the new. So in *El Dorado* I tried not to take too much advantage of the jungle, the Indians, the wild animals. . . . The important thing here is what happened among the Spaniards themselves: their power struggles; why and how they killed each other. That is the main theme.

PC: *A constant theme of Carlos Saura. Is* El Dorado *an* auteur *film?*

CS: (Thinking a bit before answering) I'm not a good narrator of stories, rather, I'm an investigator of images. I always want to tell *my* story, not a story. My way of making film, on the other hand, isn't anything revolutionary. I just pay attention to my temperament. I try to be faithful to myself. The kind of cinema that interests me carries the strong imprint of its author on it and I try to do a little of that too. Each film is a new experience that requires new motivations, but what the years also do is give you a lot of jobs. Stylistic complexity no longer attracts me. I've become somewhat lazy. I leave that to the young ones. Let them do pirouettes with the camera. I prefer to space out my efforts, to conserve energy. Specifically in the case of *El Dorado*, my intention, and that of all who have collaborated with me in its making, has always been to adhere to the historical reality, to the chronicles. With the material in these chronicles there is more than enough to make a thousand and one films.

PC: *No inventiveness then?*

CS: More than inventiveness, I've allowed myself certain liberties. But I insist that the ideal for me has been to not bring any of my own creativeness to the original story. That is, if there's a helmet, let it be a helmet from the period; if there's a sword, let it be one from the period; if there's a ship, let it be the same kind that was used then.

It seems to me that the inventiveness is in other things, if it is there, which I don't know. But it's not in what can be seen at a glance. That's my opinion, and it's fine that way.

PC: *Well, but someone could feel cheated. You know, someone who is looking for* El Dorado *to be an adventure film with lots of action, like the previous ones, or like* Indiana Jones.

CS: I don't think that the kind of deception that you are talking about is going to happen. All of the information I give in the film is truthful. El Dorado doesn't exist, everyone knows that. Maybe I think that we're all still looking for El Dorado. Right? And if we were to find an El Dorado there always would be many people who would say it wasn't the real El Dorado, that there's another much better one. El Dorado is a fantastic utopia invented by man. A crazy dream. It's not logical for me to have invented an El Dorado in the middle of the Amazon jungle, with solid gold cupolas and marble streets. My film is something else entirely. I have conscientiously studied the historical-geographical frame in which it takes place and I have done the script simultaneously. You can't forget about the existence of five or six chronicles that tell the adventure. They are written by different authors, many of whom were part of that very expedition, and they all agree on the fundamental details. They are an extraordinary source of information. What I tried to do was get to the heart of the story. I tried to clean up the texts and give a logical interpretation to the events that are not sufficiently explained in the chronicles: the feelings, the characters intimate thoughts, the deep motivations for their actions. . . . The chronicles only give the cold hard facts, and what I had to do was to try to understand what lies beneath them, which is what various novelists—Ramón J. Sender, Abel Pose, Oslar Pietri—have done before me.

P C : *And Werner Herzog?*
C S : *Aguirre, or the Wrath of God* is a beautiful film, but filled with inaccuracies and anachronisms. It's not the same thing.

P C : *Did you essentially find yourself attracted to the character of Lope de Aguirre, as had happened to the writers you mentioned and to the German filmmaker?*
C S : I don't find Aguirre disagreeable, but neither is he very likable. (laughter) I don't know. He's not one of those hero's hero. At any rate, I've tried, if not to justify him, at least to understand the reasons for his actions. I've never firmly believed what's written in the chronicles about him. They portray him as a ridiculous little man who was hateful, criminal, murderous, implacable, and evil, partially because the chroniclers wanted to show Philip II that Aguirre and no one else was to blame for all of the bad things. It would have been totally different if his adventure had succeeded. You have to read all of the history between the lines, finding the consequences for yourself. My Lope de Aguirre, the one in the film, was a man who had many reasons for doing what he did: also keep in mind that it was a brutal and barbarous era and in those days they didn't have any help from anyone. They were left

to their fate, knowing nothing, desperately fighting against hostile and unknown surroundings. I think that he was obliged to do those things. In a way he transformed an expedition in search of a legendary territory into a revolution against Spain, into the creation of an independent kingdom. It's a brilliant form of madness! And in that way Aguirre was a true pioneer. What I especially like is the immediacy of all of his decisions, that instantaneous energy, that boldness. . . .

P C : *It certainly was a shame that Omero Antonutti's voice had to be dubbed.*
C S : You're telling me! Above all, keeping in mind the marvelous diction Omero has in Italian: beautiful, precise. . . . The same thing happened with Lambert Wilson, an actor capable of modulating his voice in French in incredible ways. It's part of making co-productions! What can you do? What I can say is that this film required wonderful actors for several roles, and I had them. I wouldn't change any of them.

P C : *Talk to me about the two female characters in* El Dorado, *who were linked by their mixed-blood* mestiza *status.*
C S : Doña Inés is one of the key characters in the whole story, at least from my point of view. She is a strange woman who, according to the chronicles, lived with the same captains who collaborated in the death of her legitimate husband and head of the expedition, Ursúa. They don't specify her reasons, but I think that she acted that way out of revenge. She is a woman who had Indian blood in addition to an unstable pseudo-European mentality. Deep down I think that she retained the great love she had for Ursúa throughout her life, and that she was carrying out her revenge in a silent, slow, and tenacious way. The only one who realized her tragedy was Aguirre, who did well in not having "relations" with her. For that reason, I think, he ended up killing her, but that doesn't justify his action. A bit of the same thing happened with Elvira, Lope de Aguirre's daughter, who also had Indian blood and consequently also had a somewhat special mentality.

P C : *Are the first scenes in* El Dorado *a dream by Elvira?*
C S : Among other things, yes. It's based on historically verified legends and it's an idea of El Dorado that's very much in accord with the Indian imagination. These images perfectly correspond with what Elvira could have

thought. It's a conception that's a bit materialistic, very poetic, and very rooted in the subconscious and in the popular traditions.

P C :   *Does Shakespeare have anything to do with* El Dorado?
C S :   Well, apparently not, but that seems incredible because this story is a true tragedy in the vein of *Macbeth,* with constant power struggles, pre-medi-tated murders, unleashed elements of nature, etc. . . . (laughter)

P C :   *At any rate, the relationships of all the characters are tremendously elemen-tary—primitive.*
C S :   In general those men—I'm referring to the ones in the real expedition—were like that, I would imagine: very elementary, very primary. The people who went to America were people without education, second sons who were left without an inheritance and had to emigrate to seek out a living. It's a very complex matter to talk about like this, but I think that when these peo-ple left to conquer new territories, Spain was still emerging from the Middle Ages. The majority of them didn't go there so much to get rich and come back as they went to remake their lives. The idea of a "round trip" voyage wasn't fixed in the mind of those people. The British were much luckier because they found North America, a rich land that has everything. The English pragmatism was a fundamental element in the consolidation of colo-nialism. Despotism always has resulted in a greater sense of practicality: to make the most of things and to get advantages out of difficulties. Despite everything, I think that Latin America, with its many faults, still has to mature and bear fruit. The United States has given all that it had to give of itself while the Latin American countries haven't even begun to get going. That's my impression.

Continuity, Rupture, Remembering: The Spanish Cinema During Franco's Time

MECHTHILD ZEUL / 1988

MECHTHILD ZEUL: *I have come to the opinion that in present-day Spain there is an indifference to Francoism, even to the point of denying that there ever was such a thing. However, even in the 1960s, you attempted in your films to make graphic and denounce specific examples of Francoism's development and consequences within people themselves—father, mother, child—in their manner of loving and hating, in the way they try to feel and function as a family. Can one say that you attain this through the depiction of memory?*

CARLOS SAURA: To some extent, yes, but I would not say it for all films. However for a large part of my films, remembering is important. What you are saying is certainly correct. There is a kind of wish, a kind of necessity perhaps—I don't know—in the present Spanish situation to forget the most recent history a bit, as if one might say: "Nothing happened here, one must forget, it would be best if everything should disappear from the scene." I've always proceeded from the idea that this is a big error, a deception. Therefore, I advocate the theory that one is morally obliged to forget nothing. What one must do, perhaps, is to overcome some remembrances, that is to say, to overcome the negative parts, things that were terrible, and attempt to make sure that such things are never repeated. That's valid not only for Spain, but for the entire world. I believe that morally one is not permitted to forget anything. Forgetting seems to me to be absolutely stupid. On the contrary, the saddest thing is that we are not in a position to remember every-

From *Frauen und Film* 44/45 (1988): 25–32. Reprinted by permission. Translated from German by Vernon A. Chamberlin.

thing we might wish to remember. This is valid, at least for me, because forgetting is very simple. Unfortunately we forget with great ease. Therefore, when I was making my films during the Franco period, I worked a lot with remembering, much more so than today. Of course I worked with a remembrance that is very much modified, for one can never say that he has made a simple autobiographical film. That is just not valid. There was always a decoding of memories, a decoding which had been sought by me. Such a version seems to me to be very much richer, for it opens up other possibilities for penetrating deeper into a matter and attaining new perspectives. Especially memories of the Spanish Civil War, without question, play a role in this, because I experienced it as a child from ages four to seven, in Madrid as well as in Valencia, and also a bit in Barcelona. My family was always traveling. My father was a secretary to the Finance Minister and, therefore, my family followed the movements of the Republican government. A large part of my life is colored by these memories, which are very strong. Today I don't know if all that still holds true for me, but several years ago, especially during Franco's time, I worked a lot with these memories. So much so that a clear, visibly anti-Franco political attitude evolved. Things are not so simple that we can say that any one of my films was truly a political film, or an unmasking, or had such-and-such a message. I've always rejected the simple things. Indeed, I believe that there is this unmasking, but there are also other things in my films. I have always been interested in focusing on the Spanish family, because it occurred to me that there are still remnants from the Middle Ages in it, that the Spanish family is conceptually a pyramid: father, mother, and only then the children. In the Spanish family there is an almost puritanical rigidity. This is found of course not only in Spain but also in England, Germany, and Sweden. They are, however, very different from Spain. The family structures of communication are more complicated here than in the Anglo-Saxon world.

There are a lot of family tentacles, relationships which are often negative. This is my contradiction. In Spain and in all the Mediterranean countries there is a relationship among fathers, mothers, and children, which is not so true for the north European countries, and it is not so frightening there. Here there are cutaneous relationships, relationships which have to do with the bodily contact with the children, with the one being protected, until one becomes quite mature. At forty we are still children. It's a contradiction, for the family cohesion also contains positive elements. There is a part, however, which is very dangerous. The children can't become independent of the parents, because there are bonds of pressure and friendship which have been established. There is a deficit in Spanish society, that is to say, the individual is forced, morally and emotionally, to stay dependent on the family and, in order to solve life's problems, he must have recourse to the family as a whole, to parents, to cousins. Family ties are very strong, because they are made of flesh and blood.

M Z :   *I should like to come back to what was said at the outset, that you had shown Francoism on the screen, how it had manipulated itself into people, into the family. Could you agree with my hypothesis that the family is your theme, as well as the theme of the film directors of the 1940s?*

C S :   Yes, the family. One can say that I, for my part, think there is a contradiction in regard to the Spanish family. It's a disaster. There is a negative side; but also a positive one, that is to say, the warmth, the protection, all that we may wish for ourselves. The negative part is the pressure which the family exerts on people in general. This is implicit in the tradition of Catholic Spain: respect for the military, the government, the king, and the monarchy. The Spanish mother is in general "the great mother." Like the mother in *Mamá cumple cien años* [Mother Turns One Hundred], she is symbolic and of aristocratic nature. There is a pyramid of power, in which the king always possesses the absolute, and the army always serves to protect the king. However, this is a hierarchy that belongs to a time which has passed.

M Z :   *I have the notion that in films such as* Reina Santa *[The Holy Queen] and* La Lola se va a los puertos *[Lola Goes from Port to Port] the women indeed have a lot of power, but they are lonely women. They are women to whom one grants no sexuality.*

C S :   This is a Mediterranean culture, a culture which attracts me very much, for I'm a bit Mediterranean. It, however, contains a great contradiction: the wife appears to be—and really is—a bit enslaved, a bit controlled, placed behind the male. Perhaps it's going too far to speak of the male; rather one should say the husband. However, she has—and this is the great contradiction—much power within her support base. That base can be large or small; it can be the realm of the house, it can be the children—above all it is the children. It's a control phenomenon within the Judeo-Christian tradition, typical for Mediterranean culture, and in the course of time it will disappear.

The mother controls the rearing, the manner of thinking, and the essential being of her children.

M Z: *And you criticize that?*
C S: Yes, I criticize it, for it seems to me to be a monstrous thing. I'm against all this. However, there exist within me contradictions in this regard. The relationship between mother and child attracts me. For example, the physical aspect attracts me. I like the sensuous attraction between mother and child. It seems wondrous to me, although for me as a man, this kind of relationship is possible only whenever I have lived a long period of time with one of my children. But I see this sensuous contact as rather between the mother and her children; this surprises me, but I don't mean that this is an exclusively Latin sensibility.

M Z: *You are referring in this respect somewhat to the relationship between the little girl and her mother in* Cría cuervos *[Raise Ravens].*
C S: That is a relationship which is a little ambiguous. On the one side, it's a very intense relationship, very strong, but it exists under the reign of frustration. The great problem, which is especially serious in this situation, is that we have a mother who is unsatisfied, a mother who is not herself fulfilled. That's very common. Generally speaking, both women, as well as we men, have not fulfilled our potential. It becomes evil when our frustrations are displaced onto the children. I don't want to speak of complexes, which is something we see very frequently in our Mediterranean countries. Domineering mothers very much impress on their children that they want them to be what the mothers themselves can not be. That also happens with the husband, but it's much clearer with the wife.

M Z: *The husband fulfills himself in other ways?*
C S: Yes, in other ways. In the case of the mother, it's far clearer because her control and domination over the children is much more direct and much more immediate.

M Z: *I should like to come back once again to the subject of remembering. Could one say that those of your protagonists who cannot and do not want to remember have no future, that remembering is a prerequisite for change, for a new beginning? The three men in* La caza *[The Hunt] can't remember, rather they are internally driven to kill one another. For remembering in the service of an action, that is to say, to get information about money deposited in Switzerland, the family itself in* El jardín de las delicias *[The Garden of Desires], ends up, like Antonio, similarly enchained (figuratively speaking).*

cs: Yes, I proceed from the assumption that anyone without remembrances and past experiences is a nonentity. Everybody is that which he has lived, and if he loses this, he remains naked, without any protection, devoid of everything. Therefore I always insist that one can not deny that which he has lived; his memory must stay animated. I think that one should dedicate time to remembering, that one must attempt to regain everything out of the past. Experiences and consequences should be pulled out of the past.

mz: *In order to conclude my questions about remembering, could you tell me what significance Imperio Argentina has for you? Her voice is heard in many of your films.*

cs: There's a series of songs from the 1930s that were sung continually during the Civil War, and those were her songs. There was a whole list of women singers, but Imperio Argentina was very popular. Everybody sang her songs, the militia everywhere, at the front too. One sang the songs of Imperio Argentina, Estrellita Castro, and Angelillo. The songs of Imperio Argentina link me to a very sad and melancholy remembrance. Independent from that, she has a wonderful voice. It's pure, clear, simple, and crystalline. And besides that, all her songs have something sad. When other women sang her songs, they sounded completely different.

mz: *You mean the style and manner in which she sang her songs?*

cs: Yes, both. I like very much the songs I chose for my films; there are two or three, one is "Recordar", the others are "Rocío" and "Mari Trini." There are others I like a bit less, but these three are exceedingly beautiful. When I search out music for my films, I don't do it in conjunction with memory, but rather because I like the songs.

mz: *And you search them out yourself?*

cs: Yes, yes, to be sure—absolutely. In addition, regarding music, I am somewhat crazy. Most often, when I write a script, I determine what music is to be used. I like music very much, I'm a music lover, but maybe I'm no expert. My mother was a professional pianist, but she gave that up when she married. During my entire life I've liked music very much. I'm in love with music.

MZ: *And the pictures—probably you do the cutting yourself?*

CS: Yes, I am one who understands himself to be an *auteur*, although this word causes me anxiety because it's so grand. When one says *auteur*, it sounds as if one is expressing something boastful, being kind of a big dictator. Of course I've always struggled with that and always wanted to be the *auteur* himself in regard to the responsibility for my work. It can be good or bad, but I never shove the blame for my work onto other people. My work is mine, it makes no difference whether it's good or bad, the responsibility is mine. In this sense, of course, I try to control everything.

MZ: *Even the cameraman?*

CS: Yes, everything. I work with people I trust, that is to say, they are people more or less like myself: for example, Teo Escamilla, who has worked with me a lot. He's very intelligent and very sensitive. It's easy for me to work with him. The music, however, in each film is a special challenge. I always try to seek out the music that suits the film best of all. Often I even try to work together with a musician, often in Spain with Luis de Pablo, who is very well known. However, I have always attempted to choose music that I like.

MZ: *You have told me that the subjects of your films are similar to those of the 1940s as regards the family. For example, in* La caza *you turned upside down what* Botón de ancla *[Brass Button] has in a positive way; that is to say, a healthy male friendship which is threatened by a woman who brings mischief and unmasks a male alliance as imbued with vanity and cruelty. Women are not the only cruel ones, as the films of the 1940s wanted to make a person believe. Rather reciprocal male cruelty, and cruelty also against women, were among the assumptions that enabled Francoism to function.*

CS: (laughter) To be sure in the case of *Botón de ancla* friendship stands above everything else; there is the sacrifice of one friend for another. I've never believed in these things. It seems to me to be a lie, and belongs to the cultivation of the feel-good. It's typical for the American film, the feeling of friendship, the sacrifice of one friend for another—for example in the case of John Ford—that he will give up his own bride. I've never believed in this form of friendship; it's possible only if deep down there is a homosexual relationship. There always exists a homosexual relationship in the case of these deep friendships, both between women as well as between men. It's not so pure and clean as one would want to make believe. Besides, it's not a question of clean or dirty, and purity and cleanliness constitute really a stupid concept. In the case of *La caza* the three friends belong above all to a circle of political friends and have shared similar experiences with one another. They are perhaps not so much friends in the deep sense of the word, but rather three men who do business with one another.

MZ: *Also in* Botón de ancla *indeed no deep friendship really binds the three.*
CS: I remember *Botón de ancla* as a feel-good film. Such things give me great anxiety.

MZ: *A thesis I have developed concerning the role of the woman in the films of the 1940s is as follows: there is a friendship between men, and the woman is evil and moreover remains so. She brings discord and disturbs the friendship. In* La caza *one sees that it's not the woman who is malicious; rather, it's the men.*
CS: And moreover, if it were the woman who destroys the friendship, that would seem interesting to me. The woman who disturbs is interesting. And the woman who disturbs such a friendship, has every right to disturb it. There's a Spanish film type of the Franco epoch, which I don't remember very well. Feudal slogans are dispensed there. These were provided with official approval and proclaimed as the only way to conduct oneself in life. It was typical for Francoism that the moral norms were rigid and there was no possibility of existence outside these norms, although they were in reality mendacious and make-believe. These moral norms had no relationship to everyday life as it occurs in other countries. These films corresponded to the official life; they were intended to show behavioral norms in which people were good, and those who were bad, were entirely bad. One could not be good and bad at the same time—there was no ambivalence. I remember my first film, *Los golfos* [Hooligans] from 1959. There was a guild that was to analyze this film, in order to judge it, and a member of this guild told me that we should change the ending. I remember very well the sentence: "Dirty laundry must be washed only at home." That's the way one says it here; possibly they say it so the world over. Things that were not favorable for the establishment—it was better not to show them, rather hide them at home.

In this way, one can explain that many films of this epoch showed only what had been well washed.

MZ: *And what happened with the ending of the film* Los golfos?
CS: It was presented, but they cut a lot.

MZ: *And how was it with* La caza?
CS: In the case of *La caza* we had problems with the film script; they cut a lot after the film was already made. During this time I always had problems with the films. The censorship of the film scripts was the uncertainty. We simply wrote something and handed in whatever they wanted, but the other script, from which the film was made, we kept to ourselves. Then later we filmed what we had retained. Elías (Querejeta) was always much cleverer than I; he always handed in the false film scripts.

MZ: *And what happened when they saw that you had filmed something different from what you had proposed?*
CS: What is depicted says much less than what has been written. And subsequently it was not at all so noticeable. Moreover, it was often ridiculous what was cut, trivialities, everything was arbitrary. Most of all, they cut at the beginning of *Llanto por un bandido* [Lament for a Bandit]. Here there were executions of nineteenth-century prisoners and Luis Buñuel played the executioner. Otherwise they cut rather little. To be sure, we always worked under the pressure of censorship, and we wrote things we thought might pass. However, censorship here functioned like everything else in Spain. You already know that. Frequently they relaxed a point, and then suddenly it was ordered to be strict again. There were ridiculous things. For example, if in the film script it said, "The man and the woman sit on the couch," then that was crossed out, because one did not know what they might do on the couch. You would have to write, "A man and a woman sat on the couch and looked tenderly at each other." But I can say, regarding myself, I did what I wanted; even if something was cut, it was certainly my work, my responsibility.

MZ: *I should like to come back once again to the similarity of the themes in your films and those of the 1940s. When I saw some of your films again, I had the notion that you had crept into some of your characters, as if you knew them from the inside. Also you knew how to investigate the connections between the individual family members out to their smallest branchings, and to present this visually. For example,* El jardín de las delicias *seems to me to be a photographic negative of* Mariona Rebull. *Against the total refusal of the son to maintain the family business, there is, in the case of Sáenz de Heredia, the obedience of the son in his duty of preserving the family enterprise.*

C S :   Yes, my films are the total opposite of those of the 1940s. Moreover, one must take into consideration that the director of *Mariona Rebull* was an establishment man. He was a Francoist and a Falangist, and was absolutely in agreement with Franco. From this point of view, of course, it's obvious that he exhibits an attitude that was exemplary for Spain's firmly united and hierarchic society: sons have the obligation to continue the work of the father and must sacrifice themselves for this. Everyone in this film must sacrifice himself, only we don't know at all for whom.

M Z :   *I have seen several of your films once again. Can one really say, as I mentioned initially, that you denounce what we could see in the films of the 1940s?*
C S :   Yes, in my films I show the Spanish family, which was rigid, apparently standing still, and incapable of further development, even as one deceived himself that everything was functioning wonderfully. In reality, everything was a lie. There was a horrendous mendacity. There was a pernicious Church, with a perpetual lie, which always agreed with Franco and had actively taken part in the war. My films are a rejection of this calamitous coalition. I attempted to separate what fascinated me about the family, and the relationship between mother and child, from what a political system made out of it. That is to say that they controlled this relationship through laws and that there was no longer any possibility of change. Everything was already stipulated regarding this false and mendacious structure, which had nothing to do with reality. That is what fascism amounted to for me.

M Z :   *But certainly wasn't Francoism something that existed not only externally to every specific person, but also within people themselves?*
C S :   It penetrated into people themselves and still sticks in many in this country and in other parts of the world. It sticks above all in the wish that nothing be changed. It's the corroboration of rest and peace, which one attempts to attain beyond maximum comfort, even if one thereby sacrifices people, in any way one might like. For me Francoism was a frightening time;

I have a very bad remembrance of it. It was a negative time, and the only thing attained has been the further delaying of Spain's incorporation into the modern world. To be sure, it really did not contribute anything. Now that the process has turned itself around, those who won the war are really the losers.

M Z: *I should like to turn to the actors. I am astonished to see that male and female actors who were part of a formerly Fascist and reactionary cinema are today recognized actors who are doing good cinema with progressive ideas. So it seems that there is something like continuity where in reality there was rupture.*
C S: Yes, that is true, and it seems to me to be a miracle. I'm in total agreement with what you're saying. There is a whole series of examples of it. I've worked with Alfredo Mayo, for example. However, in my opinion, the actor has less responsibility within a work, within a film than does the director. From a moral point-of-view an actor can represent different causes, which really don't touch his inner essence directly. An actor can be a leftist and work in rightist films, always to be sure under the assumption that they're not excessive in their ideology. I have often reflected on that, because otherwise one really cannot explain how people of the Left like Fernando Rey or Paco Rabal, who was a member of the Communist Party, can make rightist films. Fernando Fernán-Gomez was always less leftist—he was rather a Liberal, who slowly came little by little to hold progressive positions—but really he was not much of a politicized man. He made extraordinary progress. Fernando Rey was the son of communists and his father was a captain in the Republican army, and I believe they even had his father shot. Paco Rabal was a man with very leftist ideas. Certainly, however, they all also had to survive, and as long as the roles in the films were not extreme rightist, they just accepted the roles that were offered to them. To be sure there were also exceptions. There also were actors who did not accept the roles that were offered to them.

M Z: *From what you say, I extrapolate that when it comes to responsibility, you differentiate between the actor and the director?*
C S: Yes, in every case. There were, for example, actors like Alfredo Mayo, who were always rightists, all their lives. He was, however, a marvelous human being, a wonderful person. Whenever you spoke with him, he seemed very liberal; I believe he wasn't an extreme Francoist.

M Z : *But didn't he indeed participate in a police raid?*

C S : Yes, in his youth he was more of a Francoist than later. The director has much more ideological and moral responsibility than the actor. In contrast and by way of example, a makeup artist or a hair stylist can have extreme rightist ideas, but still can do outstanding professional work. The actors, in any case, do only what the director allows. The directors must openly answer for their ideas, the actors not.

M Z : *What you say is certainly surprising, for Alfredo Mayo indeed was, as is well known, the number one actor in the Franco cinema. Can one perhaps say that the role that was given to him in* La caza *is the photographic negative of the role of José Churruca in* Raza *[Race]?*

C S : You may be correct, but the most important thing was that Alfredo Mayo was a very pleasant human being, pleasant in his manner of thinking, which was rather open when one dealt with him directly. For us and others of that time, he was an idol comparable to Jean Gabin in France.

M Z : *And that is why you worked with him?*

C S : He was a daredevil, very handsome, loaded with energy, not especially intelligent perhaps, but that didn't matter. He and Amparo (Rivelles) worked all night a few times—especially Amparo, what an actress. She was like him—also full of energy and desire to enjoy life. I have worked with actresses who made films in Franco's time, but I worked with them above all because they were good actors. I also worked with Pepe (José Nieto), who was a man of the Right.

M Z : *Can you say that directors like Sáenz de Heredia and Rafael Gil have influenced you?*

C S : We didn't consider the films of either of them at all. That was our form of protest. Both were men of the regime, Sáenz de Heredia above all. His triumph was not our triumph. He was a Falangist and a lieutenant of the Right, and naturally he made only films that repeated exactly the norms and values of Francoism. Many say that he was a good film director, that he was an orderly director, but I did not like his orderliness. I reject him totally. Perhaps I should have concerned myself with him, but I truly reject him. He's very alien to me.

MZ: *What would you say concerning whom you have learned from?*
CS: We were self-taught, no one taught us, there was no one. If someone says that I had things in common with Luis Buñuel, I would not say no, but really I am self-taught.

MZ: *Let's come back once again to the film directors of Francoism. Would you say that they were all like Sáenz de Heredia?*
CS: Yes, that is surely true. They were men of the regime. They liked it, they felt at home there. Perhaps there was one exception. That was Edgar Neville. Although he was a rightist, he was very well-educated. Perhaps that really doesn't say anything, but at least he was reflective. The others didn't do any thinking, they just felt at home.

Interview: Carlos Saura

ANTONIO CASTRO / 1996

Carlos Saura always says that he doesn't like interviews because what are more interesting are the analyses of his works—something that to his way of thinking I can do better than he can—rather than the "impressions" that the author can provide. He justifies himself by saying that, besides, he is one of those people who doesn't rewatch his films very often, and this makes it difficult to remember things about his own films. Also, he doesn't consider himself to be a brilliant interviewee, something which is completely proven false by the interviews themselves, this being at least the fourth I've done with him. For that reason, it's hard for him to get himself going, but once he does, he feels comfortable and the interviews flow quite well.

ANTONIO CASTRO: *The pretext for this interview is the 100 year anniversary of Spanish cinema. Do you think that this type of commemoration serves a function or is it just a perfectly useless ritual?*

CARLOS SAURA: Well, you have to excuse me, but I think that it is completely useless. But at the same time I believe that it is interesting and that it does have to be done. Its practical function is to allow some officials to do a type of retrospective of cinema from their country and to allow us to see the films of Buñuel under better conditions than we have seen them before. For this type of thing, yes, it serves a function. But as a rehashing of cinema, I think not. I think that we are at a very interesting point now because it's

From *Dirigido por* 249 (1996): 52–67. Reprinted by permission of *Dirigido por*. Translated from Spanish by Linda M. Willem.

total chaos. And no one is trying to put things in order. Things are continuing as disordered as ever.

AC: *When you filmed* Los golfos *[Hooligans] did you pose to yourself the possibility of your being in the forefront of a type of generational change-over?*
CS: When I filmed *Los golfos*, I didn't pose anything to myself. The only thing that we wanted was to make films, and also, each within the realm of his possibilities, to contribute to changing the system of government in Spain, which seemed to us to be this enormous entity that did not let us tell the stories we wanted and kept us from expressing ourselves freely. Keep in mind that I was learning while I was making films. For me, each film is a new adventure, and perhaps for that reason I have embarked on adventures that seem foolish to some people, but I hope to continue doing it anyway.

On the other hand, I'm not interested in having a style. I've never wanted to have a style. I only limit myself by always continuing to do what I like the most. In this sense I have changed since the time, almost forty years ago, when I went all over the province of Cuenca by myself with a camera. Now they offer me things, and I am lucky enough to be able to pick the one that I like among the various ones that are of interest. Now it's easier for me to make films than before.

AC: *Your first film was produced by Films 59, which was new and owned by Pedro Portabella.*
CS: That was for personal reasons. Portabella was a friend of my brother and was from a family with money. He was an intelligent man, interested in culture and art, and it was proposed that he make a low-cost film for which we hardly got paid anything. I think I received 25,000 pesetas as director, but of course those were other times. And he accepted, and at the same time contacts were established with Marco Ferreri to make *El cochecito* [The Little Car], also produced by Portabella and some independent producers from the Basque Country. *Los golfos* was a very simple film shot in a few weeks, half improvised. Mario Camus and I wrote the dialogue on the spot.

AC: *Formally, despite being a film made with little money, it has some very interesting innovations, above all in the structure, that refer to the French New Wave, but when the French New Wave was just appearing, so that one can't speak about influences.*

c s : I endeavored to make a film with some pronounced, very large ellipses, very direct, very quick, with a very documentary tone. I had originally come from documentaries, and I didn't feel all that strong in plot-driven films. At that time I had a meager literary background. Well, maybe not that small, because I had read a fair amount, but I had written almost nothing, and that's another thing that has evolved over the years: I've become more of a writer, even to the extent where now I write with a certain ease. At that time writing was enormously difficult. It was something that was almost impossible, and that's why I always tried to surround myself with friends or collaborators who were better writers than me, like Mario Camus and Daniel Sueiro, for example. But the really beautiful thing about the film was adapting the ideas we had to the actors and the circumstances that arose. Keep in mind that the majority were untrained actors without any experience. We did it all right there on the spot. We rehearsed a scene and depending on what happened in the scene, we rewrote the dialogue. To make a film with an intense and fast pace, the opposite of a psychological film or even the costumbristic films of the time.

A C : *I wasn't referring to that. If within Spanish cinema, the documentary tradition had disappeared after the Civil War, in many other European countries it still remained alive. I was referring to a rupture produced by a form of editing a film that leaves the scenes at the half-way point, without putting an end to them, without completing their development. And that doesn't have anything to do with the documentary, where that would be due to shooting difficulties.*
c s : From the beginning that was absolutely deliberate on my part. From the beginning I set out to make a very choppy film. And the proof is in the fact that it was shot precisely. It wasn't a case of me shooting entire scenes that were later cut in half, but rather, that from the beginning I only shot the scene to the mid-point. So whatever was taken out was done by the censors, not by us.

A C : *I say this because, apparently, the style of* A bout de souffle *[Breathless] arose as a consequence of the fact that there wasn't any way to edit the film.*
c s : Well, I've always been convinced of the relationship there is between the problems you have and the solutions you come up with in your films. The clearest case is Russian cinema. The close-ups were imperative because their cameras had cords, with little freedom of movement, and that required

them to shoot very close-up. It could be that something similar happened in *Los golfos* and *A bout de souffle*.

AC: *But you're saying that in your case it was absolutely intentional.*
CS: There is a very curious anecdote, because we went to Paris to do the mixing. *A bout de souffle* premiered, and we went to see it. The film surprised me and I thought it was very beautiful, but I remember that the others who came with me didn't like it at all. When I returned to Madrid, Marco Ferreri had already started *El cochecito*, and at that time he was having major technical problems. No one knew what to do with the scenes. He had minimal technical resources, and he always was quite dazzled by the way I moved the camera. I said to him, "Look, I just saw Godard's film, and he solved it in a great way. He put Coutard in a wheelchair and that's how he shot the whole film." And it seemed a fine idea to him, and all of *El cochecito* was made that way. I myself, before starting film school would do a tracking shot with my little camera by lying on a rug and having others pull me.

AC: Llanto por un bandido *[Lament for a Bandit] is stylistically very different.*
CS: You see, that's because after making *Los golfos* I was supposed to have made *Young Sánchez*, based on a short story by Aldecoa. And we began to work on it, but I wanted to do something else. I wanted to use longer shots, to make the film in color if possible. . . . I tried to make *La boda* [The Wedding] but it couldn't be done. We reached an agreement with Dibildos to make *Llanto por un bandido*, which was a completely different film in all respects. It was in CinemaScope. It was more contemplative. But the film was then destroyed by the editing in Italy. It was a matter of it being a much slower, more contemplative film.

AC: *As I recall, the influences and references came through Mizoguchi, who was as far away as can be imagined from* Los golfos.
CS: Yes, Mizoguchi, and also something of Kurosawa, although Kurosawa was not well known at that time. As with almost all my films, it is a different exploration. The editing has no correspondence at all to what the idea of the film was. The producer didn't like my editing and they cut up the film. It was an unpleasant film, because they forgot all about me. They had promised me many things and didn't give me any. They abandoned me with some wonderful actors and with a minimal crew and equipment, and with no possibil-

ity of doing anything. I had a bad time because I didn't have the resources. It has been the only film in which I didn't have adequate resources for what I was going to shoot. Aside from that, I remember that film and there were things that I liked a lot. Some things were ruined, but others are still there.

A C : *There is a clear pictorial inspiration that was not in* Los golfos.
C S : It was an attempt to reconstruct the aesthetic world of Goya. Meticulous work was done on the costumes. Little money, few resources, but I think it worked very well.

A C : *The people you socialized with at that time—Aldecoa, Carmen Martín Gaite—were much more literary figures than film makers, among which there only was Mario Camus.*
C S : That has always happened to me. Rarely have I surrounded myself with film people, I enjoy their company while I am working with them, but not in everyday life. Having another perspective, always speaking with people who can share a different perspective, that's very good. My best friends are writers or doctors or scientists, people who don't belong to the world of cinema, and for a long time both Mario and I attended the literary gatherings at the Gijón and especially at the Comercial, and we would meet there every night for quite awhile, with Aldecoa, with Ferlosio, Jesús Fernández Santos, Josefina Aldecoa, Carmina Martín Gaite, etc. They were very clever people who knew a lot, and what I did was listen. I have always had some very big literary gaps because even though I began to read a great deal at that time, writing seemed extremely difficult, almost impossible.

A C : *But at that time did you want to write?*
C S : No, no. It's my impression that everything I have done has been to be able to make better films. If I was interested in music, as I still am, it's to find which themes and melodies I can use in a film. When I read, it is inevitable that I make a cinematic transposition, even when it hadn't even crossed my mind to make a version for film. The same thing happens to me with theater. I'm an extremely bad theater viewer. I sit down to see a play, and although it may be marvelous, I can't manage to get into it completely. I stand back and see myself thinking, "That would be much better if the camera were located there and the face of the actress was seen, etc." And I convert almost everything into what I like and what interests me the most, which is cinema.

I remember that Aldecoa had just come back from the United States, very impressed by the Beat Generation, and he brought things that hadn't entered Spain yet. It was a new type of youth, a new way of seeing the world, very connected to the world of drugs, with many of the authors being alcoholics, like Ignacio himself. They were very clever people.

A C : *New variation on the following: your encounter with Querejeta, and you left Camus to begin doing scripts with Angelino Fons.*
C S : Sure, because Mario became independent. He decided to do *Young Sánchez*, which we had begun to write together but I wasn't convinced. . . .

A C : *Before that, you had done the script for* Muere una mujer *[A Woman Dies] together.*
C S : The truth is that we didn't do it together. The idea for the script was mine and Mario asked me to let him do it because I didn't want to. I gave all the materials to him, and then in the credits I appeared as co-scriptwriter, but my participation was limited to what I just told you.

We presented *La caza* [The Hunt] as a type of military operation. It was a matter of putting everything together again and organizing in a logical way. I made the firm decision never to make a film if I didn't have adequate resources at my disposal to be able to shoot it, regardless of whether it cost a lot or a little. Second: to try in whatever way possible to shoot the film following the order of the script, something which I continue to do and which, above all, leaves the final part open for me to resolve at the last moment. Third: to surround myself with colleagues of the highest quality without caring if they were disagreeable, but assuring myself that they were the best. If on top of that they were nice, all the better. It was a matter of making everything the best it could possibly be technically. As of *La caza* I no longer allow anyone to interfere in my work. *Los golfos* was a loose, youthful, passionate film, and one with extraordinary results for what it was. *La caza* was a very thought-out film. It is better to be told that you have a dolly of only five meters, but you can use it when you need it, than to be told that you have everything in the world, but it wasn't true. In this sense, it was the beginning of a completely new stage and also of a certain freedom of movement. And a total autonomy.

A C : *In addition, it was your most clearly political film to that date.*

cs: Below the surface. But so was *Llanto*, and if you push me, even *Los golfos* too. But you are right, there were more elements there: the war appears, a generation that had made and had won the war, including being part of the Blue Division. They are characters that I know well. Then there was a kind of confrontation with a younger guy . . .

AC: *Played by Emilio Gutiérrez Caba . . .*
cs: . . . for whom this entailed a discovery of the horror, of finding out that things were not as he thought they were. There was a certain naiveté on his part about life, which in a way was shown to us.

AC: *The Lorenzo of* Nueve cartas a Berta *[Nine Letters to Berta], by Patino, seems to be a cross between this character and those played by Jacques Perrin in the films of Zurlini.*
cs: You know that my cinema has been accused, sometimes with good intentions but mostly with bad ones, of being "symbolistic." I don't care. It seems very good to me to make symbolic cinema or metaphoric cinema. I like the metaphoric better because it seems richer to me. For example, in *La caza* I tried to bring out a series of elements, consequences, or symbols, which were there, but they were not to be taken directly as symbols.

AC: *They don't have a direct correspondence.*
cs: That's it. They are there. Some are relatively fortuitous, but only relatively.

AC: *But what I meant to say was that Emilio in your film and Patino's became a representative of a new generation, that was yours. I'm not sure if that was planned or not, but that's what happened.*
cs: I think I remember that I liked his innocence, his bewilderment at his elders, at their assuredness, and then to show how everything starts falling apart.

AC: *And the discovery of sexuality?*
cs: Certainly, but for me the most important thing is his relationship with the older men, the certain fascination he feels for them. He doesn't have a clear ideology. It's a film that I remember with a good deal of affection, and one that served me well.

A C : *It's curious, because the film did well all over the world, but in Spain it did poorly.*

C S : Well, that has happened quite often with my films, like *Carmen*, one of the most financially successful films in the world, and in Spain it was just so-so. Or *Cría cuervos* [Raise Ravens]. You never know the reasons.

A C : *In thinking of possible films to make, has public success influenced you, or have your foreign sales provided a cushion against that influencing you too much?*

C S : I think that if my movies had not been sold abroad, I would not have been able to continue making films. But remember that *La caza* is a film made in four weeks, on a ridiculous budget, without a focus, and in a dreadful summer heat, and if we made any profits, however small, it was good business because it cost almost nothing. That is, success isn't in how much money is brought in, but rather, in the relationship between cost/revenue.

A C : *Certainly that has been talked about. But what always is cited as a strange case is Eceiza, who made four films with Querejeta that didn't make any money, but that didn't seem to cause the slightest problem.*

C S : I mean that if you make a difficult, experimental film, and it doesn't sell, you won't make the next one, or it will take a lot of work for you to do it. Elías was very clear with us on this point. If a film failed, part of our creativity would be called into question. Perhaps we could weather one failure, but never two. In terms of Eceiza, that's something else. He had an arrangement with Elías. They were long-time friends, partners too I think, and it was another story altogether.

When I tried to make *La caza*, I took it to a bunch of producers, and despite the fact that it was very cheap, nobody wanted to make it. I took it to six people, and only Elías told me, "Look, we'll do it." I've always been an advocate of making film in my country, with my culture, and trying to see if it could be advanced just a little bit at a time. To always try to open a breach. There also were a lot of people who helped us. They were camouflaged and were on the left, and when they could, they lent us a hand. They were marvelous people who even got burned in the attempt. That's how Bardem survived, and thanks to them we were able to make films. Not Berlanga. Berlanga always had the right-wing press on his side. He had García Escudero and the entire right-wing press.

A C : *That's true, except for* El verdugo *[The Executioner], which had lots of problems.*

C S : But that was already different. Azcona was there. My memories of that time are not good ones. Censorship did us a lot of harm, and now they have the gall to say that it wasn't dangerous, that it didn't matter. Another idea is that my films were convoluted and difficult to understand because it was a way of not confronting the censors. That is a half-truth, which almost always is the worst kind of lie. On the one hand, it is true that you couldn't deal directly with certain subjects, but on the other hand, dealing with things in an indirect manner has always been something that I've liked a lot, to use the interpretation as a game, etc., etc. But the thing is that I like that way of narrating, and that's why I have continued to use it after censorship ended, because it seems to me that it was used in Golden Age Spanish literature where one thing is told to you while at the same time another is also being said. It seems richer, more interesting, more fertile. It makes you think more. Taking an oblique approach to something not only doesn't seem to me to be a defect, but on the contrary, it is an extraordinary virtue, making things more complex, not so direct and simple. And if I haven't always used it, it's because the producers don't like it all. But I have done it and will continue to do so. But at the same time I'm aware that it is a possibility, but not the only one.

A C : *Is it true that* Peppermint frappé *is a film that was going to be shot in English?*

C S : That's completely true. It was Elías's idea; he told me, "Look, this film has to be made in English because it is very expensive and that is the only way we can sell it." We all turned white. He told me he would have an advisor on hand to translate, and they translated the script into English. I remember that we shot the first scene in the studio. It was a scene between López Vázquez and Alfredo Mayo. We were all very serious in spite of the joking that had gone on behind the scenes. As soon as I gave the order to start, Alfredo Mayo said, "Pretty roses," and we all let out a big laugh. There was so much joking around that Elías said to stop shooting in English. We continued shooting in Spanish. I think that Luis Cuadrado fell off his camera from laughing.

A C : *Stress es tres, tres [Stress Is Three, Three] is one of your strangest films, and from what I remember, one of your least successful.*

c s : The truth is I don't remember much about that film. It was a very improvised film.

a c : *Shot in black and white after* Peppermint frappé *had already been made in color.*
c s : Well, the thing is that I don't remember why the film was made in black and white. It certainly wasn't because of me because, unlike so many people who feel the opposite, I always have wanted to work in color. The problem is that it was much more complicated, and it wasn't treated well and it worked out badly. It was a story of a group of people on a car ride to Almería. We began to shoot, a bit quickly, the episodes that took place during the trip and what happened at the arrival. A very simple little film.

a c : La madriguera *[The Burrow] inaugurates in a systematic matter something that already had appeared episodically in some of your films, and which we already have spoken about before, namely the use of performance, of the theater, of showing one thing to say another.*
c s : The film is a game. It's a type of closed circle with two people in one place. It was a kind of *tour de force* for a couple. I was very interested in making that film.

a c : *It seems to me that it is one of the most interesting films in terms of the issues raised, and one which received the worst treatment.*
c s : One time I was surprised by a women who asked me, while I was parking my car in Madrid, if I was Saura. I said yes, and she told me that she had seen *La madriguera* and that she thought it was a marvelous film. And she didn't understand how I could have portrayed her life with such precision. I said that she should excuse me but I had not the pleasure of knowing her until a few minutes before. I was left completely dumbfounded. Or maybe some couple should indeed lock themselves up to the point of destruction. The idea was that a couple isolates themselves from the rest of humanity— supposedly because that way they will know each other better—and what this greater knowledge implies is the destruction of the relationship, which in life happens quite often.

a c : *That is notably pessimistic.*

C S : Yes, but it happens very frequently. Sometimes it's not good to know too much about a person. It's preferable for some dark zones to remain. If all is known, it's dangerous.

A C : *Do you think that what also could have contributed to the audiences cool reception was the fact that the main couple was very alien to the Spanish audience?*
C S : Not just alien, alien in the extreme. I liked it a lot because I always liked Bergman's films. Well, not just Bergman's films, but Nordic cinema, of Dreyer, etc. But bringing in a Swedish actor was Elías's idea, not mine.

A C : *In order to shoot the film in English this time.*
C S : Per Oscarsson was a marvelous actor, a perfect actor for a Dreyer film. He was a kind of meticulous Calvinist, and then with Geraldine, Anglo-Saxon, it was a very interesting couple, but not at all Spanish, which never mattered to me. What happened was that it was a difficult film from the beginning. It was a film that was absolutely minimalist, that went beyond even what we had seen in *La caza.*

A C : *How did your work with Azcona develop over time?*
C S : Well, there is a great deal of misunderstanding about this. Rafael's work on *Peppermint* was very small, although very important in the sense that the script had already been completely written when he joined us. What happened was that it was very long and poorly structured, and we weren't able to fix it. I had already tried to work with Rafael before because I would have liked to have made *El Jarama* by Ferlosio with Elías. I don't know what happened, but we didn't do it.

A C : *I think I remember that there is a scene in* Los golfos *that is clearly taken from* El Jarama.
C S : That could be, because I liked it a lot. And the things that I like, I take and I use, and I don't worry too much about it. In this sense I'm like Borges, who you know says that everyone who cites Shakespeare is Shakespeare. Our obligation is to "vampirize" everything and make it our own. And I'm not at all shy about doing so. But let's continue about Azcona. In *La madriguera* he already had contributed many things, along with Geraldine who incorporated elements that were autobiographical or from friends of hers. From that point on Rafael and I worked together on a series of films very harmoniously.

Later that was spoiled a bit. But *El jardín de las delicias* [The Garden of Delights] was the first really harmonious effort.

AC: *To what point was* Peppermint *a more or less camouflaged adaptation of* Abel Sánchez?
CS: Of course it was. It really has many elements of *La boda*, which was a direct adaptation of Unamuno's *Abel Sánchez*, and which couldn't be made. I like that novel by Unamuno a lot even though Unamuno's novels are a bit like theoretical hypotheses.

AC: *Like theorems.*
CS: Indeed, almost theorems. But the idea for that novel is lovely: the jealously of two friends. And *Peppermint* is very much inspired by Unamuno.

AC: El jardín de las delicias, *despite having many problems, was a big success with the public.*
CS: I've always said that this film was inspired by a real event. I have a neurologist friend who told me one day that he had a patient with a similar situation to the protagonist in the film. He had had a type of heart attack that had affected his brain. He had lost his memory. And since he was a man who didn't trust people, he kept all of the facts about his bank accounts in his head, and no one but him knew them. He was a man who controlled millions, and then it became a matter of getting him to remember the necessary information so that they could know where the money was. It seems that they called someone in Sweden, or wherever, and they also staged some small performances to try to stimulate the recovery of his memory. That's all I know about the matter.

AC: *We already have here some themes that are crucial to your work: memory, remembrance, and performance as forms of stimulation, which we already have said are in* La madriguera. *On the other hand, many silly things have been said about this film, like whether it is a representation of Franco, which to me seems out of place.*
CS: I can assure you that I never thought that this person could be Franco. What is true is that when he was hunting, and he said, "Yes, yes," that was a reference to Franco, but he wasn't Franco.

A C : *At specific moments there were specific references or specific jabs. But that's a long way from saying that the protagonist is Franco.*

C S : There were some ironic things, just to play around. There were lots of things that I liked about this character, but what I liked the most was that this man—who was a real shark when he was healthy—was a charming, sensitive, and gentle person when he was sick, which usually happens. And I also took advantage of something about Juan March. As you know, he had a terrible accident on the La Coruña highway and he died as a result of the accident. And there appeared in all the newspapers the lovely sentence he said when he entered the hospital: "Do whatever you want with my body, but don't touch my head." That, along with what I just told you about, was the basis for making the film. At first the film was a disaster because, as you know, it was totally banned for five or six months, I can't remember well anymore, and Elías was very brave and risked a lot, and when they invited him to the New York Festival, it went there, where it was a big success, and they realized that it wasn't that dangerous.

A C : *Ana y los lobos [Ana and the Wolves] has the appearance of a moral story.*

C S : It is a story. It's a moral story with three characters that are archetypes and that are in line with the Spanish theater of the Golden Age, and also with modern theater because the theater of the absurd—Beckett, Ionesco, and even some things by Arrabal—are in this vein. Those characters, where each one represents something, that's where it comes from when they say my cinema is symbolic. *Ana* is a story and all stories are symbolic. Each character represents something. The mother is the mother, the governess is the foreigner who comes and who is an innocent and basic character bewildered by that performance she is continually seeing. The soldier is the soldier and the mystic is the mystic, the erotomaniac is the erotomaniac. It's a film that I like as an idea because it comes from the literary tradition of *costumbrismo*.

A C : *La prima Angélica [Cousin Angelica] became more famous for its extra-cinematographic problems than for its cinematographic ones.*

C S : Yes, the truth is that I never thought it would become such a serious thing to have the Falangist with his arm raised up high, which was clearly done on purpose, but as a joke. And what's more, we were convinced that it was going to be cut by the censors, but we put it in just in case. The film was enormously successful all over the world. I just arrived from Argentina where it was a tremendous hit. And that's very lovely. The truth is that cinema is not made for the general audience. First it can't be and then it shouldn't be.

A C : *It's that there isn't just one audience; there are many kinds of audiences.*
C S : Sure, I have always said that. The only thing you can be sure of is doing what you want. For that reason, since *La caza*, I've followed that course no matter what. Nevertheless, I do like a lot of things. Plus, I'm almost certain that if I like something, someone else has to like it too. But I can be wrong about that because sometimes it works and sometimes it doesn't. I would say that what really impresses me is when you go to a country—wherever, the USA or Canada or Latin America, which is closer to ours—and a marvelous woman stops you on the street (as happened to me when I was making *El sur* [The South], the Borges adaptation) and she says to you, "How wonderful! You have made the most beautiful and sensitive film that I've ever seen in my life, it's *Elisa, vida mía* [Elisa, My Life]." The fact that someone thinks I have given her something important in her life, to me justifies having made the film. Now I know that's something you can't ever say to a producer, but deep down inside me, that's what I believe.

A C : *It's curious, but cinema has the great ability to deeply affect people. It's capable of getting to the core of a person rather easily, much more so than a painting or literature. Perhaps in this respect it is only surpassed by music.*
C S : Well, I don't know. We are getting into profundities, which scares me. Perhaps cinema is a closer reflection of some moments in the life of mankind. But it's hard for me to go beyond that point. When I was younger, films from the thirties seemed horrible to me. But now in Argentina I have been watching the films of Libertad Lamarque, of Hugo del Carril, and of tangos, and I think that they're not at all dated—perhaps I'm speaking nonsense—but there are some actresses and actors that continue to be pretentious and even invisible, but on the other hand, others achieve a modernity that surprises you. I think that in cinema everything is yet to be seen. Things have been accepted and rejected in an apparently definitive way, and I think that this is totally provisional and that the assessment of many films and many filmmakers will still go through numerous cycles. Hugo del Carril has been a discovery for me. He is surrounded by antiquated actors, but he is, for me, modern, handsome, fantastic. He has been a great surprise.

A C : *In* La prima Angélica, *it is the first time that you use an old person to play a young one.*
C S : At times I've been told that this has an antecedent in *Fresa salvajes* [Wild Strawberries] by Bergman. I don't think so. What Bergman had done is different from what I did.

A C : *Well, there is a very similar thing with the character played by Viktor Sjöström, but it is not the same thing.*
C S : Exactly, it's not the same thing. I believe that it is the first time in cinema that an adult adopts, let's say, the form of a child and acts like a child. In Bergman, there is a distance. There is a man who looks and sees like a child. But he is not a child. He enters into a world of infancy, but he does not act like a child. On the other hand, here he does act like a child. López Vázquez plays with the girl, and suddenly he is a boy, but he sees himself as an adult, and that seems pretty logical to me.

And the first idea about this came from a reflection of mine. And it is the mirror. When you look at yourself in the mirror, you can see yourself at all ages. The mirror can bounce back your image. In the best of all cases, the image that you see will be the image you remember in the mirror from when you were young. In the worst of all cases, you are seeing yourself. This game in which you can imagine yourself as you were as a child, because you remember it or because you have seen some photos, that is where the origin of that image lies. The idea—it's a very literary image, I'd even dare to say a bit Borgesian—is that one is all ages. One isn't Carlos Saura in 1906, but also in '59 and '68 and, of course, in 1936.

In literature this is done very frequently. You write, "I was eight years old when I was with my mother," and an adult is writing. He—José Luis López Vázquez—isn't seeing himself as a child but as an adult. But it seemed to me to be an interesting dimension of that film. There are a lot of intuitive things in that film.

A C : *That you later develop in* Cría Cuervos *and* Elisa, vida mía.
C S : Exactly. And in *Dulces horas* [Sweet Hours], where the game is even greater. Now it's delirious. I would say it perhaps is my most daring film, although it wasn't understood very well during its time either.

A C : Cría cuervos *seems to me to be one of your best films.*

CS: It's a film that has given me a great deal of satisfaction. They gave it the Special Jury Prize at Cannes; it has made a lot of money; it has sold well; and I think that very little is left to be said about it.

AC: *I think that in a cinema like yours, where there is no gambling without risk, at times what is aimed at is more interesting than what is obtained.* Cría cuervos *is a much more finished film in that the sketches are more clearly outlined, as if this were the end of a stage.*

CS: Well, I wouldn't say no. Actually, that could be. The curious thing is that it began very badly. In Spain it had some negative reviews, just dreadful ones, the kind that are destructive. Like the one in *Triunfo* by Fernando Lara that asked why I didn't go down to the metro to find out what life is really like in Madrid instead of making *Cría cuervos*. He said that it was an idealized film, that it didn't interest him at all, and that people like that didn't exist. They were like reproaches arising from a Marxism that had been strained through a colander. I was never able to understand why he did such a thing. And then suddenly they selected it for Cannes. It was shown on the first day of the festival, which as you know is the worst day along with the last one, and they gave it the Special Jury Prize. They didn't give it the Palm d'Or because the Coppola film, *The Conversation*, was there, and they were under a lot of pressure.

AC: *How much do you think that the song by Jeannette contributed to the success of the film?*

CS: I think a lot, because it is a song that sticks in your head. I liked it a lot, and that's why I used it. And the curious thing was that it was an uncatalogued song. And it was a success throughout the world. And later, when I would fly Air France, they would play the song for me as soon as I stepped into the airplane. At times I was tempted to run away.

AC: *Did the success of* Cría cuervos *allow you to make* Elisa, vida mía?

CS: Well, yes. Elías told me then that I could do whatever I wanted. And since I always had wanted to make a more personal, more experimental, more difficult film, I decided to make *Elisa, vida mía*. And it seemed to be the right time to make it. It's a film that I like a lot, and I think that it has some very strange and disquieting areas. Perhaps from that point on I have been making a different kind of cinema.

The bad thing is that the road I took with *Elisa*, and later with *Los ojos vendados* [Blindfolded Eyes], is a road that is progressively becoming more narrow, and I'm not going to be able to continue taking it because the producers totally refuse to make this kind of film. I would like to go even farther, but I can't. I recognize that there is a road block, especially now, and not just in Spain, but all over the world. It also was because there is a certain weariness of certain types of art films, which were very unsuccessful and very pedantic and were complete failures. Then the producers leaned toward the safe and reliable—the remake or the literary adaptation—to run the least amount of risk. The film, *Elisa*, did very well for me. It won awards everywhere and it got a lot of recognition, which was almost unthinkable because it is a very difficult film.

A C :   *I think that* Los ojos vendados—*a film also in this vein, though to a lesser degree—received much less acclaim.*
C S :   Much less. I guess that people also get tired. *Dulces horas* was even less of a success. Perhaps some day I should examine these films to see if they are not as interesting as I think they are, or to look for reasons why the public ended up getting tired of this kind of cinema. Perhaps it's because new generations appeared that, as always, are very destructive, especially at the beginning, and are ready to crush everything that came before them. I'm remembering now the appearance of Trueba and Boyero. It's curious because they were people who came right at me and at other directors who, like me, made a particular type of film, and it was all done in order to defend another type of film, which didn't need defending anyway. I remember the terrible reviews of Bergman's films, saying that he was an imbecile, a metaphysician, a moron. It came to the point that Trueba made a little movie that was called *Coñan Sonatem* [Pubic Sonata]. I suspect that they regret all that now, but at the time it hurt me a lot. It also caused me a lot of harm and kept me from following the path of making bold, exploratory cinema.

And yet I was lucky because at that time I made a film like *Deprisa, deprisa* [Hurry, Hurry], which was a success all over the world, and it is the type of cinema that I have always wanted to make and which I always return to. It pertains to a more city-oriented cinema, more current, more like *Los golfos*. Now it's the same with *Taxi* or with *Dispara* [Shoot/Outrage]. I like to see how Madrid changes, especially the slums. They gave *Deprisa* the Golden

Bear at Berlin. It was well liked everywhere, including Spain. And the other thing that worked out very well for me was the "musical film."

I always wanted to make a musical film, but I didn't know how to. I think that it stems somewhat from my time as a photographer at the Festival of Granada. My mother was a pianist and I had had a musical education since I was little. I had always liked dance. Flamenco has been one of my life-long loves. When I was young I wanted to be a flamenco dancer. I even gave classes. I've been a motorcycle driver. I see the musical film as parallel to the fiction-based film, although they sometimes are mixed together as in *Carmen* or *El amor brujo* [Love, the Magician], even to the extent that I'm not capable of working on two projects at the same time. I just can't. The paranoia only works for one project. But when I make a musical film, I find that I can do it.

A C :   *Let's get back to chronological order.* Mamá cumple cien años *[Mama Turns One Hundred] is a return to* Ana y los lobos.
C S :   Yes, I think about ten years had passed, Franco had died, and I wanted to do the same metaphor of *Ana*, but applied to the current time period: how the country had changed, how the young people were freer.

A C :   *It's curious, once again, that the two films are very similar in concept and theory, yet they were received so differently. To what do you attribute the greater success of* Mamá?
C S :   Well, I don't know either. Perhaps it's because Rafaela Aparisio is emphasized more. This film was such a success that permission was requested to make a theatrical play out of it.

A C :   *The use of music in your films is getting more varied.*
C S :   For me the music is extremely important in the films. I had a big discussion with Luis Buñuel about this subject, but it was useless because he was deaf and didn't really know anything about it. When I write or when I'm shooting, I see the scenes with music. The music almost always comes first. It's previous music. And I think that this has been happening since *Los golfos*. That's where there was a petenera [popular Andalusian song] played on the guitar by Perico el del Lunar and sung by Rafael Romero, one of the great singers of the era. He also sang and was an actor in *Llanto por un bandido*, and he was a friend of mine. That is, I almost always have made films as if they were musicals, but not like American musicals.

A C : *You are referring to when music is the catalyst for something.*

C S : It's the catalyst, but it can turn into the protagonist. And it's not the usual American music, of accompaniment, but rather, something very specific.

A C : *This obliges you to use more and more existing music and less original music.*

C S : Yes, but because even when I used original music—in *La caza* or *Peppermint*—with Luis de Pablo, who is an excellent musician, I felt quite uneasy about saying to Luis, "Look, here I want a Vivaldi, and here I would like a Mozart, here a Beethoven quartet." Luis's great talent did it for me, composing "in the style of." But it seemed to me like a bad solution. I decided to choose the fragments, out of all the marvels there are in music, which interest me for my films. It's even to the point where sometimes there is a fragment of a Brahms concerto in *El sur* that repeats as a leitmotif. It's a theme on the cello that appears for ten seconds and never appears again, and I take it and convert it into a basic theme of the film. It's a manipulation of a classical theme.

A C : *But the problem there is that the tempos are set.*

C S : No, because I can make variations and manipulations like the one I just told you about. In addition, in *Taxi* the musical compositions don't end, they get shortened, or they don't finish during the sequence and go on to the next one, and nothing happens.

One of the problems of the musical film—and here we get into something that is more complicated—is that if you adapt Antonio Gades's *Bodas de sangre* [Blood Wedding], you can't do it like it's presented on the stage, because simultaneous actions occur on the stage. In the theater that doesn't matter because you are seeing things on a plane, you are seeing it all. But in the cinema you have to choose a part to tell well. Even to the point where— along with the editor Pablito del Amo, Gades, and the musician—we took apart the music, we repeated measures, we changed the order of things, we duplicated musical compositions, we modified choreography, etc., etc. With *Carmen* all of the choreography was already done for the camera because we all had learned from our previous experience. Music is a tyrant. It can destroy something for you or it can give you tremendous power. *Dulces horas* to me is a musical film, even though it doesn't appear to be one. In *Dulces horas* the music articulates the whole film. Ravel's music articulates all of the scenes.

A C : *We've arrived at* Deprisa, deprisa. *You have spoken about how every little while you feel the need to make a more current film. How do you bring that about?*
C S : Without any prior conceptions. All of a sudden, a topic appears, I like it or they offer it to me, and I make it. I never know why I do things, but neither do I worry about it in the least. In this case, it's a type of need.

A C : *How did your meeting and subsequent collaboration with Emiliano Piedra come about.*
C S : I knew him a little because he had distributed some of my films. One day he called me and said that he wanted to make a film with me. At first he was very vague. It had to do with an episodic film, one of those with Gades. I made my excuses, and he told me to at least go see *Bodas de sangre*. I hadn't seen it. And at one time the Americans had offered me *Bodas de sangre* to make with a lot of money and resources, and I turned them down because I was afraid of all those white walls and dancing gypsies. I went to the National School of Dance where they did a kind of show for us. I said yes. But the work lasted only 20–25 minutes. I thought that with some sort of prologue it could last somewhat longer, but I wasn't even sure about that. But we decided to charge ahead. He rented a studio set in Cineart and reconstructed it the way I asked him to, with a section set aside for make-up. A script never existed for this film. We did a rehearsal and went around taking notes. And it ended up being an hour and ten minute full-length film that was tremendously successful all over the world. Emiliano, who was a very warm kind of guy, had some economic problems, and after that film he was able to get out from under them. If he hadn't died, we would have continued making films together.

I entered into the world of the musical film with this obsession of mine to be able to fit the camera to the music. I wanted the camera to be one of the dancers.

A C : *That is a cinema that requires a great deal of precision.*
C S : Of course. But that is one of the most marvelous things about working with true professionals. But we are talking about only one type of musical film, because there is another type, as in *Sevillanas* and *Flamenco*, which comes from a totally different direction, based entirely on improvisation.

I contend that the musical film is one thing and the plot-based film is another, although at times they can coincide. In the musical film you become an absolute *voyeur*. In the fictional film, at minimum, you create some characters, a story that you develop. Not in the musical because knowing nothing of choreography, what you are is the perfect *voyeur*. You have to place the cameras and look to see what is the best way possible. And the big responsibility is theirs, not yours. And this is a relief because you are seeing brilliant artists dancing just for you. You become the only spectator.

But there are stages. That happened more in *Bodas de sangre* than in *Carmen* because in both *Carmen* and *El amor brujo* there was much more of my creativity—not because I wanted to, but because there was a story, and more of my participation is essential once you get beyond a lack of content.

A C :   *We are at* Antonieta.
C S :   It's part of my Ibero-American experiences.

A C :   *Which are few. There's* El Dorado, *and if we count TV,* El sur.
C S :   It's an hour-long film made in 35mm and it's like a movie. To me it does count.

I'm in love with Latin America. It must be the adventurous side of me. And now I'm going to make *Tango* in Argentina. I like the people. I enjoy working there.

But let's return to *Antonieta*. Until *Bodas de sangre* I had not accepted a project blatantly unrelated to me. I thought that if a film director wanted to be an *auteur*, he should be responsible for as much as possible. The script for *Antonieta* had been written by Carrière, who was Buñuel's scriptwriter and a good friend of mine. It was an assignment that Gaumont in France had given me. They told me to pick between three things. One was the *Carmen* that Francesco Rosi then did, something else that I don't remember, and *Antonieta*. It seemed the most interesting because I wanted to shoot outside of Spain in some Latin American country, and I liked the script. I think that if there is a mistake in this picture, it's Isabelle Adjani. I tried for a Mexican actress, but the conditions of the production required her to be French and famous. Among the ones that they told me about, Adjani seemed the most appropriate. Soon I realized that this girl didn't know anything about the country, lived isolated in Mexico, didn't go out on the street, and never came to understand her character well. And that she was a stupendous actress. In spite of everything, it was a positive experience for me.

AC: *The thing that comes most to mind when I talk about* Los zancos *[The Stilts] is that it is an odd film.*

CS: Yes, and I don't remember much about it. I think there is a fundamental flaw because the idea that I had didn't become realized. I wanted to establish a chemistry between Fernán-Gómez and Laura del Sol, and there was no way. And not because they didn't want to, but because they were too different. And I would have liked there to be something more sensitive between them. I wanted to establish this as the last love between a person, already old, seventy, an intellectual, and a young girl, but understood as an *amour fou*. In the film this passion doesn't come through. It's proper, but it doesn't have that force, that bestial loving of an older man, a bit out of his head for a young girl, to the point of destruction. That was the drama of the film, and I don't think that it became that important.

AC: *Let's go on to your second Latin American experiment,* El Dorado.

CS: It's a film that I like. It's exactly what I wanted to make. *Los zancos* could have been something else, but not this film.

AC: *Why do you think it was treated so badly?*

CS: I don't know the reasons very well. I think that the publicity was bad, talking about the film as the most expensive one in Spanish cinema. And I think that a contributing factor was that Andrés Vicente Gómez at that time had very powerful enemies at the newspapers, at *ABC* for example. If it had been made after the ones about Columbus, maybe that would have been the proper moment. But, as always, the truth is that I don't know.

Some intellectuals stuck their noses in the film, and there even was a letter from Carlos Seco that I answered very sharply. In the letter he talked about how it was an insult to Spain, how it denigrated the Spanish conquerors, that there had been famous examples of heroic deeds. I answered that this was the history of Lope de Aguirre, and that he should read the chronicles again because everything was there.

In contrast to what it may seem, I was very faithful to the chronicles. It's a film with very little invented, some of the ending and a bit more.

I like the film a lot although I recognize that it is a bit atypical in structure and construction. But because I wanted it to be that way. The character of Aguirre emerges little by little because the main character at the beginning of the film isn't Aguirre and little by little, from underneath Aguirre starts appearing after twenty minutes have passed. I believe that it responds very well to what I think this expedition was.

AC: *And why a film and a series?*
CS: I didn't make a series. I made a three-and-a-half-hour film. But for commercial reasons the film had to stay 120 minutes long. With a lot of heartache, I made the cuts so that they wouldn't mangle it even more on me. But I will always consider the longer version to be much better than the short one. And later from these three and a half hours they got four chapters for television, repeating the ending of each chapter or making a summary so that the audience could follow it, but without touching it.

I haven't gone back to see it, but I'm convinced that this film isn't bad.

AC: *Is* ¡Ay Carmela! *a type of substitute for* Esa luz *[That Light], your pending film about the Civil War that you have not been able to make?*
CS: No, not at all. They are two different things. *¡Ay, Carmela!* was a proposal by Andrés, who took me to see a theatrical play. I went rather reluctantly, but I became enthusiastic about the play, and I told him I'd do it. And I said something foolish that I later upheld. Everyone thought that what I liked about *¡Ay, Carmela!* was precisely the playing with time by having a character come from the beyond. That is what I liked the least about the play. I told Andrés that I'd do it but only on the condition that it would be a linear narration. Because I just couldn't see it. That part about Carmela coming from the beyond and telling the story of what was happening seemed to me to be fine as a theatrical device, but I thought it would have to be done in a more open manner, with new characters. And I proposed it to Rafael Azcona, with whom I had not worked for a while, and after two days of disagreements, everything began to go very well and we did the script. We changed a lot of things. For example, Gustavete, who is hardly mentioned in the play, here is raised almost to the position of a protagonist. Also the Italian. And it was a fantastic shoot. The film was a great success.

AC: *And for that reason you could make your next film,* La noche oscura *[The Dark Night].*
CS: I have a special preference for that film, which almost nobody liked. It seems a bit pretentious, but from time to time I've wanted to make a type of cinematic essay about a particular person. For example, Lope de Aguirre, San

Juan de la Cruz, Borges, and Goya, whom I want to do and will do someday, and I have a script about Philip II that I'd like to do some day. And rather than an essay about his entire life, it always is a fragment of his life that seems essential to me and which in some way explains his life and allows me to use the imagery of the era, and above all, imagination, inquiring into the truth about what the character was like. The size of the film doesn't matter.

With *La noche oscura* I tried to do this. I've always been enamored of San Juan de la Cruz, since I was little. I've always been dazzled by those nine months that he was incarcerated in a miserable cell in Toledo, martyred by his companions because he would go barefoot. They also had transgressed. It's very Buñuelian. The life of San Juan does not interest me, but I'm very interested in those nine months that he spent in isolation, without eating, practically naked, in frightening heat and horrible cold, and being taken downstairs every Friday to have them beat him to see if he'd repent, and he never did repent.

I became very well informed on the subject, and I came to the clear conclusion that the only way to survive there was because that man had found a way to communicate with the world beyond. Therefore, the poems were not written by him, but by God. And that seemed such a nice idea, having them dictated by God, that I wanted to make the film as if it were that way. It was a disaster. It was only liked at the San Juan conventions. All of the Carmelites considered it to be a very profound and interesting approximation, but secular.

On the other hand, there were people who tried to attack me for San Juan's sake. First they said he should be left as is and couldn't be touched; that he was closer to God than to men. And I never understood that. If he was a man, he would have to be closer to men, that's what I'd say. . . . I think it was the worst disaster of my life.

AC: *But a relatively inexpensive film.*
CS: It wasn't that inexpensive. It could have been so but the construction of the sets kept the film from being inexpensive. It was a disaster that I am very, very proud of. They say that disasters are useful because you learn from them. That's a lie. You don't learn anything. What happens is that you stay perplexed because you don't know what the reasons for such a disaster could be. I have a diary in which I wrote after finishing *Carmen*: "And now what are we going to do with this film," and it went around the world.

That said, I have to recognize that for me it was a big stumbling block because I could have continued making films with Andrés, and after that things got more complicated. Andrés got a bit scared. And I would have preferred to continue along that line. My *Goya* is somewhat on that road: an isolated person in the last moments of his life, in Bordeaux, with his mind lost, not knowing his name, sometimes remembering things but only partially. That road has been cut off a little, but I hope I can recover it.

A C :   *Your third Latin American occasion is a curious adaptation of "El sur."*
C S :   Well, as you know, the script was not mine but Víctor Erice's. I had already arranged it beforehand with Andrés. I remember it among the films for which I hold a special affection. *El sur, La noche oscura, Los ojos vendados, Elisa, vida mía* are very delicate and very personal films.

A C :   *You almost never have talked about* Maratón.
C S :   Once again, it was an essay. They offered it to me with very little time. We had spoken a lot before, some two years before, and I had said yes because I've always liked athletics a lot. It's fascinating to see the effort of the people. Then I forgot about it because Hugh Thomas was going to do it. Apparently something went wrong, and at the last moment they offered it to me again, and they sent me a script about eight hours long. It was very good, but it didn't have anything to do with what I ended up doing. It encompassed all aspects of the Olympiad: the economic aspects, the medicines used, etc. Given the shortness of times, what I did was fasten myself to the Olympic games themselves. That is, I looked for the best cameras, and I put together a marvelous crew. I collected a great deal of footage. The first edit I made took four hours. But since I was contracted to make something two hours long, we had to take out many things. What remains is a type of musical. What I don't understand is that it hasn't been exhibited, it hasn't even come out on video. It's absurd and I think that something strange has happened. With the start of the Atlanta games, it was the opportune moment to launch it.

A C :   Sevillanas.
C S :   Is a different product. It's taking the musical to a realm that is difficult to move toward. And later *Flamenco* is like the culmination. It's a matter of looking for the ultimate purity: giving the most power possible to the music

and the dance, where there is nothing to interfere. And at the same time the scenic space—I'll call it that although it isn't, but since there isn't any set, I don't know what to call it—with the light and transparencies collaborates in this spectacle. It's a matter of isolating the dance in a place that both does and doesn't participate.

Manolo Sanlúcar, who knows more about this than I do, helped me to pick out the groups. And as you can see, we are once again dealing with a minimalist proposition, which is something I really like a lot. It's a rectangle of illuminated *panós*, and nothing else. It's a musical in its purest state. What confers the rhythm to the spectacle is the linking of the diverse elements. Nothing else. Nothing to do with the historiography of the sevillanas or anything like that. It was an enormous success.

A C :   *Was* Flamenco *done under the same set of assumptions?*
C S :   Only to a certain point. It's a more complicated matter because sevillanas is a small concept, but flamenco is delicate and very difficult to deal with. And I always approached it with a lot of fear and caution despite the fact that I've liked flamenco since I was little. I worked hard, I studied a lot, and I got very good advice. And I think that it is a further step, but as I told you before, it seems to me that it will be very difficult to continue in this direction because we have almost reached the limit.

A C :   *How did Vittorio Storaro's participation come about?*
C S :   Well, curiously it wasn't my idea. It was the idea of the producer, Juan Lebrón, who was annoyed one day because none of the directors of photography that we wanted were free. He said: "Well, bring in Storaro." He contacted him, and he told him, "Fine, with Saura, and since he knows me."

He had been a member of the jury that awarded prizes for television, and *El sur* had been presented there. And it walked off with all the awards, which no one knows about in this country. But in brief, since I had to go to Japan because they had bought *Dispara* and it was going to be judged at the Tokyo festival, which is held in Kyoto, we arranged to meet in Kyoto. I brought him all of my sketches, and he said yes. We've already made two films. We are going to do *Tango* because I've wanted him to participate from the very beginning of the project, and he came with me to Argentina. And it's possible that we will do *Pajarico* [Little Bird] together, but that all depends on the

American film he has pending. He is a marvelous person with whom I have formed a great friendship.

A C : *In what way is it different working with Storaro than with the other Spanish directors of photography?*
C S : I've worked well with them all. Storaro has the advantage of being a humanist, of having a broad cultural foundation. He's a man obsessed with photography and color, but he has a global concept of things. It's uncommon to find a technical collaborator with that sensitivity, who is not limited exclusively to the specific concepts of his profession. Besides, he is not at all a *prima donna*, he's quick at doing the lighting, and he has a different sense of light. One thing I like a lot is that Storaro uses light dramatically within the scene. I'll explain. What he normally does is not just light a scene but modify the light over the course of the scene. It's extremely interesting. He has a system of illumination that allows him to raise and lower the intensity of the light at the moment that interests him. He can achieve fantastic things.

A C : *It's like adapting to film the system of lighting used in the theater, where that is done too.*
C S : Right. I hadn't realized that. Well, it gives excellent results. Like me, he's interested in doing something out of the ordinary. That's something that unites us. And now I've done *Taxi*, which seems like something normal because I've been able to do something more. In *Tango* I imagine that we will be able to do much more, and in *Pajarico* I can't say. *Goya* will go still farther. Like him, I think that what I wouldn't crave is to make a conventional, costumbristic film or a regular Spanish comedy.

A C : *What is that little bit more in* Taxi*?*
C S : You'll have to see it to tell me yourself.

A C : *I'm planning to see it, but until I can, you'll have to talk about it.*
C S : To some extent it's the music, and a certain dramatic boldness in the structure of the film. It's a film that can approximate *Los golfos*, *Dispara*, *Deprisa*. I don't really know. It's a rhythmic film, the complete opposite to a reflective film. It's a film in which things happen and where the characters,

who are very young, are not reflective. They don't have the time to reflect on things.

AC: *We have started to talk about* El sur *twice but we stopped in the middle.*
CS: It could be that the appropriate time hadn't arrived. It's a very amusing story. While I was making *El Dorado*, Andrés told me that he wanted me to make some of Borges's stories that he had the rights to, for a television series. The idea was that I would either make them all or choose the one I liked the most. I told him that I was crazy about Borges but I didn't know how I'd be able to do a Borges story on film. I read the stories and told him that I just couldn't see it. Time passed and he asked me if I wanted to make one of the stories, "El sur," with a script by Víctor Erice. I was very intrigued because Víctor had done *El sur* another time, and I told him to send it to me, and I found that he had made a really good script out of a two-page story. I accepted but reserving the right to make minor changes, and under the condition of going to Buenos Aires to get used to the surroundings. Víctor told me that he was very happy that I wanted to make the script, and I got down to work. But at the end of three days Andrés called me to say that Víctor wanted to do *El sur*. I told him fine, no problem. But he added that Víctor was now writing another script—*La muerte y la brújula* [Death and the Compass]—and said that I could direct it. He sent it to me. It was an unfinished script, but very good. I told him that he'd have to start thinking about making a film because it already was almost an hour and a half long. Andrés said that he'd think about it. He called me back after three or four days to say that Víctor didn't want to make *El sur*, he wanted to make *La muerte y la brújula*. And by then I was irritated and I told Andrés to decide once and for all what it was he wanted me to do. And Andrés decided that I should make *El sur*.

I went to Buenos Aires and was there for ten days. And I wrote a completely different script. He's a character from the present who in some ways is Borges, but he isn't Borges. Everything I used was Borges's materials. Furthermore, Argentina at the time I was filming still was like postwar Spain, with the libraries falling apart and the buildings destroyed. There was a certain poverty. I thought it was the perfect climate for what I wanted to do: to make an essay about Borges by way of an intervening character. I really like how it turned out. I like the game, that ambiguity that's there underneath.

A C : *You began to direct opera a while ago. How have these experiences gone for you?*

C S : Great directors have offered me operas to direct: Abdado, and I don't know who else. Because of *Carmen* mostly. And I always said no because it scared me. But when they proposed that I do *Carmen* I thought that it was indeed something I could do. For that I was prepared. The first time was for the Paris Opera because Barenboim, the pianist, called me, but it all went to hell because they threw him out. Then they called me from Stuttgart to make *Carmen* with my brother, Antonio. And I did it. And later, a year ago, in June, almost to the day, we were in Spoletto to do *Carmen*.

It has nothing to do with cinema. On the other hand, I really felt like filming how one makes a *Carmen*. But I already had made my *Carmen*.

A C : *Will* Tango *follow the line of a musical film?*

C S : Yes and no. I want to go back again to a plot-oriented film: to *Carmen*, to *El amor brujo*, not in the same vein as *Flamenco*.

The Apprenticeship of Life: Interview

ANTONIO CASTRO / 1998

ANTONIO CASTRO: *One of the most curious things about* Pajarico *[Little Bird] is that it's filled with new people. For quite a while you've had a kind of crew of regulars, and now you are working with new people, except for Palmero and a few others.*

CARLOS SAURA: Sometime ago I decided to change these regulars, whom I respect a great deal, like Teo Escamilla, Pablo del Amo, or Pedro del Rey. But I think change is also very good. It's very healthy.

AC: *Including the cinematographer, who is essential for you.*

CS: Pedro López-Linares had worked with me before. Not in film, but he had done two operas with me, the two *Carmen* operas that I had directed with my brother Antonio, one in Stuttgart and the other at Spoletto. I'm pleased with how he works. Also, he is a very warm person, and he's been a good friend of my son Carlos for many years.

AC: *For the first time, before making the film, you published a novel.*

CS: Well, let's call it that. To me those words frighten me, but let's say that we can categorize it as a type of short novel without many pretensions, that I wrote because I've always felt that it was more pleasant to read it as a narrative than as a script, but always with the idea of making a film. And that's a habit I've had for some years now, although this is the first narrative that

From *Dirigido por* 265 (1998): 37–39. Reprinted by permission of *Dirigido por*. Translated from Spanish by Linda M. Willem.

was published. That way you can describe the landscape more or spend more time on the psychology of the characters, and it's all easier and more comfortable to read.

Right now I'm writing a script entitled *Querida, ¿me alcanzas el cuchillo?* [Darling, Can You Get Me the Knife?], and I'm also writing it in narrative form. Then the last step is a lot easier. You have to clean it up a little, but not much. It also has the additional advantage of helping to avoid, as on other occasions, the lack of understanding by the producers, because the script, at least the kind that I write, is very dry, very severe, very visual. I even write the script in almost a diagram form. Each point is a diagram. It's not written or thought out that way, but it's the way I visualize it, and it turns out that way in the end, although I sometimes change things.

A C : *But you can only do this when you write it by yourself and when it's not commissioned.*
C S : Of course, under other conditions I wouldn't dare, although it could perhaps work out in a collaboration, but I've never tried it.

A C : *Why* Pajarico *now?*
C S : Because I owed a debt to my Murcian family. I've wanted to do something like this for years. When Javier Castro, *Taxi's* producer, asked me if I had something prepared, I told him to read that, but thinking it wouldn't interest him. Nevertheless, he read it right away, called me the next day, and we made it immediately. I had a series of memories, of images, of odors in my mind, and also of characters.

A C : *The film is structured in three parts that correspond to the three uncles and to the time that Manu stays in the house of each.*
C S : And to the different floors that he passes through. There is a climb for the boy. He begins climbing floors, until he arrives at the last one where his uncle Emilio lives. Well, not really the very last one, because in addition to the three floors there is the terraced roof and the basement. It is, if you like, the universe in miniature.

At the beginning it isn't a story where many things happen, but rather, a film of characters who are not together except at the beginning and the end, at the meal and at the cemetery.

A C : *To my mind it's your most personal film of the last few years, even to the extent that I have the impression that you are speaking at times through the voices of some of your characters, different characters at different times. For example, when the uncles meditate on art.*

C S : Look, that doesn't happen only here but in many other films. The truth is that up to now I have not made an autobiographical film. But in the broad sense of the word autobiographical, well there are many that indeed are.

A C : *And clearly this one is much more so than* Taxi.

C S : Certainly, because it is more personal and more intimate. But as far as art is concerned, I do think those things and many other things too. I don't just like *Las Meninas*, which is a marvelous painting.

A C : *Along with some of Uncle Fernando's opinions.*

C S : And those of Paco Rabal.

A C : *Why did you use epilepsy as something that encompasses the whole family, although in different ways?*

C S : Well, I don't know. For the absences I suppose. But there aren't any epileptics in my family. What's certain is that it has always seemed very magical to me. You already are aware that there exists the *petit mal* and the *grand mal*, some seizures that last hundredths of a second and others a long time. As you know, I certainly am a person who is very concerned about the brain. I've studied a lot, and I have friends who are neurologists.

A C : *And I suppose that everything concerning the iris and the eye in this film also falls under this concept.*

C S : Undoubtedly. Everything concerning the eye is very close to our work, to cinema and photography. The brain is fascinating. The character most affected by the epilepsy is Aunt Margarita. And it's not known whether the girl is epileptic or not, but she is magical because she is capable of predicting things, or seeing them while they are happening even though she's not there.

A C : *There is a joke concerning that character who had no choice but to become a volunteer. Her Falangist boyfriend, the one with the heavy step, is called Federico Sánchez.*

CS: It came to me naturally, but not very wickedly. I was looking for a name and that one occurred to me and it amused me. For that reason I used it.

AC: *The film insinuates—through the differences between the grandfather's story and that of Aunt Margarita—a possibility of incest between the grandfather and his daughter.*
CS: That's not known, but it actually is possible. Furthermore, there is the confrontation between an upright Republican like the grandfather and a Falangist like Federico.

AC: *Margarita is said to have magic powers, but nevertheless, the one who does indeed have them is Fuensanta.*
CS: It's another example of the superiority of women. Fuensanta is the one that guides the boy, who has a very slow awakening. On the other hand, you already know my way of thinking: women are more clever, they are the ones who manipulate the lives of others. And Fuensanta at a very young age realizes that she can manipulate Manu, and he lets her manipulate him, fascinated by a girl who has powers and who is very strong and very magical.

AC: *Uncle Juan uses all the things he works at to try to solve his sexual problems.*
CS: Like so many people. To me this character is very appealing because he's a very sensual man with a marvelous outlook on life. Everything is fine with him and he isn't in conflict with either his natural surroundings or with people. He is a very affectionate type, very Mediterranean.

AC: *In contrast, his wife spies on him and although we know hardly anything about her, we have the impression that she is an embittered person.*
CS: She's jealous and tormented because Juan is a womanizer and is surrounded by very beautiful women. But Juan does everything very naturally. There's not any of that Nordic spying. He has a very direct and simple concept of sexual relations, at the other end of the spectrum from his wife.

AC: *What about the drugs in the film? The topic is insinuated, but that's all.*
CS: To some degree it's the presence of danger, a new way of seeing the life of the young that is very different from the apparent tranquillity of the provincial city.

A C : *Curiously, the only sexual act we see is between homosexuals and is spied on*
by children.
C S : I wanted this scene to have a cinematic treatment that is similar to heterosexual acts. For example, in the use of the music. It's not sentimental
music, but it is lyrical music, the kind that normally is used for heterosexual
couples, but never for homosexual ones.

A C : *Does Fuensanta have anything to do with* La prima Angélica *[Cousin*
Angelica]?
C S : It's a very complicated question. I suppose that there is some connec-
tion, but I haven't worked it out for myself.

A C : *In both cases the girl cousins are the ones who guide the boys.*
C S : Could be, but what I'd do is connect Fuensanta more easily with the
girl from *Cría cuervos* [Raise Ravens], in a different way of course.

A C : *The character of the grandfather is more complicated than it seems. Some-*
times he confuses his son with his grandson, but it seems that at other times he
does it on purpose, that he uses his lapses of memory, that he plays with them.
C S : He is a character who is in a limited position because of his age. He's
fading, but at the same time, he's blackmailing the family. And this is the
game that older people play when they lose a bit of their sense of reality,
sometimes they're absent and other times they're extremely lucid. Also he
has a lot of the Arab in him. He's a great storyteller.
     Besides that, he wants to be the main character. He won't let anyone
around him be the main character while he's there. He is a very domineering
character. Much more than it seems. He's somewhat above good and evil.
The structure of the family is very male dominated. The grandfather enjoys
a special respect. Next is the oldest brother, Uncle Emilio, who is the one
who brings the family together.
     Aunt Lola is reminiscent of one of my aunts, a stout, busty woman who
would hug the children in the family as if she were a Great Mother. I like her
a lot. I really like it when she goes through the corridor navigating like a
great ship that has to support itself on the walls so as not to fall.

A C : *Nature is important, but only at the beginning and at the end—when they*

find him in the park, the grandfather wants to go to the sea—does it have a real
importance in the film?
C S : Yes, at the beginning, with the countryside, it's speaking to us about a
type of communion between the characters and space. I think that in comparison with what happens in my mother's family, the Murcian family is
more extroverted, more Mediterranean, I'd almost say Asian.

A C : *What is the function of the character who plays "the magician" in the film?*
C S : It's a story that Rabal told me about a character in Aguilas, which is
where Paco was born and where he spends the summer. I included him. It's
difficult to say what his function is, but he's one of so many visionaries in
the world who believe that they are God. And it's not so strange. Deep down
Jesus Christ was convinced he was God, and he wasn't because a man can
never be God.

A C : *It seems like a deeply felt film.*
C S : Well, it tries to be a more poetic film. As you know, I'm not a person
who is enamored of his work, and yet, I feel very close to *Pajarico*. I think
there are things that went very well, the way I wanted them to be. I like the
world of *Pajarico*.

A C : *Would you say that you have a more emotional relationship with this film*
than with the rest of your works?
C S : Well, it's very possible. It turned out to be more intimate for me.

A C : *That's why the film is dedicated to Lali and Anna.* (Interviewer's note: Lali
refers to the actress Eulalia Ramón who plays the role of Aunt Margarita and
who is Saura's current companion. Anna is the name of their daughter).
C S : Exactly, because it's something that comes from deep down inside me.

Tango According to Saura

PAULA PONGA / 1998

PAULA PONGA: *How long have you been thinking about making a musical about the tango?*

CARLOS SAURA: The idea didn't come from me. It came from an Argentine director, Juan Carlos Codazzi, and I told him yes immediately because I've always liked Argentine folkloric music: the milongas, the tangos, the valsecitos.

PP: *How did this fondness originate?*

CS: I grew up listening to the tangos of Gardel and Imperio Argentina on the radio. At the time of the Civil War the tango was very popular. My father was a real fan. I remember him singing tangos around the house, when he was shaving. My childhood memories are filled with tangos.

PP: *And do you know how to dance the tango?*

CS: Yes, pretty well, but in the European way. That is, in a straight line, which is easier than in circles. Like in Bertolucci's films, which is fine for Europe but is a kind of insult for someone from Argentina.

PP: *You could have made more of a documentary, like* Sevillanas *and* Flamenco, *but you opted to combine the dance with a fiction, with a dramatic plot. Why?*

From *Fotogramas* 1859 (1998): 94–96. Reprinted by permission. Translated from Spanish by Linda M. Willem.

C S : Perhaps out of the need not to repeat the same format, to seek out new paths and to delve a little deeper into what I had already done before. In a certain way, *Tango* is the child of *Carmen*. It's closer to *Carmen* than to my other films, although it does pertain to *Flamenco* in terms of structure, sets, lighting. In my opinion, it's a step beyond *Flamenco*. And besides that, it seems to me that the tango lends itself well to making a story about emotions, which is part of the tango itself. Because the lyrics of tangos—although they don't appear much in the film—always have that tone of tragedy, of emotions, of death, of stabbings.

P P : *The story of a man, abandoned by a woman, in an emotional crisis, taking refuge in his job of preparing a film about the tango—this plot-line gets mixed in with the dance, but in the end everything turns out to be a fiction.*
C S : Everyone can interpret it the way he wants to. It's all the same to me. The plot corresponds almost exactly to what is being sung at the beginning of the film, which talks about disillusionment. The protagonist begins to read a script and he himself becomes the protagonist of the script. It's he who comes up with the elements that then start appearing as images. It's all a game: a story that can exist or never did exist. That's a little of the idea: a film or a project of an unfinished film. And the camera is all around, omnipresent. And the disillusionment that was sung about corresponds to the disillusionment of this character, emotionally in a state of crisis, but saving himself through his work, as happens so often. Because I'm one of those people who believes that if an emotional crisis coincides with a professional crisis, you might as well shoot yourself, but generally work helps to cure emotional maladies.

P P : *What criteria guided you in the selection of the tangos?*
C S : My intention, and that of Lalo Shifrin, was to dig a bit deeper, to see that there are very distinct ways to show how one can dance the tango, not only the traditional one, but also a tango oriented toward the future, including being choreographed by the dancers like in the scene where Julio Bocca appears, and not only in pairs. In the film there are three fundamental kinds of music that are the ones that make up the tango: the Creole waltz, different from the Central European one; the milonga, probably of Spanish origin; and from them both arose the tango. And those are the three basic rhythms. The inclusion of the "Va pensiero" was Vittorio's suggestion. I had a very

clear chorale image of the immigrants, a type of homage to immigration, and on a trip from Los Angeles to Buenos Aires, Vittorio kept listening to *Nabucco* and suggested it to me with all of the humility that characterizes him. I wasn't completely sure, not even after hearing it several times, but upon seeing it in the rehearsals, I liked it, and it seemed to me to be a fitting homage to Italian immigration, since all the other elements in the film were Spanish.

P P :   *To what extent is* Tango *autobiographical?*
C S :   All that pertains to the process of making a film about the tango: the casting, choreography, music, scenery, etc. The rest is very much invented.

P P :   *The protagonist doesn't hide his fears: the passage of time, emotional emptiness, loneliness.*
C S :   He's a lucid man, in my opinion; disoriented, like everyone, and he's doing a job he likes a lot, setting things up to carry out the project. He's in a time of personal crisis, that age of collapse, as he puts it—and which was referred to in one of Scott Fitzgerald's stories—that age starting at forty where one looks back and realizes that he hasn't done any of what he could have done, and that it's too late to get it all back. In a way he is his own critic. He saves himself because he falls in love with another woman.

P P :   *The protagonist also says that he doesn't have the slightest idea of what's going to happen to him, which is something that you recognize happened to you while preparing the movie.*
C S :   It's not that it happens to me, but I seek it out. What I detest the most is knowing what I'm going to do. People think that my mind is very structured, but it's not true. Perhaps I do indeed know what I'm going to do, but I don't want to know. What I like best is having the sensation that I'm going to invent something new every day, to direct something that's alive, and the script doesn't have to be made of iron, and the film doesn't have to be perfect. It has to be like life, with good things and bad things. What I like is to leave open areas rather than follow a script exactly. I don't believe in iron-clad scripts. I want the script to be something alive and to develop over the long creative process of making a film.

P P :   *Does it bother you that you are recognized more as a creator of images rather than a narrator?*

c s : That *is* my conception of cinema. I don't believe in using literary works for films. I like literature a lot and I do like to write, but that literature isn't good for making a film. What needs to be clear are the images, the mystery of coordination between the movement of the camera, the performances, the stage sets, the lights, the music. And all of that can't be written down. If it could be, there would be no reason to make a film.

P P : *Tango's protagonist says that he doesn't accept interferences in his work. Have you always made the films you wanted to make? Have you never made anything you didn't want to?*
c s : Never. On that point I've always been inflexible. And perhaps for that reason I've made thirty films. Neither have I ever accepted any cuts, and so I've had problems when they tried to make cuts because of censorship or for other reasons.

P P : Tango *is also a political film. One of the dances alludes to the crimes of Videla's dictatorship, and it's said that the torturers played tango music very loudly during their tortures.*
c s : Yes, it has a political aspect because the protagonist has lived through a horrible period of Argentine history, that still is having serious consequences. That has left its mark on an entire generation of Argentine people, and I didn't want to ignore it. I know the topic of torture well because I studied it in depth when I made *Los ojos vendados* [Blindfolded Eyes].

P P : *There is a delightful statement in the film: "The past is indestructible. Things return. Above all, the idea of abolishing the past."*
c s : Yes, it's by Borges, whose work I really immersed myself in when I made a movie about him, *El sur* [The South] in Argentina. I've always been influenced by Borges, almost since when I began to make films. No one has said that, but I'm saying it to you. There is always something Borgesian in my films. I really like the labyrinthian game of time, of temporal leaps, of what we talked about before about the scripts that don't get written—all of which cinema seems to me to be particularly well equipped for.

P P : *There's also a comment about the role of women. The protagonist says that he hopes that women don't follow men into their confusion.*

cs: Yes, it's something that I've thought about for many years and is a topic that preoccupies me. I believe that women are in a position to teach men what shouldn't have been done, to not follow the same path as men, but take another one—mind you, I don't know which one—but not to commit the same stupidities that men have: work, alienation due to work, with children and without them.

pp: *Have you ever taken refuge in your work at times of emotional crisis?*
cs: Not just once, but many times. And since I already know how to do it, it works like a dream. Emotional problem? Work like crazy, and if you can, get out of there.

pp: *Which do you fear more, a creative crisis or an emotional one?*
cs: I've never been afraid of having a creative crisis. I don't say that in a conceited way. I've had some difficulties when producers didn't want to make something that I did want to make, but not for any other reasons. Perhaps it's out of foolishness, but I've always had some project in mind that I could launch, and even several things at the same time. Besides, there are films that I'm making now that should have been made years ago, like *Pajarico* [Little Bird], or my next film about Goya.

pp: *And what's happening with* Esa luz *[That Light], your project about the Civil War?*
cs: The Goya project will come first but—and I say this out of experience—all things that you believe in end up being done. Sometimes you can't get something started and it seems like a catastrophe to you, but it's also good for time to pass in order to reflect on and adjust things, etc. I'm a bit fatalistic, but I'm always optimistic about work. If I didn't make films, I'd write, and if not that, I'd do photography, and if not that, well, something else. *Esa luz* is progressing, but it's a very complicated film, very expensive—some 1,500 million pesetas—and if I don't have sufficient resources, I don't want to make it. Sometimes I get lazy about it, but on the other hand, I'd like to leave it as a type of testimony, almost like a testament. Not about my life, but about the war. I don't think that there has yet been a serious film about the Spanish Civil War.

pp: *Do you think that people who are not fans of tango will enjoy your film?*

C S : It seems to me that *Tango* is a show worth seeing, and if I find it so, then I think it can be for many other people. I'm the first one who feels like applauding when I see Copes, Julio Bocca, Cecilia Narova, or Carlos Rivarola dancing, and it's not because I made the film, but because they are marvelous. The only thing that I've done has been to observe them dancing and to try to make it powerful with the camera.

The Image and the Word: A Conversation with Filmmaker and Novelist Carlos Saura

LINDA M. WILLEM / 2000

LINDA M. WILLEM: *In* Goya en Burdeos *[Goya in Bordeaux] you focus on the last stage in the life of the painter and you allow him to tell his own story through his conversations with his daughter. Why did you decide to structure the film this way?*

CARLOS SAURA: Maybe it's just because I liked this time in Goya's life, in Bordeaux. It seemed to me to be a particularly sorrowful exile for such an elderly man who had lived practically always in Spain. There is a very interesting book on Goya, called *Goya en Burdeos*, where this entire stage of his life is analyzed. It's a very lovely, exhaustive study with lots of material. I read it several years ago. And it seems interesting to me to analyze the relationship of Goya in Bordeaux, in exile, living with two women: his ex-mistress, or his mistress, that's not very clear, but she's a woman much younger than he by some forty years; and with Rosario, his daughter, and it isn't even known whether or not she is his daughter, but to him she is. Well, that's what I liked: the relationship between this old man, his young mistress, and the girl, in a foreign land, and structuring it around his old age and the conversations he has with his daughter.

LMW: *The mental processes of your protagonist—their memories, fantasies, hallucinations—are of fundamental importance to your cinema. Throughout your career you have developed various ways of representing this subjectivity, especially*

Madrid, July 7, 2000. Translated from Spanish by Linda M. Willem.

in order to show the presence of the past in the everyday life of the characters. Goya
en Burdeos *seems to be a further step in that direction.*

C S :   Well, it's a very free film, a bit atemporal. Time passes almost as if it
were looking for a rhythm, a narrative form rather than a logic. There isn't
much logic. At first when I proposed the film, the idea was that it would start
during his old age and end at his birth. It was a much more logical process.
All of the stages of his life were more clearly marked by time, but always
going backwards. But then I realized that it was too rigid, so I thought it
would be better to look for a more visual rhythm, a visual narrative rather
than being obligated to follow a rigid temporal order. That gave me more
freedom. I thought about how he was an old man with lapses of memory,
not always sure of where he was, and then he has times when he is very
lucid, like what sometimes happens to elderly people. That's what gave me
the pretext to be able to intermix dreams and memories as if it were all one
and the same time: the time of birth, the time of death, the time of everything in life being the same, all time mixed-up in the mind of a person.

L M W :   *Something that seems new to me in this film is how you have Goya speak
to himself through conversations between the old Goya and the younger Goya. I
don't think that you have used this type of stylistic device in any of your previous
films.*

C S :   In mine, I don't think so. This is the first time. And why not? This man
at the end of his life sees himself as a young man. It's something that happens to me. I don't try to remember many things from my youth, but when
I do, I see myself as if I were right there. Of course it isn't me, but in a way it
is me. It's rather confusing. But in this case, I liked the mixing of Goya as an
old man and Goya as a young man, and the answering of one to the other,
responding to what the other says, like in the scene where the young Goya
says that his masters are Velázquez, Rembrandt, and nature, and the old
Goya says, "and imagination," which is something that Goya never actually
said, but I liked as an idea.

L M W :   *In the scene where Goya speaks about Velázquez's* Las Meninas, *he says
that it is "beyond all palpable and physical realism. It is a part of another reality,
one that is born of painting, the deforming mirror of life, a magical reality where
everything is possible." Do you think that this type of imaginative reality that*

belongs to the realm of painting also pertains to other forms of visual representa-
tion, such as theater and film?

C S : Yes, because this is really something that I came up with. Goya hardly
wrote anything, just very little, so there are many things that I invented.
This is a statement that I'm making mostly about cinema. It's a very personal
statement. I don't know if Goya would have said that. But I do think that if
Goya had lived now, he would have been a film maker instead of a painter
because the imagination can be explored in fantastic ways through film. Literature is marvelous, and it can express itself through images in ways that
film can't. But what literature can't express is this mixture of sounds and
music with images. Literature can't approach this. If you write, for example,
that someone is listening to the Fourth Symphony of Brahms, first it's necessary for the reader to know Brahms's Fourth Symphony, which is something
rather doubtful, and then the reader has to stop reading to go and listen to
the symphony, which probably won't happen. In cinema, the music, the
sounds, are all present and they collaborate with the image. This is very
important in the formation of a complex chorus, even what is beyond opera,
in my opinion.

L M W : *It's very interesting that you mention that because the recent novel* La ley
del amor *[Law of Love] by the Mexican writer, Laura Esquivel, comes with a music
tape for the reader to listen to at certain points in the novel, as a way of trying to
achieve this kind of integration.*

C S : Yes, but for that sort of thing, it is better to make a film. Many novels
these days are influenced by film, the dialogues, the narratives, the ways of
explaining things are all influenced by cinema. Today it is unthinkable to do
what Flaubert did in *Madame Bovary*, spending eight or ten pages describing
the clothes at a wedding. In photographic images we can do this in an
instant. Each age has its own language.

L M W : *It's very interesting how you incorporate Goya's art in your film, especially
in two scenes: first, during the festival of San Isidro, and later in the long scene
depicting the war. But what impresses me the most is the theatricality of these
scenes, due to your use of an obviously artificial backdrop with actors moving in
front of it, as if it were a theatrical performance. Why did you present these scenes
in this way?*

c s : Well, because I didn't envision them in a naturalistic way. Instead I preferred something coming more from the imagination: to construct a reality from elements that are not always from that reality. Like the festival of San Isidro, which as you know is a very small painting. But it is truly beautiful projected as an enormous backdrop, more than 100 meters, and with people in front it is very theatrical and very operatic. But at the same time, I was aiming for there to be a strangeness about it, so when the viewer sees it, it seems somewhat naturalistic, but it really isn't. It's like a new view of reality, like another world, a different world. The entire film works at doing this: to create everyday life that is real while at the same time has a strangeness to it which forms part of its theatricality. What I thought was that since I was dealing with an artist, I could allow myself greater freedom to make a pictorial film, with colors, where everything has a more theatrical feel, more of a feel of the canvas, even a bit static at times. This is a very personal process of mine that I have been carrying out since *Sevillanas*, which I did quite awhile ago, and later in *Flamenco* and *Tango*, and now this is somewhat an evolution in the structure of the plastic elements. In *Goya* there is an evolution in the creation of spaces that are not naturalistic but can be so in another form, with light, etc. It's a game, even a personal game. But at the same time, it is the way that I see Goya's world.

L M W : *The war scene reminds me a lot of the dance in* Tango *dealing with the political violence of Videla's dictatorship, not only because of its theatricality, but also because of the presence of a female eyewitness to the horrors. Did you plan for there to be a relationship between these two scenes?*
c s : Yes, there certainly is a relationship, but I'm not sure what it is. When I wrote this scene, I was thinking of it having a relationship to *Tango*, but what kind, I don't know. In *Tango* this scene is conceived of from the point of view of a dance. It's a ballet, even though it may not seem like it. There's music that follows the actors throughout the scene. The whole thing is studied first through the sound of the music and then through each of the dance elements, which is very much like a ballet. Perhaps this is the first time that this type of ballet—with specific examples of cruelty—is depicted in film. But at the same time it's very expressionistic. In terms of *Goya*, it does seem very similar, but the performance is different. It isn't a ballet, or rather, it is a ballet of a different sort. There are different time periods represented, first the repressions, then the flight, which resembles the flight of people in all

wars, and in all civil wars, people fleeing from the fear and the terror, something we saw quite recently in Kosovo. Brutality, violence, shootings, it's all there. In Goya the scene is aesthetically presented differently, but the idea itself is linked to Tango. In terms of the eyewitness, in Tango her point of view is more specific because she is the protagonist of the main story. In Goya she is a little girl who is looking here and there for her mother and her father. She is peripheral to the main story. I didn't dare to put Rosarito in that role; I was a bit afraid. Perhaps I should have.

L M W : *Something very striking in* Tango *is the presence of illuminated screens, with all of the effects of light, shadow, color, and image that they allow. These screens are also seen in* Sevillanas, Flamenco, *and* Goya en Burdeos. *Was your use of these screens influenced by your director of photography, Vittorio Storaro?*
C S : Yes, most certainly. The first time I used them was in *Sevillanas*. These screens were semi-transparent and done mostly in black and white. There was very little color, practically none. These screens really precipitated the inclusion of color. Vittorio is a man who is used to working in color. As you know, the Spanish school of colors is a school more of grays. I've always liked browns and dark colors, and when I started working with Vittorio, I wasn't convinced about using colors that seemed too violent for the film. But, little by little, he began to convince me that they were marvelous, that it was a new way of seeing everything, that colors were very important for indicating the situations and even the spirit. In this sense, Vittorio and I have worked very closely. He is a wonderful person and a good friend.

L M W : *And in addition to colors, sometimes there are images on the screens, such as Goya's etchings.*
C S : Yes, everything was done in a studio with plastic materials that were semi-transparent and photographed. In a way this is an evolution of what we tried before, in *Tango* for example. I wanted to go further and I convinced Vittorio to come with me.

L M W : *In your films, you sometimes take a story you've told before but retell it in a different way, as if it were a variation on a theme, similar to what is done in classical music. The manner in which the story is told seems more important than the story itself. A good example is* Tango—*which to me is a reworking of* Carmen—*where you were able to explore certain themes and ideas all over again in a different way.*

c s : I agree. I think that's true. When I first thought of writing *Tango*, I had in mind something like *Flamenco*, something without a plot. But when we went to Buenos Aires and I began talking to lots of people, I realized that I needed a story, and the story I thought of was very similar to *Carmen*. It's true, yes. I don't know why. *Tango* is done in another way—it is different— but it's true that I always like to tell a story from the point of view of a theatrical director or someone who is mounting a number because there is so much freedom to use the elements out of order. I don't have to resort to telling the story of the opera *Carmen*, which would have been very boring. For me, precisely what is inventive in *Carmen* was that I was able to put the elements from the opera where I wanted them, and I used them in a different way, not like in the opera. For example, there is a leitmotif I used. And with *Tango* and *Goya* it's the same. It's this freedom. And above all what I like is the mounting of a theatrical work, the mounting of a film: the rehearsals, the preparations, the whole structuring process, that is what interests me the most. The performance itself is less interesting.

L M W : *In fact I was going to ask you about that. In all your dance films*—Tango, Flamenco, Sevillanas, El amor brujo, *[Love, the Magician],* Bodas de Sangre *[Blood Wedding], and* Carmen—*you show what goes on behind the scenes, revealing the studio setting and showing the dancers, singers, and musicians practicing. Why do you include these preparations rather than just focus on the performances?*

c s : For many reasons. First, because it's more interesting, seeing the corrections and the effort involved. Also, because the dancers are more natural; they are working hard at something to learn it. I've always been very influenced by the American film *42nd Street*, which is a marvelous film, but what I like most about it aren't the performances but the rehearsals. I remember when I was a photographer at the Festival of Granada and I was always at the rehearsals. I really liked how the dancers would work and sweat and exert themselves physically—all the effort that went into doing these things. When I go to a theater and see *Swan Lake* with someone like Nureyev jumping into the air, it all is very magical, but I don't care for it at all. But if I got to see Nureyev sweating during a rehearsal, that I'd enjoy.

L M W : *At the beginning of* Tango *Mario has a fantasy in which he kills his ex-*

wife, and the scene is exactly the same as the end of Carmen: *the way that he stabs her and how she falls at his feet, etc. Did you include this scene to remind the viewer of* Carmen?

c s : No, well, maybe. But what really interested me about the beginning of *Tango* was that in the first few minutes everything was explained about the film. That may not be clear but that's O.K. with me. What happens is that Solá, as the protagonist, is seated at the table talking about the script, which is my own script for *Tango*, and he is reading the first scene. So in a way you can look at everything that happens as being what he is writing in the script, and the people are the ones he is introducing in the story. I like this way of opening the film. As for killing his wife, that could be part of the story he wants to tell. We don't know if the story is real or not, if what is happening is real or if he thought it up. Killing his wife would be logical because she left him and he is depressed and at the point of killing himself, not knowing what to do with his life. Buñuel has a lovely saying: "Thoughts never break the law," that is, they never sin, which means that it is fine to think about killing your wife or father or whomever. In life there are many people we may want to kill (laughter).

L M W : *In* Tango *there is a scene where Mario looks at a boy, who is also named Mario, in a classroom. This reminds me of the scene in* Dulces horas *[Sweet Hours] where the protagonist, Juan, looks at a boy in a park, but the difference is that in* Dulces horas *the boy is Juan as a child, whereas in* Tango *it isn't clear if the boy is Mario from the past.*

c s : He could be Mario from the past, as a memory of himself. I left it unclear because I wanted it to be ambiguous. It's something that could be contemporary because today in the school of Buenos Aires it's like it was in Spain from the 30s and 40s. The schools are like from the past. I thought that he could be Mario seeing himself as a boy, or he could be a different boy entirely. I left it like that, very mysterious.

L M W : *Another recent film is* Pajarico *[Little Bird]. The concept of this film is very similar to that of* La prima Angélica *[Cousin Angelica]: a boy spends time away from his parents in the home of some relatives, where he falls in love with his spunky cousin. But the tone of the film is very different.*

c s : Yes, indeed. The first one dealt with the war and the postwar period, whereas the second one is more Mediterranean. It's a type of homage to my family in Murcia. It's made up of my memories and fantasies from this part of Murcia and the Levant, which is a very beautiful and sensual region, much different from *La prima Angelica*, which is more like Castile.

L M W :   *In* Pajarico *there are clearly supernatural elements—the uncle who levitates in the air while playing the cello, the aunt who sees religious visions, the cousin who can see the future with eyes that have an unusual structure—but the entire family accepts these supernatural events as a normal part of everyday life. This is very similar to what happens in the magical realism of Latin American literature. Did you think at all about that while making the film?*
C S :   No, not really. What I was thinking of was my family (laughter), which is a rather surrealistic family. There are things that I didn't even include because my family wouldn't have liked it. In all families there are some people like that, a bit magical and mysterious. No, I didn't think about that. The world of García Márquez is something I like. *Cien años de soledad* [One Hundred Years of Solitude] is a novel I enjoyed reading, but it is typical of Latin America. The imagery in my film is found in the Spanish tradition. It's a game of reality, but within reality itself. It's all reality but also an escape. The uncle levitates, well, why not? He is transported by the music. And the girl, well, she is somewhat like my own daughter, who has now lost her powers, but when she was little, she would say, "Something is happening in this house," and she would be right. The cat would have escaped or been in a fight, something like that. She could predict things. So I sort of copied this idea for the character.

L M W :   *At the end of* Pajarico *you use a voice-over with Manu speaking, which transforms the film into a retrospective story. Why did you do this?*
C S :   Well, I don't know. Because it occurred to me that way. I played with this idea before in a different way in *Cría cuervos* [Raise Ravens]. The events of the film—Manu in Murcia—are occurring in the present and the voice-over is from the future, his reflection on the present from the future. In *Cría cuervos* the time scheme is the same with Geraldine reflecting on her childhood. At times it's a bit irrational. You can't think too much about it. For example, in *Dulces horas* in the final scene the boy is seen as an adult with his mother, but you don't know whether it is his mother or if it is the actress. I like the idea of characters from various time periods being brought together.

L M W :   Dulces horas *is my favorite film of yours, precisely because of the complexity of its narrative levels and temporal planes.*

C S :   It really is a lovely invention: the construction of a family. I really liked it, and it was complicated. But no one in Spain liked it; in Germany and elsewhere they did, but not in Spain.

L M W :   *Returning to* Pajarico, *in addition to making the film, you also wrote a novel of the same title.*

C S :   Well, it's a short novel, not like *¡Esa luz!* [That Light!]. I wrote it in order to make the film. I'm tired of writing scripts. They bore me. I prefer to write a story of what is going to happen in the film.

L M W :   *In various interviews you have stated that you consider the script to be only a provisional form of the film, and that you have no problems with changing elements of the script, particularly the ending. But with* Pajarico *the film is very faithful to the novel.*

C S :   That's because I made revisions to the novel after the film. There are some differences between the novel and the film, but they are not big ones. The way I look at a script is in terms of cinema. A script is not a literary work, and I don't think it would be good if it were because then it would be something definitive. A novel is set. It has a specific place within the realm of literature. But a script needs to be a living thing or else it would be useless. If I write a script now, I may not make the film for a year. A lot of things can happen in a year. It's not logical that everything will stay the same. Even in a month or two weeks things can change: the actors are not who you imagined, the photography is different, or the places change, or even the seasons. You planned for summer but you have to shoot in winter. The script material is always temporary. It develops over time. It gives structure to the film but it doesn't constrain it. If it did, it wouldn't be a real script. It's just theoretical and literary material used for making a film.

L M W :   *A few minutes ago you mentioned your second novel,* ¡Esa luz! *which deals with the Spanish Civil War. In reading it I was struck by the number of references not only to your life, which I expected, but also to your films. For example, Goya is mentioned several times, there is also a quote from the poem* La noche oscura *[The Dark Night], and the exclamation "¡Esa luz!" during the bombing of Madrid is already in a scene from* Dulces horas. *What relationship does the novel have with your previous films?*

C S : Well, I don't know (laughter). That's for you to figure out. It's a story that has many personal things, but it's not about my life and it has invented characters. But the whole atmosphere of the war and memories of mine have appeared in my films: in *La prima Angélica*, above all in *Dulces horas*, and in *¡Ay, Carmela!* in a different way because that wasn't mine, that was Sinisterra's. It's a recurring theme that interests me. There are images that I hadn't used yet that I use in it, and I also repeat the ones that I like. As for Goya, he is a referent in many of my films, but usually indirectly, rather than directly as in *Tango* and *Goya en Burdeos*.

L M W : *¡Esa luz! has two narrative levels, one in the present tense dealing with the events of the war and one in the past tense relating the characters' memories of those events. I find it interesting that you use the present tense to convey the more remote past.*

C S : (laughter) I have no idea why I did it that way. I just liked it. Actually, what interests me is the meeting of literature with theater or cinema. I've done opera, but I've never done theater. In *Elisa, vida mía* [Elisa, My Life] I tried to get at this idea: how a story makes a character disappear, how it changes the character, how it eats up the character in the telling. In *¡Esa luz!* it's different because there is a type of meditation on the Spanish Civil War. But it's also similar because it's a real story that I began many years ago. There is a Spanish writer, Ramón José Sender, who is also Aragonese. He used to be my mother's boyfriend, and he wrote a novel, *Requiem por un campesino español* [Requiem for a Spanish Peasant], that was later made into a film. Well, the same thing happened to him during the war, and when I heard the story, it was so very awful that I wanted to make a film about it. Not about Ramón himself, but about the terrible story of a couple separated by the war. It could have been any civil war, Spanish or American. All wars are bad, but civil wars are worse because it's a war between family members, between siblings, between friends. That's the story I wanted to tell. And Sender's story was true because his wife was shot to death. So to some degree my story is based on reality. She was in the Francoist region and he remained in the Republican zone. She was a Christian woman from a good middle-class family, and they began to make life impossible for this woman when she began to lose control, and they shot her. Those things happen in a war. You think one way and someone thinks another way, so he shoots you. Civil wars accentuate all of the miserable things—envy, revenge, hate—that are usually covered by a cloak of civilization. Similar things happened in Argentina and even Chile. This type of repression and bestial things occur during a period of brutality.

L M W :   *Since ¡Esa luz! already has been published as a novel, will you feel more of an obligation to follow the storyline as written when you make the film?*
C S :   Well, I'm not sure if I ever will make the film. I wrote the novel because I thought that the film would be complicated to make, so just in case I didn't make it, I wanted to leave my testimony about the Civil War. It has been in some of my films, but always peripherally. The only time I deal with the war directly is in *¡Ay Carmela!*, but that isn't my concept, it's someone else's. I wanted to leave personal testimony of my own. I needed to write it. I never thought of publishing it, but a friend of mine wanted me to publish it with the Círculo de Lectores, so I set about writing it in a more literary manner, more formally. I'm not sure if there ever will be a film. After having written the novel, I feel more content. It's almost as if I had already made the film. I no longer feel the need.

Interview: Carlos Saura

JOSÉ ENRIQUE MONTERDE / 2001

JOSÉ ENRIQUE MONTERDE: *How and when did the* Buñuel y la mesa del rey Salomon *[Buñuel and King Solomon's Table] project get started?*
CARLOS SAURA: Actually it didn't originate with me. I've always known that some day I'd do something on Buñuel, but I didn't have any idea about what it would be. It was Agustín Sánchez-Vidal who called me from Zaragoza and said: "Listen, do you want to make a film about Buñuel?" I immediately said yes, and interestingly enough, it occurred to me right away that Buñuel had to be in an adventure about the search for King Solomon's table. The reason is that two weeks beforehand a Swiss-Jewish producer of large scale productions told me it's likely that the table is in Spain, probably in Valencia or Toledo. So I took this lovely idea about searching for the table in Toledo, and when I spoke with Agustín, it turned out that he knew a lot about that table, which even appears in a novel he has been writing for years.

JEM: *From the start it has been conceived as a work of fiction.*
CS: Yes. Right away I told the producer, José Antonio Romero, that I wasn't at all interested in making a film about Buñuel in order to tell the story of his life. Rather, an imaginative film where we could relate what we thought about Luis—finding some contrivance to do so—that's what I was interested in.

From *Dirigido por* 305 (2001): 46–47. Reprinted by permission of *Dirigido por*. Translated from Spanish by Linda M. Willem.

JEM: *From the start such an adventurous contrivance is surprising because there are times that it resembles Indiana Jones searching for the lost ark.*

CS: Well, after a Toledan fashion. We decided that the table was in Toledo, under the Tajo river, and that he would have to undergo a series of trials, like in adventure films. That's the most traditional part, but less so at the beginning when the friendships come together and where the adventure sometimes is less prominent.

JEM: *Don't you think that the film is basically trying to have too many things in it; that it's saturated with references and interconnections among the characters? And does it seem to you that the public, which is rather ignorant about Buñuel's work, will be able to follow all these things?*

CS: That could be; I'm not saying no. But cinema in general—and it really is sad—tends to simplify things, to make things very uncomplicated in order to have time to spell everything out. I don't think it's necessary to do all of that here. But it could be, as you say, that too many things are included. On the other hand, you are completely right about the public not knowing Buñuel's work well. Or that of Dalí, or Lorca either. Or even Cervantes's work for that matter. As for Buñuel, since his films were shown at four o'clock in the morning during his centennial, they are hardly known at all. At any rate, I thought that none of that really mattered, that the story we told was over and above all of that, that it could work even if those characters were fictitious, invented. It wouldn't be the same film, but it would be similar. Imagine for a moment that I were to bring together Marx, Freud, and Lenin in search of a mammoth in Siberia. That could be a lovely film, couldn't it?

JEM: *Really, this film could be understood as one of those jokes from their days in the Residencia de Estudiantes [student residence].*

CS: Indeed, but above all it's the freedom, the not needing to make something orthodox, the ability to put into the film all of the things that occurred to us.

JEM: *But with the contradiction of a strong dose of erudition being present.*

CS: Yes, but the erudition is there for those who want to see it. Of course, I don't know if these two parts of the script fit together very well. I start with the premise that the Buñuel we present in the film is not the real Buñuel. It's a matter of us making a homage to him, but Buñuel is really Agustín and me, and therefore imagination is what's present, and that is the real subject of the film, not surrealism, which doesn't interest me in the least. It's a matter of it being a fantastic world in which Oriental influences reappear, like what already happened in *Los zancos* [The Stilts], a film in which all of the music had Sephardic roots. Don't they say that Toledo is the city of three cultures? Well come on, let's mix them into the plot of the film, let's see how the three great religions come to an agreement in order to send freethinkers to Hell. Really, Toledo still is overly burdened with the influence of religion. In fact, they didn't allow us to film in the cathedral. Everyone in Toledo supported us a lot, except for the church.

J E M :   *There are really two Buñuels in the film: the more biographical and reliable one, played very well by El Gran Wyoming, and the imaginary one.*
C S :   Yes, you're right. In a way the first one provides the foundational support for the film, since he's more real, but he's also been altered since he's been placed in the present time. He's the one who begins to think up what can happen with those actors and with King Solomon's table. From then on the film can function with greater freedom, following my mind, but it could also be the mind of Buñuel himself. I imagine that he would have found something like this to be extremely amusing. It's too bad that he couldn't have gotten around to doing it, to disassociate himself from so many things that are attributed to him. Wyoming's presence in the film was the producer's idea, stemming from the fact that everyone says that he looks a lot like Buñuel. At first I wasn't very convinced, but I spoke with him and he was charming. Then, once he was put into character—after five hours of makeup—he worked out very well, with a perfect Aragonese accent.

J E M :   *Is there, on your part, a certain fascination with the new technology that you could make use of in this film?*
C S :   Well, this film lends itself to that. If you write down that there's a child who lifts up the skin of the ocean, well, that's very difficult when you edit the script. Really, when we wrote the script, we didn't put any constraints on the imagination, even though we didn't know yet how we were going to do it. We even had doubts as to what the robot would be like, but we also thought that the one from *Metrópolis* was the prettiest robot of all, that it had a symbolic character, and that it was a woman besides! My surprise has been that I wrapped up the film at the beginning of February and I didn't have it

totally completed until two weeks ago. I've pursued the technical process very laboriously in Barcelona, taking advantage of José Hernández's work painting the backgrounds. This is the same way of working that I began with *Sevillanas* and continued in *Flamenco, Tango,* and *Goya.*

All of this is put to use in order to continue making films about characters that interest me, as were Lope de Aguirre, San Juan de la Cruz, or Goya. Now I'm interested in tackling Philip II, one of those characters who has attracted me the most and whom I have studied throughout my life. For many years now—more than twenty—I've wanted to make something about him. So the use of the screens will allow me to solve the problem of it being impossible to film right in the middle of the Escorial. They will allow me to create "another" Escorial, which is what I like.

J E M :   *What do you think that Buñuel would have said about the "recuperation" of his image by those in power?*
C S :   Well, something like what Buñuel would have said had he been here at the Quincentennial. At any rate, that recuperation, which perhaps does betray the spirit of Buñuel, is inevitable. But on one hand it's for the good because that way people know who Buñuel is. Any homage that's made to any artist lacks moderation.

Clearly, when I began talking about Buñuel during my days at the National Film School, nobody knew about him, and the first films of his that were shown there didn't interest anyone. Even some of the most prestigious critics of the time said that those films were shit. And yet, now he's "Saint Buñuel," with monuments, streets, drum rolls. So I think that the more natural tone that I've adopted is one that would have pleased Buñuel, my retaining of a certain amount of respect but without the veneration that you see everywhere today.

INDEX

A bout de souffle. See Godard, Jean-Luc: *A bout de souffle* [Breathless]

Abdado, Claudio, 143

Abel Sánchez. See Unamuno, Miguel de: *Abel Sánchez*

Academy of Motion Picture Arts and Sciences, xxii; Oscar nominations, xxi, xxiii, 81

Adjani, Isabelle, 75, 77–78, 135

After the Deluge. See Esteva, Jacinto: *Después del diluvio* [After the Deluge]

Aguirre, Lope de, 86, 98, 100, 136, 137, 170

Aguirre, The Wrath of God. See Hertzog, Werner: *Aguirre, der Zorn Gottes* [Aguirre, The Wrath of God]

Aldecoa, Ignacio, xviii, 119–20; *Young Sánchez*, 118, 120

Aldecoa, Josefina, 119

Almodóvar, Pedro, vii

Alterio, Hector, 73

Altman, Robert, 55

Alvarrán, Víctor, 73

Amacord. See Fellini, Federico: *Amacord*

Amaya, Carmen, 91

Ambiguity, narrative, xii–xiii, 17–18, 26–27, 40, 43, 48–51, 53–54, 58, 62, 76, 78, 123, 142, 153, 157, 162, 163–64, 169. *See also* Double, the (theme); Memory/remembering; Symbolism/metaphor

American cinema, xviii, 54, 80–81, 108, 132–33, 141

Amo, Pablo del, 73, 133, 144

Amor de Dios (dance studio), 91

Angelillo (Angel Sampedro Montero), 107

Antonioni, Michelangelo, xviii, xxiii, 23, 39, 81; *L'avventura*, 23

Antonutti, Omero, 101

Aparicio, Rafaela, 58, 64, 132

Argentina, Imperio, 107, 150

Arrabal, Fernando, 127

Auteur, x–xi, 30, 33, 54, 62, 66, 70, 74–75, 79–80, 99, 108, 135

Azcona, Rafael, 16, 18, 26, 38, 42, 123, 125–26, 137

Azúcar Moreno, 92

Bacon, Lloyd, *42nd Street*, 161

Baena, Juan Julio, 23

Bardem, Juan Antonio, xviii, 7, 82, 122

Barenboim, Daniel, 143

Beckett, Samuel, 127

Beethoven, Ludwig van, 133

Béjart, Maurice, 90

Beleta, Rovira, *Los Tarantos* [The Tarantos], 91

Bergman, Ingmar, 39, 57, 81, 125, 129, 131; *Smultronstället* [Wild Strawberries], 129

Berlanga, Luis García, 7, 14, 23, 36, 82, 122; *El verdugo* [The Executioner], 123

Berlin Film Festival. *See* Festivals, Film: Berlin

Bertolucci, Bernardo, 150

Bilbao Film Festival. *See* Festivals, Film: Bilbao

Billard, Pierre, 6

Bizet, Georges, 88; *Carmen*, xxii, 143, 144

Black Tulip, The. See Delon, Alain: *La Tulipe Noir* [The Black Tulip]

Blood Wedding. See Gades, Antonio: *Bodas de sangre* [Blood Wedding] (theatrical version)

Bocca, Julio, 151, 155

Bodas de sangre. See Gades, Antonio: *Bodas de sangre* [Blood Wedding] (theatrical version)

Borau, José Luis, 57–58

Borges, Jorge Luis, 125, 129, 138, 142, 153

Botón de ancla. See Torrado, Ramón: *Botón de ancla* [Brass Button]

Boyero, Carlos, 131

Brahms, Johannes, 133, 158

Brass Button. See Torrado, Ramón: *Botón de ancla* [Brass Button]

Bread Without Land. See Buñuel, Luis: *Tierra sin pan* [Bread Without Land]

Breathless. See Godard, Jean-Luc: *A bout de souffle* [Breathless]

Bresson, Robert, 39

Bronston Studios, 87

Bruno S., 28

Buero Vallejo, Antonio, 24

Buñuel, Luis, vii, xviii, xix, 6, 7, 14, 23, 24, 39, 57–58, 62–63, 64, 81, 110, 114, 115, 132, 135, 138, 162, 167–69, 170; *El* [This Strange Passion], 6; *La joven* [The Young One], 6; *La vía láctea* [The Milky Way], 64; *Simón de desierto* [Simon of the Desert], 64; *Tierra sin pan* [Bread Without Land], 6; *Viridiana*, xix, 5, 6, 24, 34

Cahiers du cinéma, x, 14, 22, 60

Calderón de la Barca, Pedro, 37, 48; *El gran teatro del mundo* [The Great Theater of the World], 48

Camus, Mario, 4, 5, 7, 116–17, 119–20; *Muere una mujer* [A Woman Dies], xix, 120

Cannes Film Festival. *See* Festivals, Film: Cannes

Carmen. See Rosi, Francesco: *Carmen*

Carmen (opera). *See* Bizet, Georges: *Carmen*; Saura, Carlos: *Carmen* (opera)

Carmen (theatrical version). *See* Gades, Antonio: *Carmen* (theatrical version); Saura, Carlos: *Carmen* (theatrical version)

Carrière, Jean-Claude, 72–76, 135

Carril, Hugo del, 128

Castro, Estrella, 107

Castro, Javier, 145

Cela, Camilo José, 62

Censorship: in France, 69; in Spain (*see* Franco dictatorship)

Cervantes, Miguel de, 37, 48, 168; *Don Quijote*, 25, 74

Chaplin, Charles, 13

Chaplin, Geraldine, xix, xx, 12, 13, 25–26, 29, 46, 49, 55, 58, 125, 163

Chaplin, Oona, 46

Chávarri, Jaime, *El desencanto* [Disenchantment], 38

Chueca, Federico, *El dos de mayo* [The Second of May], 57

Cien años de soledad. See García Márquez, Gabriel: *Cien años de soledad* [One Hundred Years of Solitude]

Cineart, 134

Cinema 2002, 63

Círculo de Lectores, 166

Ciro, 91

Codazzi, Juan Carlos, 150

Comolli, Jean-Luc, 14

Conversation, The. See Coppola, Francis Ford: *The Conversation*

Copes, Juan Carlos, 155

Coppola, Francis Ford, *The Conversation*, 130

Coutard, Raoul, 118

Cuadrado, Luis, 23, 123

Cukor, George, 81

Dalí, Salvador, 168

Dance, viii, xiii, xxi, xxii, 69–71, 84, 87, 88–95, 128, 132, 133, 134–35, 140, 150–52, 155, 159, 161

De Sica, Vittorio, xviii, 23; *Umberto D.*, 3

Delgado, Fernando, 30

Delon, Alain, *La Tulipe Noir* [The Black Tulip], 24

Después del diluvio. *See* Esteva, Jacinto: *Después del diluvio* [After the Deluge]

Dibildos, José Luis, 7, 8, 24, 118

Disenchantment. *See* Chávarri, Jaime: *El desencanto* [Disenchantment]

Don Quijote. *See* Cervantes, Miguel de: *Don Quijote*

Double, the (theme), xiii, 19–21, 47–48, 50, 61, 78, 85, 142

Dovjenko, Oleksandr, 3

Dreyer, Carl Theodor, 125

Ducay, Eduardo, 3

Dwan, Allan, 81

Eceiza, Antxon, 24, 122

Eisenstein, Sergei, 3, 63

El amor brujo. *See* Gades, Antonio: *Fuego* [Fire] (theatrical version of *El amor brujo* [Love, the Magician])

El cochecito. *See* Ferreri, Marco: *El cochecito* [The Little Car]

El desencanto. *See* Chávarri, Jaime: *El desencanto* [Disenchantment]

El dos de mayo. *See* Chueca, Federico: *El dos de mayo* [The Second of May]

El espíritu de la colmena. *See* Erice, Víctor: *El espíritu de la colmena* [Spirit of the Beehive]

El gran teatro del mundo. *See* Calderón de la

Barca, Pedro: *El gran teatro del mundo* [The Great Theater of the World]

El Jarama. *See* Sánchez Ferlosio, Rafael: *El Jarama*

El misterio de Elche. *See* Pablo, Luis de: *El misterio de Elche*

El. *See* Buñuel, Luis: *El* [This Strange Passion]

El sur. *See* Erice, Víctor: *El sur* [The South]

El verdugo. *See* Berlanga, Luis García: *El verdugo* [The Executioner]

Enigma of Kaspar Huaser, The. *See* Hertzog, Werner: *Jeder für sich und Gott gegen alle* [The Enigma of Kaspar Huaser]

E.O.C. (Escuela Oficial de Cinematografía). *See* Film School, Spanish National

Erice, Víctor, 57, 139, 142; *El espíritu de la colmena* [Spirit of the Beehive], 39; *El sur* [The South], 142; *La muerte y la brújula* (script), 142

Escamilla, Teo, 73, 108, 144

Esquivel, Laura, *La ley del amor* [Law of Love], 158

Esteva, Jacinto, *Después del diluvio* [After the Deluge], 15

Estos son tus hermanos. *See* Sueiro, Daniel: *Estos son tus hermanos* [These Are Your Brothers]

European Film Academy, xxii, xxiii

Executioner, The. *See* Berlanga, Luis García: *El verdugo* [The Executioner]

EXPO'92, xxii

Falla, Manuel de, 87, 88

Felipe II (Philip II), 100, 138, 170

Fellini, Federico, xviii, 39, 57, 63–64, 81; *Amarcord*, 64; *Giulietta degli spiriti* [Juliet of the Spirits], 64

Ferlosio. *See* Sánchez Ferlosio, Rafael

Fernán-Gómez, Fernando, xxi, 84–85, 112, 136

Fernández Santos, Jesús, xviii, 119

Ferreri, Marco, *El cochecito* [The Little Car], 116, 118

Festivals, Film: Berlin, vii, xix, xx, xxi, 16, 132; Bilbao, xix; Cannes, vii, xix, xx, xxi, xxii, xxiii, 6, 30, 34, 39, 71, 130; Montreal, vii, xxii, xxiii; New York, xx; San Sebastián xix, xxi, xxiii; Tokyo, 140; Venice, xx, xxi, 86

Film School, Spanish National, xviii, 3–5, 6, 8–9, 22–23, 34, 78, 118, 170

Films, 59, 116

Films for the Humanities, viii

Fire. See Gades, Antonio: *Fuego* [Fire] (theatrical version of *El amor brujo* [Love, the Magician]); Saura, Carlos: *Fuego* [Fire]

First Name Carmen. See Godard, Jean-Luc: *Prénom Carmen* [First Name Carmen]

Fitzgerald, F. Scott, 152

Flaubert, Gustave, *Madame Bovary*, 158

Fons, Angelino, 8, 14, 120

Ford, John, 81, 108

42nd Street. See Bacon, Lloyd: *42nd Street*

Franco dictatorship, vii, 51, 103–05, 108–14, 116, 122; censorship, vii, xiii, xix, xx, xxi, 4, 6–7, 9, 11, 14–16, 20, 22, 23–24, 29–31, 34, 37, 46, 53, 60, 109–10, 116, 123, 127, 153; state subsidies/subventions, xix, 15–16

Franco, Francisco, 111, 126–27; death, xx, 47, 51, 54–55, 132

French New Wave. *See Nouvelle Vague* [French New Wave]

Freud, Sigmund, 60, 168

Fuego [Fire]. *See* Gades, Antonio: *Fuego* [Fire] (theatrical version of *El amor brujo* [Love, the Magician]); Saura, Carlos: *Fuego* [Fire]

Gabin, Jean, 113

Gades, Antonio, xxi, xxii, 69–71, 82, 84, 85, 87, 88–94, 133, 134; *Bodas de sangre* [Blood Wedding] (theatrical version), 90; *Carmen* (theatrical version), xxi, 90; *Fuego* [Fire] (theatrical version of *El amor brujo* [Love, the Magician]), xxii

García Escudero, José-Maria, 9–10, 122

García Lorca, Federico, 70–71, 88, 168

García Márquez, Gabriel, 163; *Cien años de soledad* [One Hundred Years of Solitude], 163

Gardel, Carlos [Charles Gardes], 150

Gaumont Company, 72–73, 75, 135

Germi, Pietro, xviii

Gil, Rafael, 113; *Reina Santa* [The Holy Queen], 105

Godard, Jean-Luc, xxiii, 16, 37, 86; *A bout de souffle* [Breathless], 5, 23, 117–18; *Prénom Carmen* [First Name Carmen], 86

Gómez, Andrés Vicente, 136, 137, 139, 142

Goya, Francisco de, xviii, 119, 138, 154, 156, 158–59, 160, 164–65, 170

Gracián, Baltazar, 37, 47

Gutiérrez-Caba, Emilio, 121

Hernández, José, 170

Hertzog, Werner, *Aguirre, der Zorn Gottes* [Aguirre, The Wrath of God], 100; *Jeder für sich und Gott gegen alle* [The Enigma of Kaspar Huaser], 28

Hitchcock, Alfred, 3, 13; *Psycho*, 14; *Vertigo*, 14

Holy Queen, The. See Gil, Rafael: *Reina Santa* [The Holy Queen]

Hoyos, Cristina, 91–94

Huston, John, 57

I.I.E.C. (Instituto de Investigaciones y Experiencias Cinematográficas). *See* Film School, Spanish National

Indiana Jones movies. *See* Spielberg, Steven: *Indiana Jones* movies

Ionesco, Eugene, 127

Irish, William, 3

Italian neo-realism, xviii, 4–5, 23

Jeannette, 130

Jiménez, Juan Ramón, 91

Juliet of the Spirits. *See* Fellini, Federico: *Giulietta degli spiriti* [Juliet of the Spirits]

Kurosawa, Akira, 118

La joven. *See* Buñuel, Luis: *La joven* [The Young One]
La ley del amor. *See* Esquivel, Laura: *La ley del amor* [Law of Love]
La Lola va a los puertos. *See* Orduña, Juan de: *La Lola va a los puertos* [Lola Goes From Port to Port]
La muerte y la brújula. *See* Erice, Víctor: *La muerte y la brújula* (script)
La Tulipe Noir. *See* Delon, Alain: *La Tulipe Noir* [The Black Tulip]
La vía láctea. *See* Buñuel, Luis: *La vía láctea* [The Milky Way]
Ladies in Waiting, The. *See* Velázquez, Diego: *Las meninas* [The Ladies in Waiting]
Lamarque, Libertad, 128
Lang, Fritz, *Metropolis*, 169
Lara, Fernando, 130
Las meninas. *See* Velázquez, Diego: *Las meninas* [The Ladies in Waiting]
L'avventura. *See* Antonioni, Michelangelo: *L'avventura*
Law of Love. *See* Esquivel, Laura: *La ley del amor* [Law of Love]
Lebrón, Juan, 140
Lemus, Silvia, viii
Lenin, Vladimir, 168
Little Car, The. *See* Ferreri, Marco: *El cochecito* [The Little Car]
López Vázquez, José Luis, 13, 28, 30, 123, 129
López-Linares, Pedro, 144
Lorca. *See* García Lorca, Federico
Los Tarantos. *See* Beleta, Rovira: *Los Tarantos* [The Tarantos]
Losey, Joseph, 13, 39
Love, the Magician (theatrical version). *See* Gades, Antonio: *Fuego* [Fire] (theatrical version of *El amor brujo* [Love, the Magician])

Lowry, Malcolm, *Under the Volcano*, 74
Lozano, Manuel Rodríguez, 77
Lucía, Paco de, 91
Lunar, Perico el del, 132

Macbeth. *See* Shakespeare, William: *Macbeth*
Madame Bovary. *See* Flaubert, Gustave: *Madame Bovary*
Magdalena, María, 91
Malle, Louis, 37
Mamoulian, Rouben, 81
March, Juan, 127
Mariona Rebull. *See* Sáenz de Heredia, José Luis: *Mariona Rebull*
Martín Gaite, Carmen, xviii, 119
Marx, Karl, 168
Maura, Carmen, xxii
Mayo, Alfredo, 112–13, 123
Memory/remembering (theme), xiii, 17–18, 27–28, 40, 43, 48, 62, 103–04, 106–07, 126, 129, 148, 156–57, 162. *See also* Ambiguity, narrative
Mérimée, Prosper, 88–89
Metropolis. *See* Lang, Fritz: *Metropolis*
Michael Strogoff. *See* Verne, Jules: *Michael Strogoff*
Milky Way, The. *See* Buñuel, Luis: *La vía láctea* [The Milky Way]
Minnelli, Vincente, 81
Mizogouchi, Kenji, 80, 118
Monroe, Marilyn, 76
Montesquieu, Charles de Secondat, 27
Montreal Film Festival. *See* Festivals, Film: Montreal
Mozart, Wolfgang Amadeus, 133
Muere una mujer. *See* Camus, Mario: *Muere una mujer* [A Woman Dies]; Saura, Carlos: *Muere una mujer* [A Woman Dies] (script)
Music, xiii–xiv, 55, 57, 64, 68–69, 88–89, 91–92, 93–94, 107–08, 119, 128, 130, 132–33, 134–

35, 139, 141, 143, 148, 150–53, 158, 159, 160–61, 169

Nabucco. *See* Verdi, Giuseppi: *Nabucco*
Narova, Cecilia, 155
Neville, Edgar, 114
New York Film Festival. *See* Festivals, Film: New York
Nieto, José, 113
Nine Letters to Berta. *See* Patino, Basilio: *Nueve cartas a Berta* [Nine Letters to Berta]
Nouvelle Vague [French New Wave], 22, 23, 116. *See also* Godard, Jean-Luc; Malle, Louis; Truffaut, François
Nueve cartas a Berta. *See* Patino, Basilio: *Nueve cartas a Berta* [Nine Letters to Berta]
Nureyev, Rudolf, 161

Olympiad, Twenty-Fifth (1992), xxii, 139
Oms, Marcel, 6
One Hundred Years of Solitude. *See* García Márquez, Gabriel: *Cien años de soledad* [One Hundred Years of Solitude]
Orduña, Juan de, *La Lola va a los puertos* [Lola Goes From Port to Port], 105
Oscar nominations. *See* Academy of Motion Picture Arts and Sciences: Oscar nominations
Oscarsson, Per, 125

Pablo, Luis de, 108, 133; *El misterio de Elche*, 64
Pajares, Andrés, xxii
Palmero, Rafael, 144
Paramount Pictures, 16
Patino, Basilio, 9, 14, 24; *Nueve cartas a Berta* [Nine Letters to Berta], 121
Penthouse, ix
Perrin, Jacques, 121
Philip II. *See* Felipe II
Picazo, Miguel, 9
Piedra, Emiliano, 69, 82, 84, 87, 88, 134
Pietri, Oslar, 100

Portabella, Pedro, 4, 6, 116
Pose, Abel, 100
Prénom Carmen. *See* Godard, Jean-Luc: *Prénom Carmen* [First Name Carmen]
Providence. *See* Resnais, Alain: *Providence*
Psycho. *See* Hitchcock, Alfred: *Psycho*
Pudovkin, Vsevolod, 3

Querejeta, Elías, xix, xx, xxi, 8, 24, 46, 83, 110, 120, 122, 123, 125, 126, 130
Quevedo, Francisco de, 37

Rabal, Francisco (Paco), xxiii, 7, 112, 146, 149
Race. *See* Sáenz de Heredia, José Luis: *Raza* [Race]
Rambal, Enrique, x, 59, 64
Ramón, Eulalia, 149
Ravel, Maurice, 133
Raza. *See* Sáenz de Heredia, José Luis: *Raza* [Race]
Reagan, Ronald, 68
Reality vs. fantasy (theme). *See* Ambiguity, narrative
Reception, critical and popular, vii, xi–xii, xix–xxiii, 34, 39, 40, 56–58, 63, 122, 123, 124–25, 126–28, 129, 130–32, 134, 136, 137–38, 140, 164
Reina Santa. *See* Gil, Rafael: *Reina Santa* [The Holy Queen]
Reisz, Karel, 5
Rembrandt, 157
Renoir, Jean, 5
Requiem por un campesino español. *See* Sender, Ramón José: *Requiem por un campesino español* [Requiem for a Spanish Peasant]
Resnais, Alain, 58, 81; *Providence*, 58
Rey, Fernando, xxi, 49, 112
Rey, Pedro del, 144
Rivarola, Carlos, 155
Rivas Mercado, Antonieta, 76–77
Rivelles, Amparo, 113

Roma città aperta. *See* Rossellini, Roberto: *Roma città aperta* [Rome, Open City]

Rome, Open City. *See* Rossellini, Roberto: *Roma città aperta* [Rome, Open City]

Romero, José Antonio, 167

Romero, Rafael, 132

Rosi, Francesco, 72; *Carmen*, 135

Rossellini, Roberto, 23; *Roma città aperta* [Rome, Open City], 23

Sadoul, Georges, 5, 6

Sáenz de Heredia, José Luis, 113–14; *Mariona Rebull*, 111; *Raza* [Race], 113

Saint James of the Cross. *See* San Juan de la Cruz [Saint James of the Cross]

San Juan de la Cruz [Saint James of the Cross], 59, 138, 170

San Sebastián Film Festival. *See* Festivals, Film: San Sebastián

Sánchez Ferlosio, Rafael, xviii, 119, 125; *El Jarama*, 125

Sánchez-Vidal, Agustín, 167

Sanlúcar, Manolo, 140

Sastre, Alfonso, 7

Saura, Antonio (brother), xvii, xviii, xxii, xxiii, 90, 143, 144

Saura, Carlos

   Works: *Ana y los lobos* [Ana and the Wolves], xx, 17, 25, 28–30, 31, 33, 52–53, 55, 57–60, 63, 65, 85, 127, 132; *Antonieta*, xxi, 72–79, 82–83, 135; *¡Ay, Carmela!*, xxii, 137, 165, 166; *Bodas de sangre* [Blood Wedding], xxi, 69–71, 88–91, 133, 134–35, 161; *Buñuel y la mesa del rey Salomón* [Buñuel and King Solomon's Table], xxiii, 167–70; *Carmen*, xxi, 72, 82–83, 84, 88–95, 122, 132, 133, 135, 138, 143, 151, 161–62; *Carmen* (opera), xxii, 143, 144; *Carmen* (theatrical version), xxi, 90; *Cría cuervos* [Raise Ravens], ix, xx, 26, 29, 31, 33–35, 38–41, 42–48, 106, 122, 129–30, 148, 163; *Cuenca*, 4; *Deprisa, deprisa* [Hurry, Hurry], xxi, 65–69, 78–79, 131, 134, 141; *Dispara* [Shoot/Outrage], xxiii, 131, 140, 141;

Dulces horas [Sweet Hours], ix, xxi, 71, 129, 131, 133, 162, 163–64, 165; *El amor brujo* [Love, the Magician], xxii, 87, 88, 91–94, 132, 135, 143, 161; *El Dorado*, xxii, 86, 96–102, 135, 136–37, 142; *El jardín de las delicias* [The Garden of Delights], ix, x, xx, 25, 27–28, 33, 35, 59, 61, 63, 107, 111, 126–27; *El regreso* [The Return] (script), 5; *Elisa, vida mía* [Elisa, My Life], x, xxi, 42, 44–51, 53, 128, 129, 130–31, 165; *¡Esa luz!* [That Light!] (novel), xxiii, 164–66; *¡Esa luz!* [That Light!] (script), 37, 154, 166; *Flamenco*, xxiii, 134, 139, 140, 143, 150–51, 159, 160, 161, 170; *Flamenco* (film short), xviii; *Fuego* [Fire], xxii; *Goya en Burdeos* [Goya in Bordeaux], xxiii, 139, 141, 156–60, 165, 170; *La boda* [The Wedding] (script), 5, 6, 14, 126; *La caza* [The Hunt], xix, 8–11, 12–13, 24–25, 26, 33–35, 46, 49, 61–63, 106, 108–10, 113, 120–22, 125, 128, 133; *La madriguera* [The Burrow], xx, 25–26, 29, 47, 124–25, 126; *La noche oscura* [The Dark Night], xxii, 137–39; *La prima Angélica* [Cousin Angelica], ix, x, xx, 17–21, 26, 29–30, 33–35, 39, 46, 47, 61, 127–29, 148, 162–63, 165; *La tarde del domingo* [Sunday Afternoon], xviii, 3; *Llanto por un bandido* [Lament for a Bandit], xix, 6–9, 23–24, 26, 33–34, 110, 118–19, 121, 132; *Los cuentos de Borges: El Sur* [The Borges Tales: The South], xxii, 128, 133, 135, 139, 140, 142, 153; *Los golfos*, xix, xxii, 3, 4–6, 23, 26, 33, 65, 78, 109–10, 116–18, 119, 120, 121, 125, 131, 132, 141; *Los ojos vendados* [Blindfolded Eyes], x, xxi, 66, 78, 131, 139, 153; *Los zancos* [The Stilts], xxi, xxii, 84–86, 136, 169; *Mamá cumple cien años* [Mama Turns One Hundred], x, xxi, 52–53, 55–61, 63–64, 65, 81, 85, 105, 132; *Maratón* [Marathon], xxii, 139; *Muere una mujer* [A Woman Dies] (script), xix, 120; *Pajarico* [Little Bird], ix, xxiii, 140, 141, 144–49, 154, 162–64; *Pajarico solitario* [Solitary Little Bird] (novel), xxiii, 164; *Peppermint frappé*,

xix–xx, 5, 11–14, 25, 29, 36, 47, 63, 64, 123, 124, 125, 126, 133; *Querida, ¿me alcanzas el cuchillo?* [Darling, Can You Get Me the Knife?] (script), 145; *Sevillanas*, xxii, 134, 139–40, 150, 159, 160, 161, 170; *Stress es tres, tres* [Stress is Three, Three], xx, 12, 25, 47, 123–24; *Tango*, xxiii, 135, 140, 141, 143, 150–55, 159–62, 165, 170; *Taxi*, xxiii, 131, 133, 141, 145, 146
Saura Medrano, Carlos (son), xix, 144
Schlondorff, Volker, 81
Schygulla, Hanna, 75–78
Scripts, x, xi, 4, 5–6, 7, 10–11, 14, 16, 18, 21, 24, 26, 31, 38–39, 42–43, 47, 48, 49, 52, 63, 66, 71, 73–76, 84–85, 110, 120, 125, 134, 135, 137, 142, 144–45, 151, 152, 162, 164, 168–69. *See also* Saura, Carlos
Seberg, Jean, 76
Seco, Carlos, 136
Second of May, The. See Chueca, Federico: *El dos de mayo* [The Second of May]
Sender, Ramón José, 100, 165; *Requiem por un campesino español* [Requiem for a Spanish Peasant], 165
Shakespeare, William, 102, 125; *Macbeth*, 102
Shifrin, Lalo, 151
Simón de desierto. See Buñuel, Luis: *Simón de desierto* [Simon of the Desert]
Sinisterra, José Sanchís, 165
Sjöström, Viktor, 129
Sol, Laura del, 84–85, 91–93, 135
South, The. See Erice, Víctor: *El sur* [The South]
Spanish Civil War, ix, xvii, xxiii, 8, 10, 12, 18–20, 25, 28, 30, 32–33, 35, 104, 117, 121, 150, 154, 162, 164–66
Spanish Film Academy, xxii
Spielberg, Steven, *Indiana Jones* movies, 99, 168
Spirit of the Beehive. See Erice, Víctor: *El espíritu de la colmena* [Spirit of the Beehive]
Storaro, Vittorio, xxiii, 140–41, 151–52, 160

Sueiro, Daniel, 4, 117; *Estos son tus hermanos* [These Are Your Brothers], 5
Symbolism/metaphor, xiii, 10, 25–26, 53–54, 56, 59–60, 121, 127, 132, 169

Temporal levels. *See* Ambiguity, narrative
These Are Your Brothers. See Sueiro, Daniel: *Estos son tus hermanos* [These Are Your Brothers]
Thirard, Armand, 6
This Strange Passion. See Buñuel, Luis: *El* [This Strange Passion]
Thomas, Hugh, 139
Tierra sin pan. See Buñuel, Luis: *Tierra sin pan* [Bread Without Land]
Tokyo Film Festival. *See* Festivals, Film: Tokyo
Torrado, Ramón, *Botón de ancla* [Brass Button], 108–09
Torrent, Ana, 39
Triunfo, 130
Trueba, Fernando, 131
Truffaut, François, 37
20,000 Leagues Under the Sea. See Verne, Jules: *20,000 Leagues Under the Sea*

Umberto D. See De Sica, Vittorio: *Umberto D.*
Unamuno, Miguel de, 126; *Abel Sánchez*, 14, 126
Under the Volcano. See Lowry, Malcolm: *Under the Volcano*
Ursúa, Pedro de, 101

Valle-Inclán, Ramón del, x, 17
Vasconcelos, José, 76–77
Vega, Garcilaso de la, x, 46–47
Vega, Lope de, 48
Velázquez, Diego, 157; *Las meninas* [The Ladies in Waiting], 146, 157
Venice Film Festival. *See* Festivals, Film: Venice
Ventura, Lino, 7
Verdi, Giuseppi, *Nabucco*, 151–52

Verne, Jules: *Michael Strogoff*, 59; *20,000 Leagues Under the Sea*, 59
Vertigo. See Hitchcock, Alfred: *Vertigo*
Videla, Jorge Rafael, 153, 159
Viridiana. See Buñuel, Luis: *Viridiana*
Visconti, Luchino, xviii
Vivaldi, Antonio, 133

Wajda, Andrzej, 57
Welles, Orson, 16, 59
Wild Strawberries. See Bergman, Ingmar: *Smultronstället* [Wild Strawberries]
Wilder, Billy, 81
Wilson, Lambert, 101

Woman Dies, A. See Camus, Mario: *Muere una mujer* [A Woman Dies]; Saura, Carlos: *Muere una mujer* [A Woman Dies] (script)
Woolf, Virginia, 76
Wyler, William, 81
Wyoming, El Gran, 169

Young One, The. See Buñuel, Luis: *La joven* [The Young One]
Young Sánchez. See Aldecoa, Ignacio: *Young Sánchez*

Zavattini, Cesare, 23
Zhang Yimou, xxiii
Zurlini, Valerio, 121

CONVERSATIONS WITH FILMMAKERS SERIES
PETER BRUNETTE, GENERAL EDITOR

The collected interviews with notable modern directors, including

Robert Altman • Theo Angelopolous • Bernardo Bertolucci • Jane Campion • George Cukor • Brian De Palma • Clint Eastwood • John Ford • Jean-Luc Godard • Peter Greenaway • John Huston • Jim Jarmusch • Elia Kazan • Stanley Kubrick • Spike Lee • Mike Leigh • George Lucas • Martin Ritt • John Sayles • Martin Scorsese • Steven Soderbergh • Steven Spielberg • Oliver Stone • Quentin Tarantino • Orson Welles • Billy Wilder • Zhang Yimou